Charlie Pye-Smith was bo. ... ..e studied ecology at Newcastle-upon-Tyne and London universities. He is the author of *The Other Nile* and *Travels in Nepal*, both published by Penguin, and co-author of three books on environmental matters. He has been a regular presenter of the BBC World Service's programme *Global Concerns*; he also works for television and writes regularly for a variety of national publications.

BARCELONA:
A Celebration and a Guide

Charlie Pye-Smith

PENGUIN BOOKS

PENGUIN BOOKS

Published by the Penguin Group
Penguin Books Ltd, 27 Wrights Lane, London w8 5tz, England
Penguin Books USA Inc., 375 Hudson Street, New York, New York 10014, USA
Penguin Books Australia Ltd, Ringwood, Victoria, Australia
Penguin Books Canada Ltd, 10 Alcorn Avenue, Toronto, Ontario, Canada m4v 3b2
Penguin Books (NZ) Ltd, 182–190 Wairau Road, Auckland 10, New Zealand

Penguin Books Ltd, Registered Offices: Harmondsworth, Middlesex, England

First published 1992
1 3 5 7 9 10 8 6 4 2

Printed in England by Clays Ltd, St Ives plc
Set in 11½/14 pt Monophoto Sabon

CONTENTS

ILLUSTRATIONS

All photographs taken by the author except numbers 7, 8, 9, 19 and 21 (courtesy of Spanish National Tourist Office).

MAPS

ACKNOWLEDGEMENTS

My thanks go to the many people and organizations who provided me with help and information while in Catalonia; special mention should be made of the Consorcio de Promocion Turística de Catalunya. Bob Martinez, a native of Barcelona, introduced me to many bars, both salubrious and salacious, which I might otherwise have missed. But most of all, I must thank Sandie, whose presence added immeasurably to my enjoyment of Catalonia.

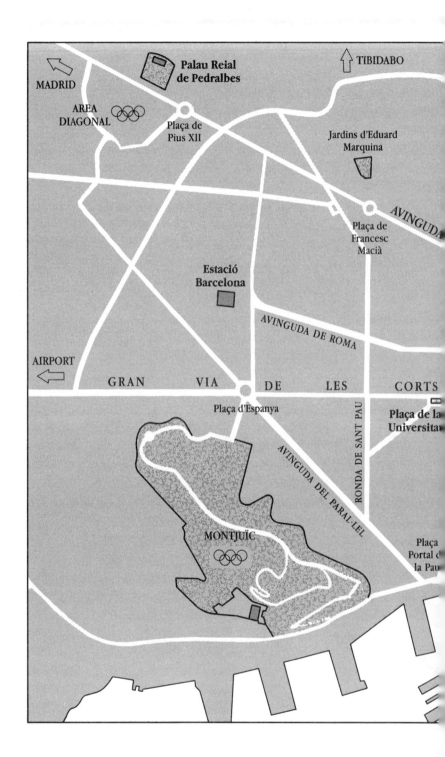

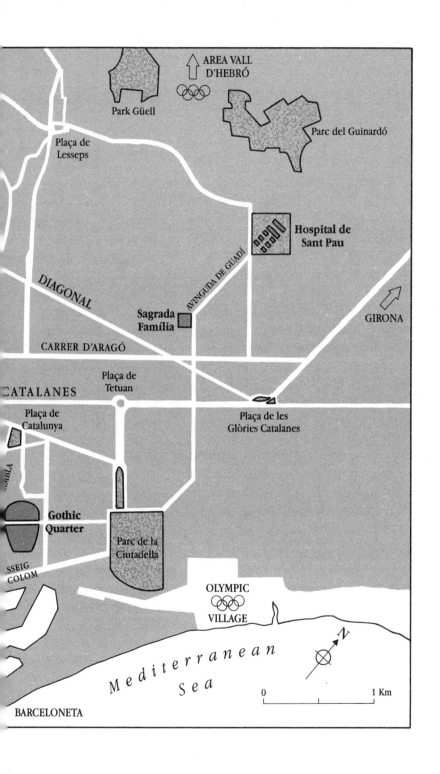

AREA VALL
D'HEBRÓ

Park Güell

Plaça de
Lesseps

Parc del Guinardó

DIAGONAL

AVINGUDA DE GUADÍ

Hospital de
Sant Pau

Sagrada
Família

CARRER D'ARAGÓ

Plaça de
Tetuan

CATALANES

GIRONA

Plaça de
Catalunya

Plaça de les
Glòries Catalanes

Gothic
Quarter

Parc de la
Ciutadella

SSEIG
COLOM

OLYMPIC

VILLAGE

Mediterranean
Sea

N

0   1 Km

BARCELONETA

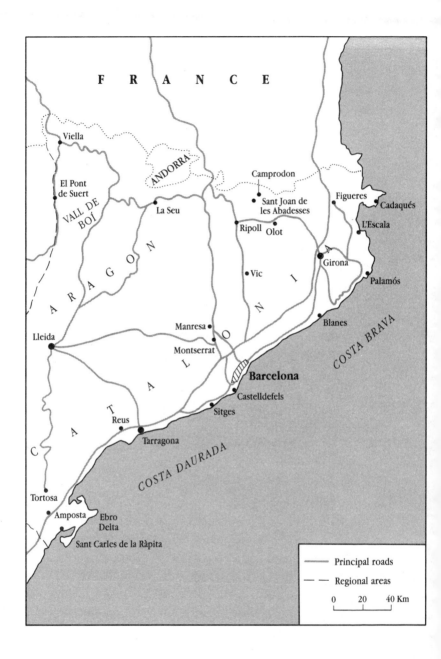

F R A N C E

Viella

El Pont
de Suert

VALL DE
BOÍ

ANDORRA

Camprodon

Sant Joan de
les Abadesses

Figueres

Cadaqués

La Seu

Ripoll   Olot

L'Escala

A R A G O N

Vic

Girona

Palamós

Manresa

Blanes

COSTA BRAVA

Lleida

Montserrat

L O N I

Barcelona

Castelldefels

Reus

Sitges

T

A

C

Tarragona

COSTA DAURADA

Tortosa

Amposta

Ebro
Delta

Sant Carles de la Ràpita

——— Principal roads

– – – Regional areas

0   20   40 Km

INTRODUCTION

This is a guidebook rather than a travelogue and should be treated as such. Chapters can be read or skipped according to your interests and needs. The first chapter is largely historical, though I suspect that most visitors to Barcelona will be indifferent to the exploits of the Romans and Visigoths. They may be only marginally more interested in the struggles for power during medieval times, but to appreciate the city and understand fully the complexity of the Catalan character, one must know something of the past. Chapter 2 is really the guts of the book and takes the reader on a tour of the streets and buildings of Barcelona. I have attempted to sample the whole range of architectural styles – from Romanesque, through Gothic to baroque and *modernista* – and where appropriate I have written about the architects as well as their creations.

There are many magnificent museums and galleries in Barcelona, few of which have decent catalogues. In Chapter 3 the contents of the main museums and galleries are described in some detail, though I have not attempted to reproduce, catalogue-like, a list of everything which can be seen. To some extent, the choices made here reflect my own likes and dislikes.

Chapter 4 is devoted to the parks, gardens and squares of Barcelona – the sorts of places in which you may wish to relax if you have spent the previous evenings investigating the contents of the chapter which follows. Chapter 5 looks at all manner of entertainment, from opera and the theatre to the old-fashioned dance halls and jazz. This chapter also describes

the folk traditions of the Catalans and the major festivals
which visitors might encounter. Some Barcelonans might quibble with the inclusion of sport in a chapter on entertainment –
football comes under the heading of religion for many – but I
have followed a discussion of spectator sport in Barcelona
with a survey of the city's sporting facilities.

Chapter 6 looks at a common preoccupation of all travellers:
food and drink. The Catalans have a very high opinion of
their cooking which, in my experience, is not entirely justified.
In this chapter I do my best to steer the visitor towards the
best of the regional dishes. Drink is a different matter:
Catalonia produces many excellent wines and champagnes,
which can be sampled cheaply in the city's wonderfully
atmospheric bars.

Catalonia is one of the loveliest corners of Europe and, its
coast aside, surprisingly neglected. Chapter 7 describes a handful of places of outstanding interest; some, like the charming
resort of Sitges, can be visited on a day-trip from Barcelona,
but most require – and deserve – somewhat longer. Each
would make an ideal destination for a weekend break. I have
been highly selective, and readers expecting descriptions of
such popular tourist attractions as Montserrat or the Costa
Brava may be disappointed by their absence. Between them,
the six areas described encompass the great variety of
landscapes and cultures on offer: from the rice-paddies and
salt pans of the Ebro Delta to the high valleys of the Pyrenees;
from the Roman ruins of Tarragona to the Romanesque
splendour of Sant Joan de les Abadesses.

The last section is a practical guide, covering such topics as
where to stay, where to eat and drink, and how to get around
Barcelona by public transport. I should point out that this
book was researched and written at a time of turmoil as
Barcelona prepared for the 1992 Olympic Games. This affected
the city in various ways. Vast construction projects were
underway, especially on Montjuïc and in the area known as
Poble Nou, where the Olympic Village has been built. At the
same time the city was attempting to come to grips with the

appalling problem of traffic congestion. It is too early to say whether the new roads, which at the time of my visits were being built, will make much difference. A further degree of uncertainty stems from the Catalan penchant for moving their museums and exhibitions from one building to another. If things are not what they seem – or where this book suggests they ought to be – then the Tourist Information Offices will be happy to help. One final point: in deference to native sensibilities, the names of streets, buildings, food and so forth are given in Catalan, not Spanish.

Within a few hours of arriving in Barcelona most visitors find themselves on the Ramblas, a tree-lined avenue of unusual beauty and liveliness. If you walk at a reasonable pace you can go from one end to the other – from the florid monument to Christopher Columbus to Plaça de Catalunya – in about fifteen minutes. But the chances are that you will take much longer, for there is always something to catch the attention: an intriguing building, or a street musician, or perhaps a political demonstration. In any case there are times in the early evening when the streets are so crowded that you can only proceed at a snail's pace. It is quieter, of course, at night, but even at three o'clock in the morning you will find people making their way home from the clubs and restaurants, or just sitting quietly beside the fountains.

There are, in fact, five Ramblas, each with its own name and possessing its own distinctive character. Rambla de Santa Mònica begins its journey away from the sea with the pretensions of being a square rather than a street. The central walkway seems too wide and the buildings on either side, though no smaller than those further up, appear timid and retiring. But soon the licentious sphincter of the Barri Xinès (China Town) squeezes the buildings closer together. Once past the Liceu (the Opera House), the stalls beneath the plane trees become more numerous: pet shops sell exotic parrots and prosaic pigeons, and the florists further up on Rambla de les Flors are decked out like chapels of rest. In the newsagents the

3

range of magazines and books is astonishing: there is plenty of pornography, but Nietzsche, Joyce and Lorca are here too, alongside daily newspapers in five or six languages.

Of the dozen or so alleys which plug the Ramblas into the surrounding city, no two are the same. One leads into a food market where you can buy everything from song thrushes to mussels raised in the local sewage outfall; another slides past an austere and untypically stiff building designed by Antoni Gaudí. Towards the top of the Ramblas the side streets head through a glitzy shopping area towards the Gothic cathedral; near the bottom, they curl through the slums where blacksmiths keep company with brothels.

When I think of the Ramblas now, I think first of the buildings: a score are memorable; nearly all are pleasing. There is the Església de Betlem with its curious, twisting-columned baroque façade, and beside it stands a handsome rococo palace, built in the 1770s for a Viceroy of Peru. Then there is the Poliorama, a theatre whose roofs are topped by an observatory and a couple of arabesque cupolas. During the Spanish Civil War George Orwell was holed up here for a few days. 'I used to sit marvelling at the folly of it all,' he wrote. 'From the little windows in the observatory you could see for miles around – vista after vista of tall slender buildings, glass domes and fantastic curly roofs with brilliant green and copper tiles.' Every now and then Orwell took pot shots at the communists who had taken refuge in the Café Moka opposite. No self-respecting communist would be seen dead there now: the Café Moka has been dressed in the cold and impersonal apparel of an international pizza parlour.

The small things on the Ramblas often please as much as the great. There is the lovely art nouveau shop front with its sinuous calligraphy on the corner with Carrer de la Petxina; and above a chemist's shop near the Poliorama a serpent embraces a child while it drinks from a chalice. A shabby little Virgin and child occupies an alcove in the façade of Hostal Parisian, and opposite the Opera House a lamp is suspended from the mouth of an oriental dragon. The wrought-iron street lamps are very fine indeed, and there are some attractive drinking fountains too.

However, it is the people who provide the Ramblas with their unique flavour. All life is here, from the stately and sedate to the seedy and salacious. Early in the morning, you can observe businessmen downing brandies before heading off to their offices; a couple of hours later, elderly ladies with dyed hair and powdered jowls meet to munch their way through sickly pastries. When evening comes the Ramblas seem to vibrate with excitement and expectation. At around the time the average Englishman is thinking of retiring for the night, the Catalans head for the opera, the cinema, the restaurants. When Rose Macaulay passed through Barcelona shortly after the Second World War she noted that 'the Barcelonese seem to shout, scream, blow horns, laugh, stare, crowd, chatter, hang out flags, all day and all night.' They still do.

The Ramblas provide theatre of the highest order, and many of its frequenters are here to see or be seen. Most ostentatious of all are the buskers: Bolivians playing Andean pipes; a 'Charlie Chaplin' mime artist; an elderly male cellist; a heavily tattooed man who treads broken glass and swallows swords; a squint-eyed lady whose bird-song imitations are as good as the real thing. Some of the buskers are perennial features; others are here one day and gone the next. Conspicuous, too, are the prostitutes who hang around the lower regions of the Ramblas, especially on the fringes of Plaça del Teatre. Ten years ago they used to gather by the score, all leg and lipstick, cajoling passers-by, smoking, chatting, laughing. Nowadays they seem thinner on the ground: apparently much of their business is done by telephone and credit card.

I notice that one American guidebook suggests that tourists should stay clear of the area. 'Many readers' it claims, 'have wisely tended to avoid the Ramblas recently because it's considered unsafe – the list of people who have been mugged in daylight is almost endless.' It is true that there are plenty of thieves on the streets (as long ago as the 1890s an English guidebook felt compelled to mention them) but your chances of being violently assaulted in Barcelona are much less than in many other Mediterranean ports. Marseilles and Naples – and, for that matter, New York – are in a different league when it comes to violent crime. You should take care, of course, especially in the Barri Xinès at night, but on no account allow fear to determine where you tread.

Once you have experienced the Ramblas – and you will continually return to them during your stay – it is time to discover other parts of Barcelona. How much you see will depend on your particular interests and the amount of time you can spend in the city. No attempt is made here to provide 'suggested itineraries', but the following guidelines may be of some help.

SHORT VISITS

2 DAYS

During the course of a day it is possible to see many of the great buildings in the medieval quarters, and it would be a shame to miss any of the following: the Gothic cathedral, the church of Santa Maria del Mar, the Drassanes shipyards, the Romanesque church of Sant Pau del Camp and the ancient hospital of Santa Creu. This little tour may sound like a religious pilgrimage, but if you make your way round these buildings you will see much else besides. Without making any great detours you could take in some exquisite squares on your journey: for example, the Plaça de Sant Jaume, overlooked by the superb Renaissance façade of the Generalitat; the tiny Plaça del Pi, a popular haunt of students and musicians; and Plaça Reial, whose neo-classical colonnades and *cerveseries* (beer houses) attract not only tourists, but derelicts and delinquents too (yes, do watch your wallet). A journey on foot between these buildings will introduce you to both the cobbled streets of the Barri Gòtic (the Gothic quarter) and the sleazy alleys of the Barri Xinès. As most buildings of interest close for lunch you will have plenty of time to refuel in the middle of the day. You might choose one of the pricey restaurants near the cathedral, or perhaps you will wash down some fish with a *porrón* of roughish wine in one of the many bars near the harbour.

If you have only one more day at your disposal, there are some awkward choices to be made. An interest in architecture will probably take you into the Eixample, the grid-pattern of streets laid down in the 19th century outside the walls of the old city. Here you will find most of the *modernista* buildings for which Barcelona is famous. The best known is Gaudí's unfinished and possibly unfinishable modern cathedral, the Sagrada Familia. This is closely followed in popularity by four extraordinary buildings on the Passeig de Gràcia, all within walking distance of the Plaça de Catalunya. Three of them – one by Antoni Gaudí, one by Lluís Domènech i Montaner, one by Josep Puig i Cadafalch – stand together on the same block. The other, Gaudí's wavy-balconied Casa Milà, is further up towards the Diagonal. My favourite building of this *fin-de-siècle* period is seldom visited by tourists: Domènech's Hospital de Sant Creu i Sant Pau, which is some ten minutes' walk from the Sagrada Familia, strikes me as being one of the closest things to perfection built this century.

Were you to spend your two days in the manner suggested above, you would see little or nothing of the city's many fine galleries or museums. Consequently, you may wish to forgo all the *modernista* architecture – with the exception, I suggest, of the Sagrada Familia, a visit to which is obligatory, even for cultural philistines. It would be possible, in the course of one day, to visit the following: the Museu Picasso (the Picasso Museum) in the old city; and the Museu d'Art de Catalunya (the Catalan Museum of Art) and the Fundació Joan Miró (the Miró Foundation) on the slopes of Montjuïc, the hill which looms above the port to the south of the city.

A Visit of a Week

I suggest that you begin your week by getting an overall impression of the city and its layout. The best way to do this is by getting above it. From the mirador of the Columbus monument you can see everything with great clarity: the green seam of plane trees snaking up the Ramblas to the Plaça de Catalunya, with the medieval quarters to either side; the Eixample beyond with the ceramic-clad spires of the Sagrada Familia towering above the grey roofscape; and in the distance, topped by a wedding cake of a church, the hill of Tibidabo, where the Devil is said to have tempted Christ with promises of earthly wealth. Turn to your left and you will see the wooded hill of Monjuïc rising up from the Avinguda del Paral·lel, one of Barcelona's red-light districts; if you look the other way, towards the north-east, you will see the Passeig de Colom, a busy, scruffy, palm-lined street, running along the quayside to the park of Ciutadella. Turn your back on the city and you have the angular sprawl of the vast harbour, with the old fishermen's quarters of Barceloneta at one end and a jungle of hoppers and cranes at the other.

There are also fine views of the city to be had from the two hills, Monjuïc and Tibidabo. There is so much of interest to see on the former that you are bound to get there sooner or later. But there is another good reason why the visitor should head for one or other, or both of these. Barcelona has two great faults: infernal noise and choking pollution. The motor car, of which the Catalans are disgracefully enamoured, is largely responsible for both. The city possesses a superb public transport system – buses and tubes are cheap, efficient and graffiti-free – yet the locals will hop in their cars for the briefest of journeys. To escape the noise and pollution you must head for the hills.

A week is long enough to form more than a passing acquaintance with a city of Barcelona's size. You will be able to see everything mentioned in the section above, though at a more leisurely pace, and this will still leave three or four days to fill. There is a variety of attractions to tempt the visitor into the suburbs. These range from the Gothic monastery at Pedralbes to Gaudí's remarkable Park Güell, a failed garden-city inspired by the ideas of English utopians, and the 18th-century garden at Horta, with its Palladian temples and shabby maze. A trip to Barcelona would certainly be incomplete without a visit to Ciutadella Park, and you should visit Barceloneta, if for no better reason than to sample the seafood in its many restaurants. There are any number of ways to pass the evenings and I know of no other city of comparable size as lively as Barcelona. It is blessed with a great many cinemas and theatres and more than its fair share of concert halls. I suggest that on your arrival you find out what events are on – either from the tourist offices or the weekly publication, *El Guía del Ocio* – and book tickets well in advance, especially for the opera, evening concerts and major football matches.

I:

THE CATALANS
AND THEIR PAST

Catalonia occupies an area of some 12,000 sq mi (32,000 sq km) in the north-east corner of Spain. Roughly triangular in shape, it is somewhat larger than Belgium, and rather smaller than Switzerland. The region possesses over 300 mi (500 km) of Mediterranean coastline, stretching from the French border to a little way south of the Ebro Delta. In the north Catalonia is dominated by the jagged Pyrenees and their foothills. The interior boasts a great variety of landscapes, ranging from irrigated plains to rolling hills clothed in pine, carob and oak. The classic Mediterranean trinity of wheat, olive and vine is augmented by vast orchards producing apricots, apples and pears. Catalonia is divided into 38 districts, or *comarques*; 11 come within the influence of the province of Barcelona, and the others are shared between the provinces of Tarragona, Lleida and Girona. The population stands at around 6 million, over three-quarters of whom live in Barcelona and its surrounding districts.

Catalonia is the most prosperous region in Spain outside Madrid, accounting for a fifth of the country's gross domestic product and a quarter of Spanish industrial output. Indeed, the Industrial Revolution first made itself felt on the Iberian Peninsula in Catalonia. While the rest of Spain, with the exception perhaps of the Basque Country, remained under the yoke of agrarian – and conservative – interests, Barcelona was developing all the attributes of a progressive, industrial society. 'Barcelona is one of the finest and certainly the most manufacturing city of Spain,' wrote Richard Ford, an English traveller who came this way in the 1840s. 'It is the Manchester of Catalonia, which is the Lancashire of the Peninsula.'

The Catalans are always keen to distance themselves from the rest of Spain, and in many ways they have more in common with their North European neighbours than with their Castilian-speaking compatriots further south. The Catalans are renowned, among other things, for their business acumen; during medieval times their merchants controlled trade throughout the western Mediterranean, and, like the Swiss, they make good bankers. Catalans are undoubtedly more efficient and reliable than the Spaniards of, say, Seville or Madrid: when they say *mañana* (or its Catalan equivalent) they actually mean it. They have a reputation in the rest of Spain for being tight-fisted, though Catalans consider themselves prudent rather than mean. However, what distinguishes the Catalans most from other Spaniards is their language; their affection for it is based not on its aesthetic virtues – it has none – but on the fact that it supports their contention that they are a race apart.

While Richard Ford admitted to a certain admiration of Catalan industry, he much preferred the more aristocratic world to the south. Catalonia, he wrote in *Handbook for Travellers in Spain*, was no place for a man of pleasure, taste or literature. He thought the lower orders brutal 'when compared to the frivolous Valencian or the gay Andalusian', and he complained that they lacked the good manners of the high-bred peasants of central Spain. Nor was he impressed by the women: 'In general they are on a large scale, neither handsome nor amiable.' But what galled him most was the belligerence of the Catalans: 'No province of the unamalgamating bundle which forms the conventional monarchy of Spain hangs more loosely to the crown than Catalonia, the classical country of revolt, which is ever ready to fly off: rebellious and republican, well may the natives wear the blood-coloured cap of the much prostituted name of liberty.' To understand why the Catalans have always considered themselves a separate people – and acted accordingly, and sometimes violently – one needs to know a little of the region's past history.

*

The Greeks set up trading colonies on the Catalan coast in the 6th century BC, the main one being at Empúries, the ruins of which can still be seen near L'Escala, a fishing village on the Costa Brava. The Carthaginian conquest of Spain, which began in 239 BC, was short-lived: having agreed with the Romans that they would remain to the south of the Ebro River, the Carthaginians incurred Rome's displeasure by attacking Sagunto, and insult was added to impudence when Hannibal crossed the Pyrenees and headed east. The Second Punic War began in 219 BC, and a year later Roman forces landed at Empúries. The Carthaginians were driven south and eventually off the Iberian Peninsula altogether. At first the Romans ruled the area from the town of Béziers, 75 mi north of the present border with France, but later Catalonia became part of the Roman province of Tarraconense, and Augustus made Tarraco, now Tarragona, the capital.

The Roman colony of Iulia Augusta Paterna Faventia Barcino – the forerunner of Barcelona – was a modest affair compared to Tarraco. It was poorly defended and, in AD 263, was destroyed by the Franks. It was later retaken by the Romans, who built thick, defensive walls, parts of which can still be seen. By the time the Roman Empire collapsed at the beginning of the 5th century, Christianity was well established throughout the region and Barcelona was a town of some significance. The Visigoths took Barcelona in 415, some sixty years before the final collapse of the Roman Empire, and their rule persisted until the Moorish invasion in the early years of the 8th century. In 801 the Moors were driven out of Barcelona by the Franks, though they held on to the areas immediately to the south and west – around Tortosa and Lleida – until midway through the 12th century. Not that peace always prevailed: al-Mansur, the vizier of Córdoba, raided Barcelona in 989; and in 1010 the Catalans got their own back by raiding Córdoba.

Barcelona's modern history really begins in the year 878. This was when the House of Barcelona – which was to endure for half a millennium – was established by Guifré el Pilós (or Wilfred the Hairy). Guifré, count of Urgell and Cerdanya, conquered and united surrounding districts once the Frankish king, Charles the Bald, had granted independence to the area. The House of Barcelona gradually extended its influence over a large chunk of what is now southern France and north-east Spain. Some areas were taken by force; some were purchased; others were taken through marriage alliances. It was the latter which brought together the territory held by the counts of Barcelona and the kingdom of Aragon. In 1137 Count Ramón Berenguer IV of Barcelona married Petronilla, the queen of Aragon, and the two nations were joined together, though each maintained its parliament and its *usatges*, or privileges. Shortly after this union took place the Moors were expelled from Lleida and Tortosa.

During the rule of Jaume I (1213–76) much land was lost to the north of the Pyrenees, but conquests were made elsewhere. The island of Mallorca was taken in 1229, Ibiza in 1235 and the kingdom of Valencia by 1238, and expansion continued after Jaume I's death, with Sicily, Malta and Sardinia all falling to the Catalan–Aragonese crown.

Jaume I set up parliaments, know as *Corts*, in each of the four confederated states: Aragon, Catalonia, Valencia and Mallorca. Representatives of the nobility, clergy and urban citizenry made up the three *braços* (arms) of the Corts. The cities had their own governing bodies, Barcelona's being the Consell de Cent (Council of One Hundred). During the following century the Corts established an administrative body capable of collecting taxes: this was the Diputació del General or the Generalitat. In 1364 the Generalitat was given a permanent home in Barcelona, and over the years its powers and functions expanded. The present Generalitat, re-established after a lapse of thirty-nine years as Catalonia's autonomous government by the new Spanish Constitution of 1978, is a direct descendant of the tax-gathering body set up in 1354 during the reign of Pere III.

Jaume I is best remembered for his policies of expansion; it was during his reign that the world's first maritime code, written in Catalan, was established. However, Jaume did much to change the shape of Barcelona too. By the 13th century, the city was suffering from appalling overcrowding and the king ordered new walls to be built well beyond the confines of the old Roman city. Over the next hundred years medieval Barcelona became a centre of Gothic magnificence, and many of its finest monuments date from that period: the cathedral, the Drassanes shipyards, the church of Santa Maria del Mar, the monastery of Pedralbes, the hospital of Santa Creu . . .

The House of Barcelona eventually ceased to exist in 1410, when the last of its line, Martí I (the Humane), died without issue. By then there were already signs that Catalonia was heading for a period of decline. Her strength and resources had been weakened by wars abroad – especially with the Genovese – and by rebellion in some of the conquered lands, while disease, rural depopulation and violence in the cities had taken their toll at home. Under the 1412 Casp Agreement a Castilian prince, Fernando I, was elected to the Catalan–Aragonese crown; not surprisingly, he viewed the world through Castilian eyes and came into conflict with Catalan institutions, as did his son and heir, Alfonso V (the Magnanimous). In 1432 Alfonso left Barcelona; two years later he conquered Naples, whose territory stretched from near Rome to the southern tip of the Italian mainland. Before he left, the Palau de la Generalitat was built behind the cathedral; and soon after, the university was founded.

The 15th century ended disastrously for Barcelona. In 1462 Catalonia rose against the Spanish king, Joan II. Eventually the rebellion was put down and Barcelona fell in 1473. Much of the city was reduced to ruins and its inhabitants were subjected to an inquisition. In 1492 the Jews were expelled from Spain – they had been persecuted for well over a century – and in the same year Christopher Columbus discovered America. Spanish eyes now turned away from the Mediterranean – which had increasingly become the stamping ground of the Turks – and towards the Americas. Under a codicil in Queen Isabel's will, Catalan merchants were excluded from the new trading opportunities to be had across the Atlantic.

Since then the relationship between Catalonia and the rest of Spain has always been uneasy, and frequently turbulent. The Catalan national anthem, 'Els Segadors', dates from the War of the Reapers (*Els Segadors*), which was really a side show to the Thirty Years War between Spain and France. A popular revolt broke out on 7 June 1640, sparked off by the poor behaviour of Castilian troops billeted in Catalonia. There were other more powerful grievances: the Catalans resented both conscription and the taxes imposed to finance the war; they also felt that the king, Felip IV, had ignored their *usatges*, or privileges. Under the leadership of Pau Claris, the president of the Generalitat, Catalonia renounced its allegiance to the king and declared itself a republic under Louis XIII of France. Twelve years later, having found that the French were also poor masters, Catalonia returned to the Castilian bosom, but Felip IV ceded Catalan territory to the north of the Pyrenees to the French.

The early years of the 18th century witnessed the long War of the Spanish Succession. Catalonia joined the English to side with Archduke Charles of Austria against the Bourbon pretender, Philip of Anjou, who was supported by the French and Spanish. The latter won, and Barcelona surrendered to Philip's forces in 1714. From thenceforth Catalonia became a province of Spain: the Catalan language was suppressed, the autonomous government institutions were disbanded and the university was banished. Some 10,000 people were evicted from Barcelona's Ribera district, and a fortress – La Ciutadella – was built on the site of their homes. From here the occupying forces were able to subdue the citizenry.

Despite these setbacks, the 18th century was a period of great expansion for Catalonia, and especially for the emerging industrial metropolis of Barcelona, where a flourishing textile industry developed. In 1778 the trade embargo with the

Americas was revoked, thus fuelling the demand for textiles and other manufactured goods. The 19th century began inauspiciously with the War of Independence, but in 1814, and with the help of the English, the Napoleonic armies were driven out of Spain and the city continued with its rapid rate of industrialization. Large numbers of people from the neighbouring countryside – southern France and south and central Spain – came in search of work, and the arrival of rail connections in the 1840s further hastened the growth of the city.

In Barcelona, as in Manchester, cotton was king. Those who profited most were the industrial bourgeoisie, and we owe them a debt of gratitude: they commissioned and supported many of the buildings and institutions which made Barcelona such a important centre, both for commerce and the arts. However, they were as much to blame as central government for the violent political events which periodically shook the city. The poverty among the working classes was considerable; crammed into appalling slums, they worked long hours for little pay, and it wasn't until 1907 that laws forbidding use of child labour were introduced. Overcrowding led to frequent outbreaks of diseases like cholera, and riots, whether caused by industrial unrest or hunger, were a common feature of city life. By 1850 Barcelona's population had risen to 180,000, and the central authorities in Madrid, having hitherto restricted settlements outside the city walls, agreed that they should now be removed. In 1859 they approved a plan by the engineer Ildefons Cerdà for a grid-pattern extension – the Eixample; work eventually got underway after the revolution of 1868, when the Bourbon dynasty was overthrown by General Prim. The medieval walls were dismantled and Barcelona gradually spread to coalesce with the outlying townships of Sants, Sarrià, Gràcia and Sant Gervasi. By 1900 the population of Barcelona was over half a million; immigration and the expansion of the city limits led it to double again by 1930.

Tension between the rich and the poor – and between the

predominantly right-wing parties supported by the bourgeoisie and the revolutionary groups which appealed to the working class – was never far from the surface. In the 1880s and 1890s the city experienced a number of bombings, including one in November 1893 at the Opera house: 20 people were killed, and many were injured, when a bomb was thrown during a performance of *William Tell*. Such acts led to Barcelona being known as 'the city of bombs', and they were invariably followed by a wave of repression. After his visit, Richard Ford had suggested that 'while they [the Catalans] tremble to disobey a monk-enjoined form, they do not scruple to kill a man.' Such respect for the cowl and cross was singularly absent during Setmana Tràgica (Tragic Week) when a strike, organized in protest at the government mobilizing troops to fight in Morocco, turned into an anti-clerical riot: over 60 churches and religious buildings were set on fire, and more than 100 people were killed.

That the Catalan language survived its proscription following the Bourbon conquest of 1714 was largely thanks to the working classes: the bourgeoisie and intelligentsia switched to Castilian Spanish, but for the workers Catalan remained the *lingua franca*. However, interest in the Catalan language among the educated classes was rekindled in the 1830s with the arrival in Catalonia of the Romantic movement, which gave rise to the Renaixença (the Catalan Renaissance). Although the Renaixença began as a literary movement – one of the pioneer spirits was the poet Jacint Verdaguer, who participated in the early Jocs Florals, the annual poetry festivals similar to the Welsh Eisteddfod – its influence spread throughout the arts and it became the seed-bed from which sprang one of the most remarkable artistic movements in recent times: *modernisme*. In the field of architecture, *modernisme*'s best-known practitioners were Antoni Gaudí, Lluís Domènech i Montaner and Josep Puig i Cadafalch. Among the artists Ramon Casas and Santiago Rusiñol were outstanding. *Modernisme* is sometimes thought of as a Catalan version of art nouveau, but it was much more than an aesthetic movement: if not quite an ideology, it sought – whether through art, architecture or literature – to reflect the region's progressive aspirations without forsaking the achievements of the past. It is no coincidence that two of the great *modernistas*, Domènech i Montaner and Puig i Cadafalch, were important figures in the political struggle for self-determination.

Catalan political history has always been a complicated affair, dauntingly so around the turn of the century with political parties mutating like fruit flies. They were less promiscuous with their ideas than with their names and most of the key groups were politically to the right. Among the more significant parties was the Unió Catalanista. This was formed in 1891, and one of its first presidents was Domènech i Montaner. The Unió Regionalista, founded in 1901, soon became the Lliga Regionalista, one of its co-founders being Puig i Cadafalch. The Lliga's right-wing views were not to everyone's taste, and many working-class people were attracted by the republicanism of Alejandro Lerroux, a charismatic demagogue from Andalucia. In 1906 an attempt was made to bring all the Catalan parties under one umbrella, the idea being that the Solidaritat Catalana would occupy the seats reserved for Catalonia in the national parliament, Madrid's Cortes. Lerroux refused to be party to the alliance, which soon fell apart.

After Setmana Tràgica, the Tragic Week of 1909, the Confederació Nacional del Trebell (the National Workers' Confederation) was founded. The CNT brought together various trade union and anarchist groups and by 1914 it had as many members as the long-established Unión General de Trabajadores. The CNT refused to deal with any political parties and was perpetually at loggerheads with the establishment. However, the yearning for a degree of self-government was to some extent satisfied by the founding of the Mancommunitat, the union of Catalonia's four provincial councils; its political powers were feeble, but it was able to carry out important projects in such fields as health, education and

transport. Its founder and first president was Enric Prat de la
Riba. He was succeeded, on his death in 1917, by Puig i
Cadafalch.

Puig was still in charge when Miguel Primo de Rivera led a
successful military coup in 1923. The Lliga Regionalista hoped
that the new dictator would help defeat terrorism (some of
which was sponsored by the CNT) and give Catalonia a
greater degree of political autonomy. Instead he abolished the
Mancommunitat and banned the public use of the Catalan
language. The dictatorship fell in 1930; a year later the king,
who had supported Primo de Rivera, went into exile. In the
municipal elections in Catalonia the left-wing Esquerra
Republicana de Catalunya, led by Fransesc Macià and Lluís
Companys, triumphed over the right-wing Lliga. Macià rather
overreached himself by declaring Catalonia an independent
state within 'the Federation of Iberian Republics'. No such
federation existed, and Macià was forced by central government to renounce – or at least tone down – Catalonia's
separatist claims. However, Madrid did allow the Catalans to
re-establish their Generalitat. The elections of 1934 brought a
right-wing government back into power in Madrid, and it
soon came into conflict with Catalonia's left-wing Generalitat.
With the support of the trade unions, the Generalitat agitated
for greater independence, and as a result its president, Lluís
Companys, and leaders were imprisoned. In 1936 there was
another round of elections. This time victory went to a left-
wing coalition: Companys and his colleagues were released
from prison and the Statute of Autonomy, suspended since
1934, became operational once more. In July 1936 a military
insurrection, led by General Franco, sparked off the Spanish
Civil War; the Generalitat helped to mobilize the people in the
fight against fascism.

For those who wish to catch the flavour of the period, two
books are indispensable: George Orwell's *Homage to
Catalonia* and Ernest Hemingway's *For Whom the Bell
Tolls*. A less partisan analysis (both writers fought on the

losing Republican side), and a more detailed study, is Hugh Thomas's *The Spanish Civil War*. Orwell fought on the front in Aragon; he also wrote about his experiences in Barcelona. One can easily spend a couple of days visiting the streets and buildings he mentioned, most of which are still standing. However, British fascination with the Spanish Civil War, especially among the literati and those with left-wing leanings, is not widely shared among Catalans, most of whom would rather forget the war and its consequences.

Orwell arrived in 1936 to find the nearest thing to an anarchist city that the world had ever known: 'It was the first time that I had ever been in a town where the working class was in the saddle,' he wrote. 'Practically every building of any size had been seized by the workers and was draped with red flags or with the red and black flag of the Anarchists; every wall was scrawled with the hammer and sickle and with the initials of the revolutionary parties; almost every church had been gutted and its images burnt . . . Every shop and cafe had an inscription saying that it had been collectivized; even the bootblacks had been collectivized and their boxes painted red or black.'

Barcelona fell to General Franco in 1939. It is not known how many Catalans died during the period of persecution which followed his victory. Some politicians escaped to France; others were executed. In 1940 the Vichy government handed Lluís Companys back to Franco and he was executed in Montjuïc Castle. The public use of the Catalan language was banned once again, and so was the performing of the Catalan national dance, the *sardana*. Franco hoped that the steady stream of immigrants, pouring into Catalonia from other parts of Spain, would have a diluting influence and further undermine the Catalan spirit. Somewhere in the region of 750,000 immigrants, many from the relatively impoverished regions of Andalusia and Extremadura, came to Barcelona in the 1950s and 1960s. A certain amount of liberalization occurred during the 1970s but it was only after the death of Franco in 1975 that Catalonia was once more able to openly flex its political muscles. Juan Carlos I was declared king and he has proved to be a great friend of democracy. A new, liberal constitution was adopted in 1978 and this allowed for considerable devolution of power.

In 1980 Catalonia's Statute of Autonomy was approved by parliament. Once again, the Generalitat was back in business. Under the 1983 Language Normalization Law, the Generalitat declared Catalan the usual language of local government and education. It also guaranteed the right to use Castilian Spanish, and to be addressed by officials in that language. It is claimed that 64 per cent of the region's 6 million inhabitants can speak Catalan, and that 90 per cent understand it. Catalan is also spoken by half the people of Valencia, the region to the south of Catalonia, and by many of the inhabitants of the Balearic Isles.

The passing of Franco was a cause for great jubilation in Catalonia, but a long period of economic stagnation was to follow. The textile industry was particularly hard hit, and unemployment rose from 2.7 per cent of the workforce in 1975 to 21 per cent by 1986. Catalonia's economic recovery, which began during the mid-eighties following a painful period of readjustment, has been boosted by heavy injections of foreign investment, especially from the Japanese. Most significant of all has been the rapid expansion of the construction sector, whose activity more than doubled during 1988; unemployment is now back below 15 per cent. By the end of the decade Barcelona was gripped by a consumer boom the likes of which it had never known. Catalans bought 200,000 new cars in 1988 alone – one for every fifteen people between the ages of 20 and 60 – and within a period of four years property prices doubled.

From time to time Barcelona puts on an extraordinary public display, to which the rest of the world is cordially invited. The first of these in modern times was the Universal Exhibition of 1888, a glorified trade fair which took place in Ciutadella Park. Among the temporary buildings constructed for the Exhibition was Domènech i Montaner's Gran Hotel International, with accommodation for 2,000 visitors. It was constructed in a mere 53 days, and among those drawn to the site was the young Puig i Cadafalch, who was later to remark that he saw here his 'first vision of that great Barcelona for which we are all working'. Puig was one of the key figures in the replanning of the city for the International Exhibition of 1929: 40,000 labourers were taken on to build the exhibition centres, many of which are still standing on the slopes of Montjuïc, and the city's metro system dates from this period. Even greater physical changes have been wrought recently during the preparations for the 1992 Olympic Games. But the significance of events such as these goes far beyond their physical impact on the city. In each case the people of Barcelona are reaffirming – often, it seems, against the tide of history – faith in themselves and their culture. Today the politicians and planners are fond of referring to Barcelona as Metròpolis Mediterrània, almost as though the city had retained its maritime influence of medieval times. Outsiders will probably forgive the conceit: Barcelona really is a remarkable city.

2:
A CITY GUIDE:
STREETS AND BUILDINGS

THE GOTHIC QUARTER

The lemon-shaped **Barri Gòtic** (Gothic quarter) lies at the heart of Barcelona. It takes about five minutes to walk from one end to the other, but one could spend days exploring the magnificent buildings and alleys in this area. The term 'Gothic quarter' is rather misleading: there are many Gothic buildings outside its boundaries, and there are many other than Gothic within. The Gothic age, which spanned some 200 years, stretching from midway through the 13th century to well into the 15th, coincided with a period of great expansion for Barcelona, which became one of the Mediterranean's foremost ports. Few cities have preserved so admirably their medieval quarters, and wandering through the Barri Gòtic's narrow streets one feels that little has changed over the centuries.

The Barri Gòtic lies within the area bounded by the old Roman walls. The Roman city occupied the hill of Mons Taber, where Augustus established the colony of Barcino, remnants of which have survived to the present day. There are some impressive stretches of wall, particularly along the northern side of the old city, and four Corinthian columns can be seen from the lobby of what is now the headquarters of the Centre Excursionista de Catalunya at Carrer de Paradis 10. There were two main streets running through the Roman city, and these met at the Forum. This remains the political centre of Barcelona with two government buildings, the Ajuntament de Barcelona (city hall) and the Palau de la Generalitat

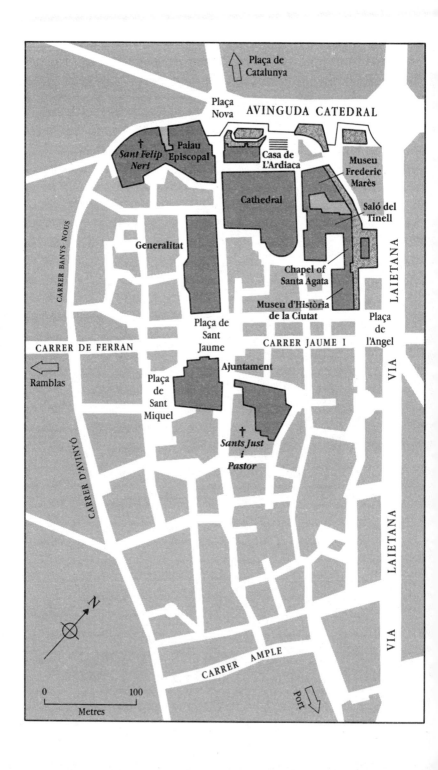

Plaça de
Catalunya

Plaça
Nova

AVINGUDA CATEDRAL

† Sant Felip Neri

Palau Episcopal

Casa de
L'Ardiaca

Museu
Frederic
Marès

Cathedral

Saló del
Tinell

Generalitat

CARRER BANYS NOUS

Chapel of
Santa Agata

Museu d'Història
de la Ciutat

Plaça de
Sant
Jaume

CARRER JAUME I

Plaça
de
l'Angel

CARRER DE FERRAN

LAIETANA

Ramblas

Ajuntament

Plaça
de
Sant
Miquel

VIA

CARRER D'AVINYÓ

† Sants Just i Pastor

LAIETANA

VIA

N

0   100

Metres

CARRER AMPLE

Port

(regional government), facing one another across the Plaça de Sant Jaume.

A good starting point for a tour of the Barri Gòtic is **Plaça Nova**. Here the only jarring sight is the modern Architects' College, which stands across the square from the cathedral. The frieze by Pablo Picasso does little to improve this ugly building. Over recent years the square and the adjoining Avinguda de la Catedral have been despoiled – albeit temporarily – by an archaeological dig which has uncovered remains from the Roman city as well as more recent sewers and drains. One of the best times to come here is on Sunday evening when hundreds gather to dance the *sardana* in Plaça de la Seu, the paved area immediately in front of the cathedral. This slow dance, accompanied by a twelve-man wind orchestra, is mesmerically monotonous and much enjoyed by both young and old (*see* page 163).

Barcelona's **Gothic cathedral**, which is dedicated to the Holy Cross and Santa Eulàlia, stands on a site which has known a succession of important religious buildings. First, there was a pagan temple; then came a church which was destroyed by al-Mansur during the Moorish raids of the 10th century; and later there was a Romanesque building, elements of which have been incorporated into the present cathedral. When Richard Ford came to Barcelona in the 1840s the cathedral looked very different from today. 'The principal façade *ésta por acabar*,' he wrote, 'is only painted in stucco, which is a disgrace to the chapter, who for three centuries received a fee on every marriage, for this very purpose of completing it.' There is now a good Gothic façade, built between 1885 and 1915 to a design of the early 15th century.

The first stone of the cathedral was laid in 1298 and the work was largely complete by 1423, when the dome was built. The cathedral has a high nave which is flanked by aisles of the same height. An ambulatory runs round the back of the altar and there are over a score of side chapels between the buttresses. Above the false transept – one arm leads to Sant Iu's door and the street; the other leads into the cloister – there are two octagonal bell-towers. In the centre of the nave there is a large choir, which to my mind detracts from the fine Gothic proportions of the cathedral; and between this and the altar are the steps down to the crypt, where lie the remains of the martyred Santa Eulàlia.

Light filters into the interior through the small windows of the clerestory. One's first, and perhaps lasting, impression is that the blind triforium is too large, and that the clerestory windows are too small to light the beautiful interior. The piers are slender and one's eyes are drawn inexorably upwards to the lofty ceiling, whose rib vaulting is punctuated by bosses of extraordinary size. Although the choir blocks the view of the altar for those entering by the main portal, it is nevertheless of great interest. The rear of the choir (the *trascoro*) is decorated with marble bas-reliefs which tell of Santa Eulàlia's life. These are the work of Bartolomé Ordoñez and Pere Villar, who were among the great sculptors of the Spanish Renaissance; they were begun in 1517. The wooden stalls inside the choir are surmounted by gilded coats of arms belonging to the Knights of the Golden Fleece, who were assembled here in 1519, for the first and last time in Spain, by Charles V and Archduke Maximilian of Austria.

One glossy guide to Barcelona suggests that 'Everything – the 26 chapels, the sacristy, the crypt with the sarcophagus of the saint, the lovely cloister – is to be carefully visited.' This, I think, is an exaggeration: many of the side chapels are of little interest other than to ecclesiastical historians (and possibly worshippers). Among the chapels, of more than passing interest is the one dedicated to San Ollegarius near the main entrance. Above the altar is a 16th-century wooden crucifix known as the *Santo Cristo de Lepanto*, which is said to have been carried at the Battle of Lepanto on the flagship of Don Juan of Austria (*see* page 55). Most of the chapels contain retables of the 16th to the 18th centuries in a variety of styles from Gothic to Renaissance and baroque. Many are in a poor state of repair.

The cathedral contains several notable sarcophagi. Special mention should be made of those belonging to Ramón Berenguer I and his wife Almodis, which are to be found to the right of the main altar. In the chapel next to Sant Iu's door lies the Gothic sarcophagus of Bishop Ramón de Escales, who died in 1398. However, the sarcophagus of greatest interest is the one in the crypt which supposedly contains the body of Santa Eulàlia, who was put to death on 12 February 304 by Dacian. Her soul is believed to have ascended into heaven in the form of a dove and her body was said to have been revealed to Bishop Frodoyno in 878 by its scent. 'The original body of Santa Eulàlia', wrote Richard Ford, 'is the gem of Barcelona; the number of miracles it has worked, and is working, is quite incredible ... Thus, June 1st 1844, when Isabel and Christina arrived in Barcelona at half past ten at night, seasick and tired, they, instead of going to bed, remained until twelve o'clock worshipping Santa Eulàlia.'

The cathedral treasury is housed in the sacristy, which is entered by a small door near the sarcophagi of Ramón Berenguer and his wife. Among the objects to be seen here is a 15th-century reliquary which is decorated with the collar of the Order of the Golden Fleece. This belonged to Charles V. The organ is situated above Sant Iu's door in the north transept; there are some curious Saracen heads, carved from wood, affixed to its base.

The Gothic cathedral is an attempt by man to imitate the celestial city, and nowhere does one feel this more keenly than in the cloister at Barcelona. It is predominantly Gothic in style, having been built in the 14th and 15th centuries, though it also contains Romanesque elements: for example, the portal of San Severo. The sounds of the cloister are rustic and harmonious: there is the constant bubble and trickle of the small fountains, and twelve white geese honk raucously throughout the day. Some believe that these geese are a symbol of Santa Eulàlia's purity; others claim that they are a reminder of Barcelona's Roman origins. At the heart of the cloister grow orange trees, oleanders and pines; there is also a small public lavatory.

Attached to the cloister is the **Chapter Hall**, which houses the Museu Catedral. It is worth paying the small fee to see a magnificent painting of *La Pietat* by Bartolomé Bermajo (1490). There are several other paintings, and a 15th-century altarpiece dedicated to Sant Bernadino by Jaume Huguet. The large marble font in the shape of a four-leaf clover dates from the 11th century and was originally in the Romanesque cathedral. There is also a wooden chair designed by Antoni Gaudí, the great *modernista* architect. You can leave the cloister by way of the Romanesque chapel of Santa Llúcia.

Immediately opposite the chapel stands **El Casa de L'Ardiaca** (the Archdeacon's House). This is a Gothic building dating from the end of the 15th century, although it incorporates a Roman aqueduct and it was built on the old Roman walls. The building, which was remodelled half a century after its completion, was constructed as the residence for Archdeacon Desplà, who commissioned for his oratory the *La Pietat* in the cathedral museum. It now contains the city's historical archives.

From here it is just a short walk to one of Barcelona's most exquisite squares, **Plaça de Sant Felip Neri**. To get there you must skirt around the Palau Episcopal along a tiny alley. Like many of the city's small squares, it is at its most atmospheric either early in the morning or late at night, when there is seldom a soul around. Dominating the square is the baroque façade of the **church of Sant Felip Neri**. The church's neo-classical altar dates from 1778. The other two buildings of note in this small square are both from the Renaissance period and both guild houses – one for the coppersmiths, and one for the shoemakers. These buildings were removed from their original locations in Plaça Lesseps and Carrer de Corribia. Behind the church, and stretching back to Plaça Nova, is the **Palau Episcopal** (Bishop's Palace), an austere-looking building whose origins lie in the 14th century but much of which has been restored and remodelled since then. Today it houses the public episcopal archives.

From here I suggest you make your way round the cathedral

to the complex of mostly Gothic buildings along Carrer dels Comtes de Barcelona and **Plaça del Rei**. The latter, as its name suggests, is the courtyard of the royal palace, the **Palau Reial Major**, which was constructed on the old Roman walls. The palace consists of a chapel, which is dedicated to Santa Agata, and the magnificent Saló del Tinell, both of which can be approached by way of a flight of stairs in the corner of Plaça del Rei. During medieval times the square supported a regular cattle market, and indeed one feels that it could do with some humanizing commercial activity today. It is enormously impressive, but somewhat bleak in character. One is immediately struck by the massive archways along the side of the Saló del Tinell and by the remarkable five-storey Renaissance tower of Rei Martí. The chapel has a slender octagonal belfry whose jagged apex is covered by sprouting weeds. Gothic gargoyles of macabre character watch down upon the square from the Palau Lloctinent opposite.

Both the **chapel of Santa Agata** and the **Saló del Tinell** are used today for temporary exhibitions. The chapel is a Gothic construction dating from 1319; it has a single nave and an ornate wooden ceiling. There is a fine 15th-century altarpiece depicting the Epiphany (the manifestation of Christ to the wise men) by Jaume Huguet. The adjoining Saló del Tinell – the great hall of the Palau Reial Major – was completed in 1370. During its lifetime it has had a variety of functions. It was used during the 15th century as a court for the Inquisition, and it was here that Christopher Columbus, returning to Barcelona in 1493 after his discovery of the New World, was received by Fernando and Isabel. Later, in 1716, it was turned into a baroque church, and in 1940 it was bought by the municipality and restored to its original form. The hall has a span of 56 feet (17 metres) and the wooden ceiling is supported by six awesome diaphragm arches. The galleried tower above was added in 1557.

The chapel can also be reached from the first floor of the **Museu d'Història de la Ciutat** (the City History Museum), which occupies the Casa Clariana-Padellás, whose entrance is on Carrer de Veguer. This admirable museum is well worth a visit, however brief, for it describes – through maps and artefacts – the growth of Barcelona from Roman times to the present day. The basement has a display of excavations of the Roman and Visigoth city *in situ*. There are narrow roads, water vats like great broken eggs, several inscriptions on stone, and a few statues. Like many museum displays in Barcelona, it is beautifully laid out but poorly labelled, and the few exhibits which carry labels are described only in Catalan. The floors above are largely devoted to the development of the city over the last four centuries. There is a wonderful display of ceramic tiles, depicting all manner of objects and activity – ships, animals, trades, musicians and so forth – and these, together with the sculptures, illuminated manuscripts, paintings and maps, bring the city's past to life. One map shows in very simple terms how the city grew. There were two stages in the medieval enlargement of Barcelona, the first taking in much of the land around the old city in the 13th century, and the second establishing a 'new town' to the west of what is now Ramblas in the 15th century. The medieval city was surrounded by walls which were still intact when Ford visited the city; they were eventually pulled down in the 1860s.

The modern city grew around the medieval core and the museum possesses Ildefons Cerdà's original plan for the Eixample, the 19th-century extension, as well as an alternative plan by Antoni Rovira. The latter actually won the municipal prize in 1859, but Rovira's plan was rejected by central government in Madrid in favour of Cerdà's. Rovira's plan envisaged a series of avenues radiating out from a large square – which was to be where the Plaça de Catalunya is now. Cerdà's plan was more prosaic, consisting essentially of a grid pattern of streets sliced through by two diagonal avenues (*see* pages 87–107).

The uppermost room in the museum contains a remarkable piece of iron machinery – a 16th-century clock which was eventually retired from the cathedral belfry in 1864. It was the fifth of the six clocks which have served the cathedral since 1401. It weighs nearly 5½ tons (5,512 kg), is twice the height of a man and some 9 feet (3 metres) across.

Another museum in this area is the **Museu Marès**, whose entry is from Plaça de Sant Iu. One of the great things about this museum – named after the sculptor Frederic Marès – is that it doesn't suffer from the sort of overcrowding which can mar a visit to, say, the Museu Picasso (Picasso Museum). In its own curious way, it is one of the most interesting museums in Barcelona. It consists of two separate parts, the lower floors being devoted to religious sculpture, the upper floors – known as the Museu Sentimental – to a bizarre collection of objects gathered together by Marès during five decades of travel and donated to the city, along with the religious art, in 1940. The crypt beneath the museum has a mix of sarcophagi, statuary, columns and so forth, many from the Roman and Visigoth period, but note too the fine Romanesque portal rescued from the church of Anzano in Huesca and reconstructed here. Of particular interest are the thousand or more examples of Spanish religious sculpture on the first floor, dating from medieval times to the end of the last century, mostly depicting Christ on the cross. The exhibits are well labelled and provide a tour through the changing tastes of the last millennium – from the sombre and contemplative Romanesque Christ, through the agonized Gothic to the syrupy baroque.

If one still had any doubts that Marès was an obsessive collector, these are finally dispelled on entering rooms 31–47 of the Museu Sentimental. Here you can peruse his collection of everyday objects: door knockers, door handles, floor nails, scissors, weights and balances, compasses, cigarette cards, navigation equipment, tarot cards, cigar labels, matchboxes, pipes of every size and description (including one with Beethoven's face), keys, dolls, penny-farthings, snuff boxes, fans, jewellery . . .

There are several other buildings worthy of mention in this area. To the east of the Museu Marès, and bordering the Plaça del Rei, is the **Palau Lloctinent**, a Gothic building completed in 1557 with a Renaissance courtyard of great beauty. The palace was originally constructed for the Viceroy of Catalonia: now it houses the archives of the Crown of Aragon, an outstanding collection of over four million documents, the earliest of which dates from the 5th century AD. Another building of note is the **Casa de la Canonja** (the House of the Canonry) which overlooks the square in front of the cathedral. In 1546 this Gothic building became the headquarters of a charitable organization charged with feeding the poor. On the other side of the cathedral, on Carrer del Bisbe Irurita, are the Cases dels Canonges (the Houses of the Canons) which date from the 14th and 15th centuries. These were aggressively restored and remodelled in 1929. The President of the Catalan Generalitat (the semi-autonomous regional government) has his residence on the first floor. Presumably for his convenience, a handsome neo-Gothic bridge was constructed in 1928 to span the street between the Cases dels Canonges and the Palau de la Generalitat.

Carrer del Bisbe Irurita leads to the Plaça de Sant Jaume with its two superb government buildings, the **Palau de la Generalitat** (Palace of the Catalan regional government) and the **Ajuntament de Barcelona** or **Casa de la Ciutat** (City Hall). It is sometimes said that great friction exists between the occupants of these two buildings, the regional government being politically to the right, the city administration being to the left: this might be so were it not for the fact that the regional parliament sits in Ciutadella Park (*see* page 70). All the same, the palace was originally built to house the Generalitat and it remains the symbolic and emotional home of regional autonomy.

Unfortunately, it takes a considerable degree of planning to get inside, unless you happen to be in Barcelona on 23 April, or St George's Day, the only day in the year when it is open to the public. It can be visited between midday and 6pm on Saturdays and Sundays, but permission, applied for more than 15 days in advance by writing, must be obtained from: Gabinet de Protocol i Relacions Externas, Palau de la Generalitat,

Plaça de Sant Jaume, 08002 Barcelona. Guided tours last about half an hour and are free of charge. Commentaries are in Catalan or Spanish.

The Catalan predilection for mixing styles, which has its apotheosis in *modernista* architecture, has always been apparent. Both the Palau and the Ajuntament combine several styles, and they are the work of centuries rather than just a decade or a generation. The Palau is predominantly Gothic and Renaissance in character, although there are some baroque elements too. The original Gothic façade in Carrer del Bisbe Irurita was designed by the master builder Marc Safont and begun in 1416. The gargoyles, pinnacles and medallion of Sant Jordi (Saint George), the patron saint of Catalonia, were executed by the great Pere Joan. Behind this imposing façade lies a courtyard of signal beauty, again by Safont, with a loggia, or covered arcade, of pointed arches on slender columns. The loggia is reached from the lower patio by way of a broad staircase; note the sculptured balustrade. Above the loggia is an enclosed gallery surmounted by pinnacles. From the level of the loggia you can either pass into the Pati del Tarongers (the orange tree patio) – another lovely, though later Gothic enclosure – or head for the small **Capella de Sant Jordi** (Saint George's Chapel). This too is the work of Safont (1432) and it is an excellent example of Catalan *flamígero*, or the flamboyant style of Gothic, its façade decorated by elaborate mouldings. The chapel has a silver statuette of Sant Jordi, who is as omnipresent in Catalonia's government buildings as the Virgin Mary is in the region's cathedrals and churches. You will see more of the saint – or rather his shield held by angels – around the cornice of the Cambra Daurada (the Gilded Room), which was completed in 1536.

Great changes to the spirit and style of the palace took place during the latter years of the 16th century, when Pere Blai constructed the elegant Renaissance façade (overlooking what was then a cemetery but is now the Plaça de Sant Jaume) and the superb Saló de Sant Jordi (St George's Hall). Ford complained that 'the front is much admired, but, as usual, it is disfigured by square port-hole windows'. There have been some changes since his visit too: in 1860 a balcony was added to the portico, thus creating a suitable dais from which politicians could proclaim their latest victories; and a statue of Saint George slaying the dragon was placed in the vaulted niche above the portico, which had remained empty since the building of the façade. I am inclined to ignore Ford's disparaging remarks: it is an exceptionally beautiful façade, full of strength, yet essentially pure, and it looks particularly lovely at night when illuminated by the four wrought-iron lamps which stand at its base.

If you face the façade from the other side of the square you will see the cupola and lantern which rise above the Saló de Sant Jordi. This began life in 1596 as a chapel and it consists of a nave and two aisles. The classical purity of design contrasts with the opulence of the decor. A massive candelabra hangs from the lantern, and the dome and ceiling are lavishly decorated with frescoes painted by Josep Mongrell in the 1920s. These depict various events in the region's history; from an artistic point of view they are far inferior to the frescoes by Torres Garciá which they replaced. Fortunately the latter, painted in the *noucentista* style between 1913 and 1918, were removed and can now be seen in a room named after the painter beside the Saló Daurat. Mongrell's historical scenes were commissioned during the dictatorship of Miguel Primo de Rivera, who came to power after a military coup in 1923. The dictator immediately banned the Catalan flag and insisted that Spanish, not Catalan, be the language of public life. Perhaps it is only to be expected that the frescoes in the Saló de Sant Jordi should be more an expression of a united Spain ruled from Castile, than of a province perpetually struggling to free itself from outside interference.

Plaça de Sant Jaume is one of Barcelona's great meeting places: many a political demonstration has begun or ended here; every Sunday hundreds turn up to dance the *sardana*; and the annual carnival comes by the square on its tour of the old city. In 1931 Fransesc Macià announced the Catalan republic from the balcony of the Generalitat; Lluís Companys did the same from the neo-classical façade of the Ajuntament opposite.

Architecturally, the Ajuntament does not seem to hang together quite so well as the Generalitat, but at least access is not such a problem for the visitor – it is open daily. The original Gothic façade by Arnau Bargués on Carrer de la Ciutat dates from 1399–1402: note the large portal with impressive voussoirs and the excellent sculptures, especially the statue of the archangel Raphael, by Pere Sanglada. The neo-classical façade (1832–44) facing the Generalitat was the work of Josep Mas. From the internal patio two stairways lead up to the first floor and the Saló de Cent, which was where the Consell de Cent (the Council of a Hundred) originally ran the city's affairs. With its diaphragm vaulting and wood ceiling, it is very similar to the Saló del Tinell (*see* page 31). Nearby is the chamber where the present-day council meets. On the same floor is the Sala de Cròniques, whose walls are covered by some rather gloomy murals by Josep Maria Sert. In 1970 new offices were constructed at the rear of the Ajuntament: the Generalitat's guide to the region's architecture describes the addition as a 'polemical fifteen-storey building'. Enough said.

Final port of call within the Barri Gòtic should be the church of **Sant Just i Pastor** to the east of the Ajuntament. There have been religious buildings on this site since the 4th century. The present church is in the Gothic style and dates from 1342, though the bell-tower by Pere Blai was not complete till 1567. The church possesses a single, elegant nave with side chapels between the buttresses. The altarpiece is an extravagant affair: marble columns with gilt capitals supporting a hemisphere topped with a figure wielding a crucifix – just the sort of gaudy church furniture the Catalans adore. Some of the side chapels are in similarly poor taste. However, the overall impression is delightful and there is some good stained glass in the clerestory windows. The church possesses certain privileges extant to this day: for example, a dying person may pronounce a will here which is legally valid, even though it is unrecorded on paper. In the surrounding streets there are several Gothic houses with charming courtyards, but in the narrow alleys on the way down to the port poverty is much in evidence. This is a world of creaking doors, caged canaries, precarious balconies, pots of geraniums, and washing flapping in a sultry breeze.

BETWEEN THE RAMBLAS AND CIUTADELLA PARK

Midway through the 13th century the city, hitherto restricted to the small area within the Roman walls, was bursting at the seams. To cope with the burgeoning population, Jaume I ordered new walls to be built, which expanded the urban area in all directions. This was the first of Barcelona's two medieval enlargements, and it took in an area now bordered by the Ramblas in the west and Ciutadella Park in the east; the harbour formed its southern boundary and to the north the walls ran along the line of what is now Carrer de Trafalgar.

One of the best ways of getting to know old Barcelona is through its bars and churches, which sit together neatly, both in my mind and on the streets. As good a place as any to begin is in the poorer quarters of the first medieval enlargement, a couple of minutes' back from the harbour. By all accounts Carrer Ample used to be one of the smartest streets in Barcelona. During the 16th century its handsome mansions were lived in by the likes of Charles V and the King and Queen of Hungary, and as recently as a century ago the residences were much sought after by the city's wealthy industrial families. Today, however, Carrer Ample looks distinctly shabby and, in the narrow side streets which run up towards Carrer dels Escudellers, the respectable poor are forced to lead their lives side by side with dope dealers and pimps – none of which should put you off coming here.

The church of **La Mercè** looms above a small square through which Carrer Ample runs. There is nothing in its baroque façade which hints at the vulgarity inside. In the evenings old women shuffle in to light candles and rest their legs, their dowdy dresses mocked by the riotous decor: angels and cherubs hover like Christmas decorations above gilt-edged columns, while the fresco in the central dome depicts a deputation of clerics and sombre-suited Catalan businessmen being wafted up towards Christ. It is all in the worst possible taste and utterly enchanting.

Greater sobriety reigns in the nearby bars, one of which, on Carrer Reina Cristina, possesses neither name, nor seats, nor tables. Stockbrokers, whores, sailors, students, tramps – all stand in a detritus of cigarette butts and discarded newspapers while they knock back cheap champagne beneath a ceiling hung with leathery hams. In the same street as the church there is another café of great simplicity. The walls are tiled, the floor bare, the tables marble. Behind the bar are three vast barrels – red wine in one, white and rosé in the others. There is nothing else to drink, and the only food is a type of small fish, served fried. Between them, the church and the bars say much about the Catalan character. There are few races which have a greater predilection for the gaudy and the tasteless, and yet they are a thoroughly serious people: reliable, straightforward, businesslike. It is this curious mix of reticence and ostentation, of the conservative and outlandish, which gives the city such a distinctive flavour.

The church of La Mercè is named after Our Lady of Mercy, the patroness of Barcelona. It holds a special place in the affections of local people and is home to a much-venerated 14th-century wood statue of Virgin and Child by the sculptor Pere Moragues. Though modified and embellished over the years, the statue possesses a serene beauty: the Virgin has a quizzical expression *à la Mona Lisa*, and sitting on her knee is an infant Christ of remarkably adult appearance. Every September a major festival celebrates Our Lady of Mercy (*see* page 165).

Popular mythology has it that the Virgin appeared to Jaume I in a dream and ordered him to create a monastic order to

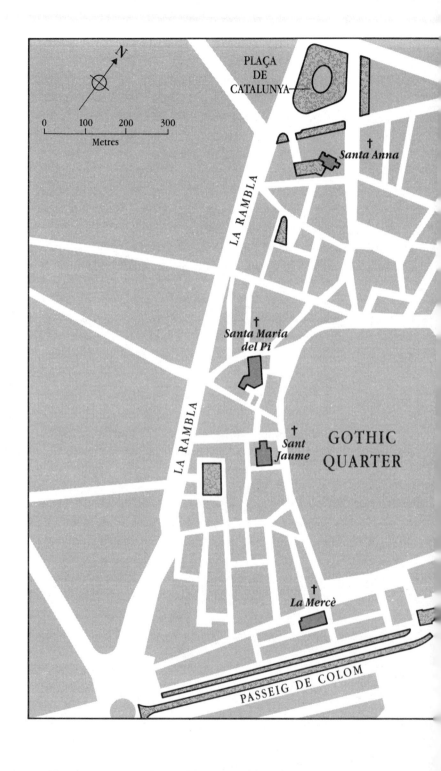

PLAÇA
DE
CATALUNYA

N

0   100   200   300
Metres

LA RAMBLA

† Santa Anna

Santa Maria
del Pi †

† Sant Jaume

GOTHIC QUARTER

LA RAMBLA

† La Mercè

PASSEIG DE COLOM

RONDA DE SANT PERE

Palau de la Música Catalana

† **Sant Pere de les Puelles**

PASSEIG DE LLUÍS COMPANYS

PASSEIG DE PICASSO

† **Santa Maria del Mar**

CIUTADELLA PARK

VINGUDA MARQUÈS DO L'ARGENTERA

help Christians captured by Barbary pirates. Whatever the truth of this, the Convent of Mercenaries was created early in the 13th century and the first church here was erected in 1267. Work on the present church began exactly 500 years later. It is frequently described as being in the style of Borromini, one of the great masters of Italian baroque architecture. This is rather misleading, for although the church undoubtedly is baroque – and thus something of a rarity in Catalonia – Josep Mas, its architect, cannot stand comparison with Borromini. Nevertheless, its curved façade, with octagonal bell-tower and dome behind, is pleasing enough to behold. The church has a single nave, a transept with dome and eight side chapels. Acres of pink and orange marble clothe the walls, and the impression of lavish wealth is in sharp contrast to the poverty of the *barri* (the quarter) which the church serves. Two pulpits face one another across the nave, each with a gilded Saracen's head fixed to its base. The side doorway on Carrer Ample belonged to the earlier church of Sant Miquel.

A short walk from here, heading west through the red-light district, is **Plaça Reial**. Somehow this stately 19th-century square manages to be both sleazy and salubrious at the same time. There is a permanent police presence, and the square attracts petty thieves and delinquents of all sorts. It is lined by some first-class drinking establishments and above the arcades are a couple of cheap hotels popular with young tourists. A Capuchin monastery which originally stood here was pulled down in 1835, and in 1848 a competition was held to attract designs for a new square. The winner was Francesc Daniel Molina, whose plans, strongly influenced by the neo-classical style favoured by the French, came to fruition between 1848 and 1859. Overlooking the square are some handsome buildings which form a continuous and uniform façade. The ground floor is fronted by an arcade of classical arches; Ionic pilasters link the first and second floors; and above the shallower third floor is a stone balustrade. A fountain of the Three Graces stands at the centre of the square surrounded by tall palms and flanked by two wrought-iron lamps designed by a then up-and-coming architect, Antoni Gaudí (*see* page 93). On Sundays there is a large coin and stamp market in the square.

Leaving the square by the Passaje Madoz will bring you to **Carrer de Ferran**, which runs from the Ramblas to Plaça de Sant Jaume. Standing like tasteless sentries guarding the street's junction with the Ramblas are two American fast-food joints. Otherwise this is a good-looking street with wrought-iron lamps suspended from the buildings, two of which are worthy of a quick glance. First, there is a shop called Wolf's, between number 7 and number 9; it is notable not so much for its merchandise – which is jewellery – but for its façade, which is pure, if somewhat clumsy, art nouveau. Further along the street, towards the Plaça de Sant Jaume and on the opposite side, is the church of **Sant Jaume**, whose façade is so self-effacing one can easily miss it. The church itself – it began life in 1394 and has been much modified since – is of little architectural interest, being one of the less noteworthy examples of religious Gothic in Barcelona. However, it stands on the site of an old synagogue and it was here, and in the neighbouring streets of Carrer del Call and Carrer Banys Nous, that there was a thriving Jewish community during early medieval times. Persecution of the Jews began during the reign of Jaume I – from 1243 Jews were forced to wear hooded capes with yellow or red circles – and by the end of the 14th century all synagogues had been destroyed. Before heading through the streets of the old Jewish *call*, you may wish to step briefly inside the church, which is named, incidentally, after the apostle rather than the anti-Semitic king (and founder of the Consell de Cent). There is a good Gothic altarpiece, but your eyes are more likely to settle on the side chapels, whose railings are 'decorated' by macabre offerings. There are plastic effigies of babies, limbs, torsos, and even little 'Swiss-style' chalets wedged between the rails: all are white, like neotenous cave creatures, and they put one in mind of death and decay.

After this it comes as a relief to enter the fine Gothic church of **Santa Maria del Pi**, which manages to dominate two small squares: its main façade towers over the Plaça de Sant Josep Oriol. The word *pi* means pine, and there is a small pine tree in the first of the two squares as well as an orange tree. The church is one of the best examples of Catalan Gothic: it is airy and uncluttered, with a wide, spacious nave. Unfortunately the surrounding buildings prevent one getting a good feel for the exterior; indeed, to see the octagonal bell-tower clearly you must retreat to the Ramblas and look back.

The church dates from 1322 and was consecrated in 1453. A relatively plain Gothic portal is dwarfed by a magnificent rose window on the west façade. This is one of the largest rose windows in the world and is best seen at night when the light streams through the stained glass. There is a single nave, some 182 ft (55 metres) long by 53 ft (16 metres) wide, and a polygonal apse with side chapels; there are also side chapels between the buttresses. The two squares are charming: there are several small cafés – one with paintings hung from the walls feels distinctly Parisian – and at weekends there is a flea market and an art fair. The streets which run into these squares should all be explored. Trendy boutiques selling designer clothes or avant-garde paintings alternate with old-fashioned shops selling hardware, *charcutéria* and delicious pastries.

The quarter nearest the Plaça de Catalunya is named after the church of **Santa Anna**, which is tucked away down a little courtyard off Carrer de Santa Anna. This is one of the oldest churches in Barcelona, dating from 1146. Originally it took the form of a Greek cross, having been built by Guillermo II, the patriarch of Jerusalem, but the nave was later extended and a dome was built above the transept. A number of chapels have been added, including a tiny one dedicated to the Black Virgin of Guadalupe. At the rear of the church there is a lovely cloister. Sitting here it is hard to imagine that one is just a few paces away from the infernally noisy Plaça de Catalunya.

All the buildings and streets mentioned so far in this section lie between the Ramblas and Via Laietana. One other building which every visitor should see before heading for Via Laietana is **Casa Martí** on Carrer de Monsió. Designed by the *modernista* architect and politician Josep Puig i Cadafalch at the end of the last century, the café on the ground floor became a famous meeting place for some of the most influential artists of the day. The café of Els Quatre Gats was founded by Santiago Rusiñol, Ramon Casas, Miquel Utrillo and Pere Romeu (*see* pages 119–21). Among the other artists who met and exhibited their work here were Pablo Picasso and Isidre Nonell. Joan Maragall read his poems at Els Quatre Gats and Isaac Albéniz gave concerts. Frequenters of the café also published several *modernista* magazines.

Via Laietana, the long straight street which was driven through the first medieval enlargement in the early years of this century, is one of the city's least attractive: it is wide, noisy and devoid of charm. It begins its journey towards the sea at the base of Plaça del Bisbe Urquinaona, slices through the old medieval quarters and eventually meets the boulevard which runs along the harbour at Plaça d'Antoni López. The **Casa del Gremi dels Velers** (the House of the Sailmakers' Guild) is unfortunately closed to the public. Built in the 1750s, it was restored in 1985, and it boasts some fine 18th-century graffiti, both inside and out. The real gem at the upper end of Via Laietana is the **Palau de la Música Catalana** by Lluís Domènech i Montaner: this is one of the most astonishing buildings of the *modernista* period. To appreciate it fully one needs to see it in the context of the entire *modernista* canon of architecture, and the Palau is described in the section on Domènech's work (*see* page 102).

Further down, Plaça de Ramón Berenguer el Gran is tacked on to the side of Via Laietana and provides good views of the buildings bordering Plaça del Rei. Santa Agata towers above the remains of the old Roman walls, and beyond you can see the upper galleries of the tower of Rei Martí, and the cathedral's belfry and spire. The statue on horseback is of Ramón Berenguer III, who played a prominent part in the cathedral's construction. Between here and the bottom end of the street there is nothing of special interest, and I suggest you head diagonally down Carrer Argenteria to the church of **Santa Maria del Mar.**

This church is possibly the finest example of Catalan Gothic architecture in Barcelona. When Richard Ford visited it in the 1840s, he noted: 'The style is very elegant, the piers airy and lofty; the painted glass very rich, in greens, blues and reds.' However, he was saddened to see that the high altar had been modernized 'with red marbles, gilt capitals, and tawdry sculptured angels'. Well, the church's interior was much improved during the Civil War when it was set on fire, thus ridding it of the baroque clutter. In one of the side chapels in the apse there is a small exhibition showing how the church looked before and after this event.

Until recently it was thought that the church was designed by Jaume Fabre, the second architect of the cathedral, but it now seems that it was the work of Berenguer de Monagu and Ramón Despuig. The church was begun in 1329 and completed just over half a century later. The central nave is slightly higher than the two side aisles and twice the width. Slender octagonal piers with simple gilded capitals soar upward to arched vaults whose bosses are painted henna-red, blue and gold. The ambulatory is especially lovely, as is the glass in the long clerestory windows. There are side chapels between the buttresses. The west front of the church is a handsome, if not particularly elegant affair. Two open, three-storey bell-towers rise from each corner, while above the Gothic portal there is an impressive rose window dating from the 15th century. The statuary in the tympanum and on the embrasures is in need of restoration and weeds sprout from the stonework further up. Inside, the church is remarkably free of vulgar ornament. There is a simple statue of Virgin and Child at the altar, behind which is a beautiful bronze *pietat* by Frederic Marès (1924).

The church is a great favourite for weddings, and most evenings you will be able to catch one. The Barcelonans do things in style: at one wedding I witnessed there were over 300 guests, dressed in dinner jackets and evening gowns. The choir sang divinely, everything was videoed, and the bride (in oceans of lace) and groom departed in horse and carriage.

The apse of Santa Maria del Mar juts into the rectangular Passeig del Born, where medieval jousts were once held. **Carrer Montcada**, which runs from the Passeig del Born to the Carrer de la Princesa, is one of the finest medieval streets in Barcelona. It began life in the 12th century, when the Montcada family was given permission to build here. From the 14th century onwards the local nobility commissioned a series of large mansions along the street, and this remained the most prestigious address in Barcelona till the late 1700s. Subsequently the rich and noble favoured Carrer Ample (*see* page 38), but the tables have turned again: Carrer Ample has gone downhill, and Montcada up. Its mansions have been carefully restored over the last fifty years, and today they house two museums – the Museu Picasso and the Museu Textil i de la Indumentària – and several art galleries. Nearly all the mansions were built in the style of civil Catalan Gothic, but there are Renaissance and baroque elements too.

Palau Dalmases at number 20 contains a 15th-century Gothic chapel, the only surviving part of the original building. The courtyard, with its exquisite baroque staircase, dates from the 17th century: three intricately carved, twirled columns support two skewed arches, and there is a fine bas-relief below depicting Neptune on his chariot. Number 25 is the Casa Cervelló-Giudice, a 16th-century house whose Gothic façade has been tampered with less than any of the others in the street. The lengthy queues further up signal the entrance to Number 15, which is the Museu Picasso. Obviously, the interior has been modified, but the courtyard is probably much as it was when the Palau Berenguer d'Aguilar – it was commissioned by Joan Berenguer – was built in the 15th century. The architect is thought to have been Marc Safont, best known as author of the Gothic parts of the Palau de la Generalitat (*see* page 122 for a full description of the Museu Picasso).

Finally, just across the street from here at number 12 is the

Palau de los Marqueses de Llio. A Gothic courtyard is embellished with certain Renaissance features, notably the doors
and windows. The Palace houses the **Museu Textil i de la
Indumentària** (the Textile and Garment Museum). There are
three main sections devoted to tapestries, clothes and lace, and
there are seasonal exhibitions downstairs. Among the things
that can be seen on permanent display are: combs (14th to
19th century); costumes from the 16th century onwards; some
superb tapestries depicting naval scenes, the Moorish army,
etc; waistcoats, dresses, suits, socks and stockings from the
18th century; military uniforms; ecclesiastical vestments; lace
and fancy needlework. There is also a room with displays of
contemporary Spanish fashion. The Museum was founded by
Manuel Rocamora, and is among the best of its kind in Spain.
However, I suspect it is of greater interest to fashion-conscious
women than to anyone else.

Barcelona is blessed with some magnificent 19th-century
markets. The finer of the two in this part of town is the **Mercat
del Born**. It no longer functions as a market, but is used for such
things as antique fairs and meetings. It is a dramatic wrought-
iron structure, dating from the 1870s, between the Carrer del
Comerç and Ciutadella Park. The other market, which is of
greater gastronomic than architectural interest, is to be found in
Plaça de Santa Caterina, near Via Laietana. Before leaving this
area and heading for the Ramblas, one other church should be
mentioned: **Sant Pere de les Puelles**, in Plaça de Sant Pere. There
are signs tacked onto the walls forbidding the playing of *pelota*,
though in truth the church has been so thoroughly messed about
that it is hard to see how it could be ruined further. The best
thing about the interior is the 12th-century Romanesque nave.

THE RAMBLAS

During the summer months many rivers and streams in Spain
are reduced to a tiny trickle of water; some even dry up
altogether, leaving a gash of sand and pebbles as a reminder of

their erstwhile purpose. The south-westerly wall of the first medieval enlargement ran alongside just such a seasonal water course, the Riera de la Malla. During the 15th century the rapid growth in population forced the city to extend its boundaries once again, and the new walls took in land to the west of the seasonal torrent, running along the course now occupied by Avinguda del Paral·lel and Ronda de Sant Antoni. With the establishment of the second medieval enlargement, the river was engulfed by the city: thus the birth of one of the most famous and beautiful streets in the world: the Ramblas. The name comes from *raml*, which is Arabic for sand. The riverbed was gradually transformed – by 1366 a sewer ran along its length – and during medieval times it was lined by a series of religious institutions. All these have gone and the present-day Ramblas date largely from the 18th and 19th centuries.

There are actually five Ramblas, each bearing its own name and possessing its own distinctive character. The Rambla de Canaletas, which leads into the Plaça de Catalunya, boasts expensive hotels and smart shops; while the Rambla de Santa Mònica – named after a vanished convent – is both the gateway to the port and the hangout of what one city guide charmingly refers to as 'the lowest strata of society'. Curiously, Barcelonans can be rather sniffy about the Ramblas, claiming that they are the preserve of oddballs and tourists. This is nonsense: come here any evening and you will see thousands upon thousands of locals ambling up and down the central walkway and inspecting the musicians, the street actors, the gaudy flower stalls and the caged birds; or perhaps they are simply relaxing on the hired seats, or heading for the Ramblas's many bars or restaurants. Richard Ford talked of the Ramblas having the most 'gape-seed', by which he meant the greatest variety of things to gawp at. The Ramblas are a voyeur's paradise: here you have free theatre of the highest order.

The Ramblas begin a mile away from the sea at the south-west corner of **Plaça de Catalunya**. In Ildefons Cerdà's original plan (*see* pages 32, 87), the Plaça was pencilled in some distance further north, midway along the present Passeig de Gràcia; Antoni Rovira, on the other hand, anticipated a vast square – over 550 yards (500 metres) long – stretching from the position of the present Plaça up towards Plaça de la Universitat. Neither had their way, and the Plaça de Catalunya ended up where it is today. Though an impressive space, the incessant rush of traffic detracts from the pleasures of lingering here too long. It was laid out in its present form from 1925 to 1927: at its heart is a wooded square with flower beds, statuary and fountains. The holm-oak trees support vast flocks of roosting starlings in winter. The statue known as 'The Goddess', situated in the corner near the entry to the Ramblas, is by the Catalan sculptor Josep Clarà. The square is surrounded by several large buildings: El Corte Inglés department store is an ugly edifice with a good rooftop café. The telephone exchange nearby played a prominent role during the Civil War, and is mentioned by George Orwell in his *Homage to Catalonia*. The exchange was occupied for a time by the anarchists, while a rival faction on the Republican side set up its machine guns in the Hotel Colon across the square. The Catalans have always injected enormous energy into their political activities and scarcely a week goes by without a demonstration of one sort or another in Plaça de Catalunya. A good place from which to observe such events is Café Zurich, a large beer hall on the corner of Carrer de Pelai.

Orwell, incidentally, was staying at the Hotel Continental when the street fighting broke out in May 1937. This is one of several hotels – it is homely rather than handsome – on the upper section of the Ramblas, the Rambla de Canaletas, which gets its name from the iron fountain beneath the plane trees. According to popular folklore, by drinking from this fountain the stranger becomes an honorary citizen of Barcelona. This section is also known as the Rambla dels Estudis, as a university stood here till 1714. On the right-hand side (I shall assume that the visitor is heading down to the port, rather than up to Plaça de Catalunya), on the junction with Carrer Bon-Succés, there is a small chemist's shop with an attractive *modernista* exterior. Note the serpent wrapped round a child and drinking from a chalice, and the art nouveau lettering of *FARMACIA* and *APOTHEKER*.

The Acadèmia de Ciències i Arts de Barcelona formerly occupied a site a little further down; the building has gone, but the Acadèmia still exists in the bizarre Poliorama Theatre. It was from one of the domes on the roof of this building that Orwell took pot shots at the Marxists holed up in the Café Moka opposite. Soon after Franco died the magazine stalls and cinemas of Barcelona were awash with pornography: an overzealous reaction, one imagines, to decades of rigorous censorship. For a while the Poliorama joined the pornography bandwagon, but later became the home of the Catalan National Theatre.

The **Església de Betlem** (Church of Bethlehem), the only remaining church on the Ramblas, is a curious building, erected between 1680 and 1732. Its best feature is the baroque façade, which is tucked away, with undue modesty, down a narrow side street, Carrer del Carme. The church presents a high, windowless wall of austere dressed stone to the Ramblas. More eye-catching is the building opposite: the **Palau Moja**, a neo-classical episcopal palace with some outstanding murals by Francesc Pla. The Palau now serves as offices for the Catalan government's Department of Culture; it also has a superb bookshop specializing in matters of local interest.

Next comes the Rambla de Sant Josep, or the Rambla de les Flors, whose central walkway is dominated by flower stalls. Evelyn Waugh thought that the Ramblas's 'chief beauty is the flower stalls, which colour and perfume the whole length of the street'. Nowadays the main smell comes from exhaust fumes; nevertheless, the flower stalls are among the Ramblas's most enticing features. If you can, come here in the early hours of the day when the women are laying out the flowers. They are far from cheap.

On the right-hand side, around the point where the flower stalls begin, is the **Palau de la Virreina**, a palace with a strong rococo influence built in the 1770s for the Viceroy of Peru.

This is used today for exhibitions: whatever is showing, it is worth paying the entrance fee just to see the building's interior.

A little way further down is Barcelona's finest market, the **Mercat de la Boqueria**. It is the food (*see* page 170) rather than the architecture that leaves one salivating after a visit here; but this 19th-century iron and glass structure possesses a certain rigid beauty. First opened in 1836, it was to be almost a century later before it got its roof. One of the most interesting stands from an aesthetic point of view is number 435–6: Fruites i Verdures, designed in *modernista* style. There is some attractive stained glass at the entry to the market. Another fine example of art nouveau, or *modernista*, design can be seen in Fca. de Pastas Alimenticias on the corner of Carrer de la Petxina. This is one of the loveliest shop façades in Barcelona.

The Rambla dels Caputxins was named after a Capuchin monastery which was pulled down to make way for the nearby Plaça Reial. Several streets converge here on the Plaça de la Boqueria, and one senses, for the first time, the rawness and energy of the less salubrious quarters further down. This area manages to be both seedy yet smart, and here you will see opera-goers in evening dress as well as hookers and tramps. In the middle of the Plaça is a round cobbled mosaic by Joan Miró: it is, like many of his large-scale public works, of questionable artistic merit.

One of the most attractive paintings of local street life in Barcelona's Museu d'Art Modern (*see* page 117) is Achille Battistuzzi's *Plà de la Boqueria* (1873), which takes in the shop fronts on the east side of the Ramblas, with the octagonal belfry of Santa Maria del Pi behind (this was used as a gun turret in the Civil War, according to Orwell). The façade of A. Foncuberta, seller of *sombreros* on the corner of Carrer de la Boqueria and Carrer de Cardenal Casañas, has been modernized, but Casa Bruno Quadras is pretty much unchanged. This building, dating from the 1880s, was the work of Josep Vilaseca: it would have been – by the standards of the *modernista* period – a very ordinary building, were it not for its extraordinary cladding of iron parasols and fans. On the corner of the building a sinuous Chinese dragon hangs over the pavement with a lamp suspended from its mouth.

A few paces nearer the sea on the same side is the Café de la Opera, a poseur's paradise with *fin-de-siècle* décor and pricey drinks. Immediately opposite is the splendid **Gran Teatre del Liceu**, Barcelona's main opera house. Ideally, one should visit the Liceu for an opera (tickets are sold in an office down Carrer de Sant Pau) but there are 30-minute guided tours too (11.30 and 12.15, Mondays to Fridays, 100 pesetas). Like many buildings in the Ramblas, the Liceu was built on the site of an old convent. Hiding behind the modest façade is an interior of wild extravagance. The Liceu opened in 1847, its construction having been paid for by 4,000 Catalans, each of whom had effectively bought a seat or box. In 1861 a fire destroyed the main auditorium, the stage and the roof, but the stairways and most of the rooms behind the auditorium survived. Josep Oriol Mestres, who worked on the Liceu earlier, directed its reconstruction. The Queen of Spain had refused to help finance the Liceu when it was first built, and she refused again when work began after the fire. Consequently, it is one of the few opera houses in the western world without a royal box.

In 1862 a performance of Bellini's *I Puritani* marked the reopening of the Liceu. In 1893 an anarchist called Santiago Salvador hurled two bombs into the stalls during a perform-ance of the *William Tell* Overture. This was to avenge the death of his confederate Pauli Pallàs, who had been executed for attempting to murder General Martínez Campos. Twenty people were killed at the bombing, and many were injured. On the main staircase there is a statue of the anonymous muse of music: the Catalans had failed to agree on whether it should be of Wagner (the great favourite here), Mozart, Puccini or some other composer. The stairs lead into the 'Room of Mirrors' with its marble floor and eclectic mix of rococo, baroque and neo-classical décor.

The auditorium is breathtakingly sumptuous, all gilt and red velvet with wonderful light fittings – originally gas, now electric – and an ornate Renaissance-style ceiling with paintings of scenes from famous operas. There are five balconies in the baroque style above the stalls. Each of the 120 boxes is individually decorated; a few are still privately owned, but most now belong to the Department of Culture.

The Liceu's acoustic qualities match those of Milan's La Scala. The theatre accommodates over 3,000 people and there are some 120 performances each year. Seats range in price from 500 to 8,000 pesetas, and virtually every performance is sold out. (For more about opera, *see* page 156.)

A few yards further down the Ramblas is the Hotel Oriente, within whose ballroom are preserved large parts of the Franciscan convent which was built here in the 17th century. The pavement café outside is a good place to take refreshments. Alternatively, you can drop in at La Castellana, a small *charcutéria* at number 41. There are a few marble tables beneath the ceiling hung with salamis, hams and beef hocks. Try these or one of the many cheeses with some local wine. Nearby, Carrer Nou de la Rambla leads past Palau Güell (*see* page 60) and into the forbiddingly seedy area known as the Barri Xinès (or China Town). The Ramblas itself begins to take on the feel of a red-light district from here south. Porn shops and peep shows alternate with gentlemen's outfitters and hardware shops. A decade ago gangs of women in mini-skirts and fishnet tights used to solicit from the doorways around the Plaça del Teatre and in bars such as the incongruously named Loch Ness. Apparently, this business is conducted mostly by telephone nowadays, and loitering crowds are a thing of the past.

The **Teatre Principal** is a shabby-looking building with a neo-classical façade. There has been a theatre here since the late 1500s; the present building opened in 1788, and it has been modified since. It is now a cinema. On the other side of the road there is a monument to Frederic Soler, one of the great figures in Catalan theatre. The last section is the Rambla de Santa Mònica, which gets its name from the monastery at the foot of the street on the right-hand side. This has been transformed into the Centre d'Art Santa Mònica. On the two occasions I have visited the Centre, I found its exhibitions of avant-garde sculpture depressingly pretentious. There was a memorable bronze statuette by Picasso, and some fine marble heads by Enric Casanovas, but the rest – including works by people who should know better, like Salvador Dalí and Joan Miró – was sadly disappointing. Nevertheless the old monastery makes a splendid space for exhibitions.

On the other side of the road is the Palau March, a neo-classical palace dating from the same period as the Teatre Principal and recently restored by the Generalitat. A narrow side street leads, a little way further down, to the unremarkable Museu de Cera (the Wax Museum). From here it is just a short walk to the Christopher Columbus monument, which is described in the section dealing with the harbour (*see* page 63).

THE MEDIEVAL QUARTERS WEST OF THE RAMBLAS

The second set of medieval walls, constructed in the 15th century, embraced the land to the west of the Ramblas. The only surviving stretch of wall – the rest was pulled down in 1856 – runs beside **Les Drassanes** (the royal shipyards). The walls followed the course described today by Avinguda del Paral·lel, Ronda de Sant Pau and Ronda de Sant Antoni. The most potent reminder of Catalonia's maritime history comes in the form of the medieval shipyards, whose long sheds look surprisingly modern when seen from the top of the Columbus monument. During the reign of Jaume I (1213–77) the Catalan navy conquered Mallorca, Ibiza and Formentera, and over the following half-century Sicily, Minorca and Sardinia were gathered to the Catalan bosom. Then, and for the next 600 years, the ships required both for war and trade were supplied by the Drassanes shipyards, which today are the largest and best preserved of their kind in the world. The central portion

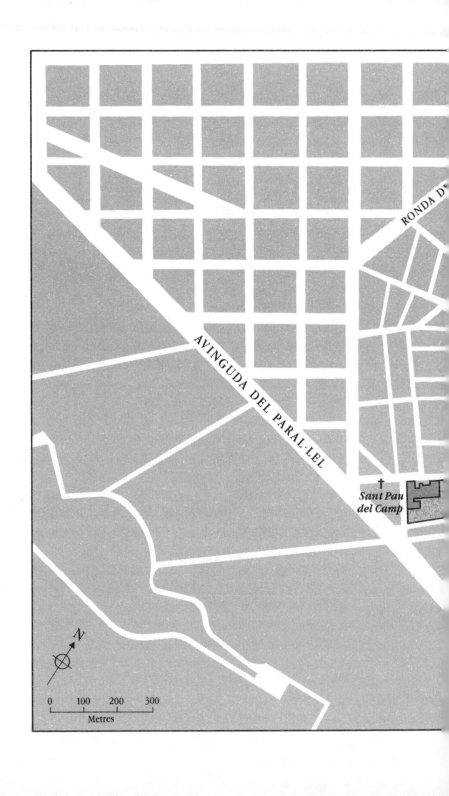

RONDA D'

AVINGUDA DEL PARAL·LEL

† Sant Pau del Camp

N

0   100   200   300
Metres

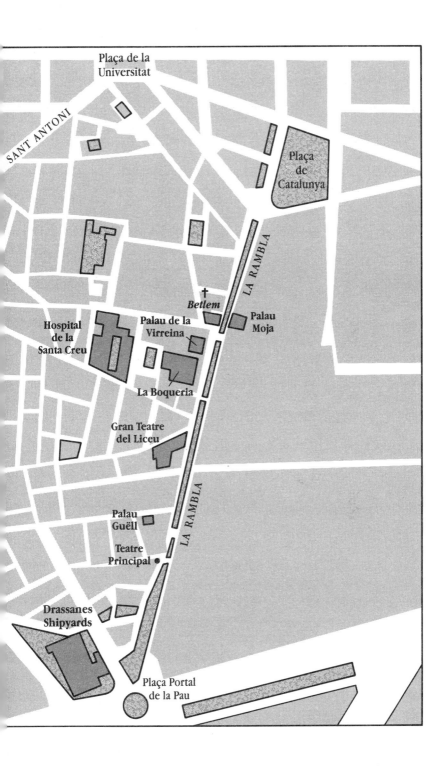

Plaça de la
Universitat

SANT ANTONI

Plaça
de
Catalunya

LA RAMBLA

† **Betlem**

**Palau de la
Virreina**

**Palau
Moja**

**Hospital
de la
Santa Creu**

La Boqueria

**Gran Teatre
del Liceu**

LA RAMBLA

**Palau
Guëll**

**Teatre
Principal** •

**Drassanes
Shipyards**

Plaça Portal
de la Pau

with its two great halls – or naves – was finished in the 14th
century. New naves were added during the 17th and 18th
centuries providing sufficient space to build 30 galleons at any
one time. Majestic diaphragm arches supported by square
piers give the Drassanes a cathedral-like grandeur. In 1663, the
Generalitat handed the shipyards over to the army, which
proceeded to fortify them and modify the naves. By the time
Richard Ford arrived, the Drassanes had been turned into an
arsenal. 'The rambling establishments and the barracks cover
a large space,' he wrote. 'The Sala de las Armas would hold
30,000 muskets, were they supplied from Woolwich: there is,
as usual, much jealousy in allowing foreigners to see the
beggarliness of these empty boxes.'

The Drassanes now house the admirable Museu Maritim
(the Maritime Museum) which is entered through the tower
near Plaça Portal de la Pau. The centrepiece of the museum is
a life-size reproduction of *La Real*, Don Juan of Austria's
flagship at the Battle of Lepanto (1571). The model was built
in 1971, 400 years after the Christian fleet defeated the Turks.
Even those with little interest in nautical matters will be
astonished by the beauty of *La Real*'s design and the splendour
of its fittings. The ship was propelled by 29 pairs of oars and by
sail. The original pendant which hung from the main mast
depicts Christ on the Cross; it is now in Toledo. The stern of
the boat is a baroque extravaganza, dripping with gilt paint,
and embellished with carvings of mythic figures: Argus, Diana
and Hercules on one side; Mercury, Ulysses and Prometheus –
the latter being devoured by an eagle – on the other. Neptune
is one of many characters depicted in the painted panels; he
also sits astride a dolphin on the tip of the long, pointed prow.

The museum contains models of a wide collection of vessels,
from Egyptian funerary boats to Brazilian canoes and galleys
built in these shipyards. Also on view are anchors, paddles,
sextants, globes, maps, portraits of Columbus and other nautical gear.

The **Avinguda del Paral·lel**, which begins its journey inland
at the Drassanes shipyards, reminds me of some ancient diva

who refuses to accept her decrepitude and insists on singing badly rather than not at all. In the early years of this century the vibrant night life led to its being seen as the Montmartre of Barcelona. In truth, it was never that picturesque, but it was probably less seedy and run down than it is today. The Paral·lel is a linear red-light district, lined by all manner of clubs, the best known of which is El Molino, which got its name from Montmartre's Moulin Rouge (this one also has a windmill above the door). There are several music halls, some of which are charmingly old fashioned, and plenty of strip joints, bars and cafés. Three tall chimney stacks, now redundant, rise dramatically above the working-class quarters to the south of the Paral·lel, which gets its name from the fact that it is aligned along the parallel 44° 44′ North. It is roughly twice the length of the Ramblas and it runs from the Drassanes up to the Plaça d'Espanya.

Near its junction with Ronda de Sant Pau is the church of **Sant Pau del Camp**, which can also be reached from the Ramblas by walking the length of Carrer de Sant Pau. This lovely church is some way off the tourist route but well worth a visit, though entry can only be gained at the time of services (Sunday Mass: 10.00; 12.00; 13.00. Weekday Vespers: 20.00). Altogether there are some 1,800 Romanesque churches and 200 Romanesque castles in Catalonia. There are tremendous concentrations in the northern parts of the province, but the small church of Sant Pau is one of the few examples of Romanesque architecture in Barcelona (others, already mentioned, are the Chapel of Santa Llúcia in the cathedral, and Sant Pere de les Puelles). For a full discussion of the characteristics of Romanesque art and architecture, see pages 113 (Museu d'Art de Catalunya) and 204 (Romanesque churches of the Pyrenees).

Sant Pau del Camp is said to be the oldest surviving church in Barcelona. It was founded some time in the 10th century, possibly before 912, which is the date on the tomb of Wilfred II. The church and associated monastery may have been destroyed during the Moorish invasion, but they were rebuilt in the early 12th century. A cloister was added in the 13th century, and there were later additions too, including a baroque belfry and some fortifications above the main façade; nevertheless, the Romanesque integrity of the church has survived. Above the main door, carved in the stone arching, are various symbols: lion, eagle and ox representing the Evangelists; starfish, birds, fish, fruit and so forth. Above these are two carvings of griffins and higher still there is a curious representation of the hand of god – a right hand with first and second fingers extended. The capitals supporting the arching are thought to be from an earlier period, possibly the 7th century. In the tympanum Christ is flanked by Peter and Paul. There is a small rose window above the door and the façade is decorated with Lombard arcuations. The church is in the shape of a Greek cross, with a barrel vault, ribbed dome and three apses. Perhaps its outstanding feature is the tiny cloister. Pairs of columns with carved capitals – depicting plants and animals and man – support unusual arches possessing either three or five lobes.

In the vicinity of the church the local authorities have demolished great swathes of tenement in preparation for the Olympics. All the same, the Sant Pau district is likely to remain its normal salacious self for some time yet. There is something poignant about the way in which many thousands of upright, God-fearing citizens do their best to lead respectable lives in very trying circumstances. It is no fault of theirs that they must share the streets with hoodlums, pimps and thieves. The streets to the south of Carrer de Sant Pau are among the most crime-ridden in Barcelona, and this, as it happens, is the way you should go if you are heading for **Palau Güell**, the only building by Antoni Gaudí in the old part of town. After walking 200 yd (180 m) east along Carrer de Sant Pau, turn right down either the infamous Carrer de Sant Oleguer, or the equally notorious Carrer de Sant Ramon, then left along Carrer Nou de la Rambla. Palau Güell, which stands within spitting distance of the Rambla, keeps strange company. Opposite there is a shop selling wedding dresses, and beside it a genito-urinary clinic and a sex-shop. The admirable Bar London is also nearby.

Gaudí (*see* pages 93–101) built Palau Güell for his patron Eusabi Güell between 1885 and 1889. It is a stiff, austere building lacking the organic fluidity associated with the architect's later works. The building combines both Gothic and Moorish elements but should be seen not so much as a pastiche of past styles but as a harbinger of *modernisme*. According to Alastair Boyd: 'Güell is reputed to have said as the construction progressed that he liked it less and less and Gaudí to have replied that he liked it more and more – the architect seems to have prevailed.' One can sympathize with Güell: it is hard to imagine living in such a building. The two large doorways, shaped like a couple of parabolic nostrils, are clad with ornate ironwork, and between them is a window grille which culminates in a chain-mail mesh of iron held in the claws of a bird of prey. In fact there is remarkable ironwork throughout the building, forming screens, light fittings, banisters and so forth. The main stairways lead up to a large room with a wide cupola. This too is pulled into the shape of a parabola; the roof is dotted with weird cone-shaped chimneys and vents covered with glazed ceramic tiles. All this seems quite restrained when compared with Gaudí's later work, but Palau Güell provides a foretaste of his future development. The lavish use of marble, ivory, carved wood and iron endows the building with a frigid, impersonal feel (it would be a good setting for an inquisition). All the same, I imagine many visitors spend as much time studying the building as they do the exhibits of the Museu de les Arts del Espectacle (the Museum of the Performing Arts), which has been housed here since 1954.

Before leaving this part of town, one should plunge back into the medieval world, brilliantly represented by a cluster of buildings around the old **Hospital de la Santa Creu**. Richard Ford may have found Barcelona 'a disagreeable city' but he was impressed by many of its public buildings. He thought the prison and poor house excellent, and the hospitals 'well-conducted'. The hospital buildings occupy the area between Carrer del Carme and Carrer del Hospital, a short distance from the Ramblas. There has been a hospital here since the 10th century; the present buildings date from 1401 when four wings were constructed round a central rectangular cloister (the baroque cross is a later addition). Each wing consists of a long nave with a wooden roof supported by diaphragm arches. Over the years other buildings accreted round the hospital and modifications were made to the original structure.

The **Casa de Convalescència** was added in the 17th century. The entrance to the arcaded courtyard boasts some beautiful ceramic tiles – predominantly blue and gold – depicting various biblical scenes, many from the life of Saint Paul. This was the work of Llorenç Passoles. The Casa de Convalescència is now occupied by the Institute of Catalan Studies, while the wings of the hospital have been taken over by the Library of Catalonia. The Antiguo Col·legi de Cirurgia was built in the neo-classical style in the late 18th century. Next to this is a small garden named after Sir Alexander Fleming, who discovered antibiotics by extracting penicillin from mould. There is a bust of Fleming erected in 1955, the year of his death, by *Los Bomberos de Barcelona* (the firemen of Barcelona).

THE SEAFRONT: FROM COLUMBUS TO BARCELONA

Barcelona is one of the largest ports in the Mediterranean. It is also one of the most introverted. Despite its long maritime history, the city seems to have turned its back on the sea. One of the obvious differences between ports and inland cities is that the former tend to be outward-looking: they gaze across the sea to distant horizons. However, Barcelona behaves like a land-locked city, with the collective attention of her inhabitants focused not so much on the seafront as on the Plaça de Catalunya and the city centre. Thoughts such as these are far from original, and over the past few years the city planners have made much of their belief that the new Olympic developments – and especially those associated with the Olympic Village in the Poble Nou area – will help Barcelonans reacquaint themselves with the sea. This strikes me as wishful thinking. Certainly, the new development with its flats, esplanades and marinas will bring some people closer to the sea (and especially those who can afford to live there); and at least the railway lines which formerly ran between Poble Nou and the beach have been taken away. All the same, I suspect that the guts of the city – the areas described earlier in this section – will remain as remote from the sea as ever.

This is not to say that you should ignore the seafront – on the contrary, half a day can happily be spent in and around the port. The obvious place to start is at the **Monument a Colom** (the monument to Christopher Columbus) which rises like an eccentric rocket from Plaça Portal de la Pau. The monument was erected for the Universal Exhibition of 1888 in honour of the great Genoese explorer, who sailed into Barcelona in 1493 following his 'discovery' of the Americas. He was accompanied by his family and seven unfortunate Indians from the island of Cuba. There is a small plaque in the cathedral commemorating the christening of the Indians. *The Blue Guide to Spain* describes the Columbus monument as 'ugly'. That is unfair. It is perhaps a rather fussy, over-elaborate structure, but that is part of its charm. Its stone plinth is surrounded by eight black lions cast in iron. The plinth itself has a series of bas-reliefs portraying events in Columbus's life, and above this is the column's polygonal base with its sculptural representations of the Kingdoms of Catalonia, Aragon, Castile and Leon. Then comes the 168-ft high (51-metre) Corinthian column, near whose base, cast in bronze, are two griffins and four winged figures. The column's capital has representations of Europe, Africa, Asia and America; above the capital a large globe nestles inside a royal crown.

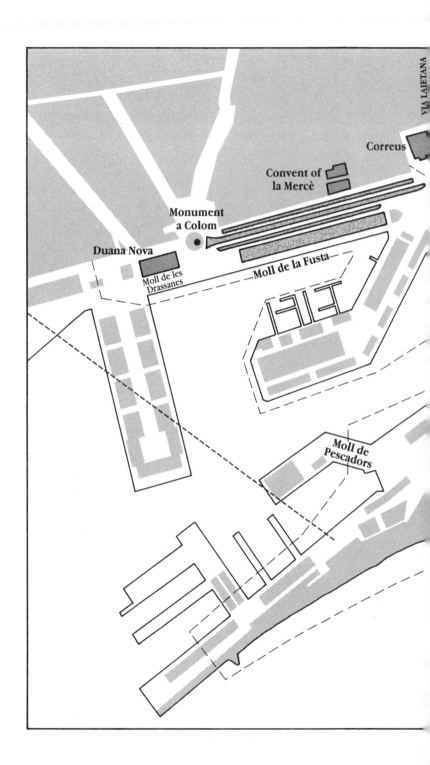

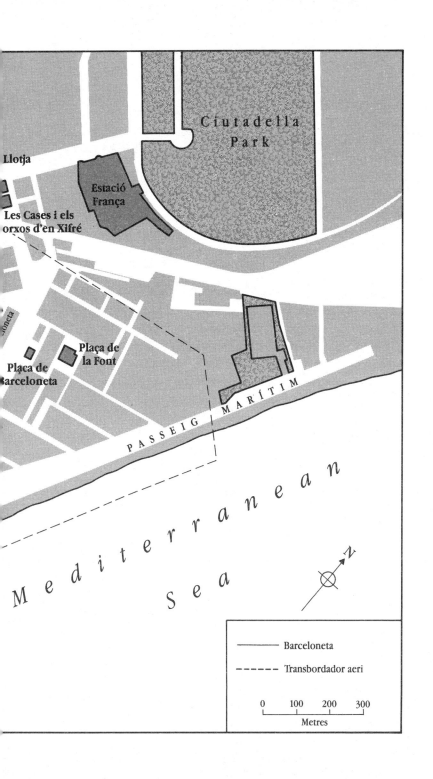

Llotja

Estació
França

Les Cases i els
orxos d'en Xifré

oneta

Plaça de
la Font

Plaça de
Barceloneta

C i u t a d e l l a
P a r k

P A S S E I G   M A R Í T I M

M e d i t e r r a n e a n

S e a

N

——————— Barceloneta

- - - - - - - Transbordador aeri

0   100   200   300

Metres

Columbus himself stands on top of the globe, his right arm pointing majestically seaward. A lift inside the column takes visitors to the mirador: from here there are superb views across the city and the sea. (*Visiting hours* 24 June – 24 September: 09.00–21.00. Rest of year: closed on Mondays; 10.00–14.00 and 15.30–18.30, Tuesdays to Saturdays; 10.00–19.00, Sundays and holidays.)

A life-size model of the *Santa Maria*, Columbus's flagship on his first voyage to the Americas, is moored nearby (*Visiting hours* 10.00–19.00). Either side of the monument are two florid buildings, neither of which is open to the public. Enormous griffins hover above the wings and entrance of the **Duana Nova** (the Custom House), built between 1895 and 1902. The **Junta d'Obres del Port**, built a few years later, looks like a cross between a French château and a wedding cake. Boat trips round the harbour go from the quayside between these two buildings (*see* page 154).

During the past few years there has been a serious attempt to beautify the quayside, and the city authorities are especially proud of the **Moll de la Fusta** (Timber Wharf), which runs from the Junta d'Obres up to Moll d'Espanya. The old sheds have been pulled down and the wharf has been paved and planted with palms. There are several cafés here and benches on which to sit. The design strikes me as being sterile, and the Moll is nothing like as lovely as the seafront at Sitges (*see* page 179). According to one guide: 'The Moll is the cruising place for Navy boys off the boats, keen to pick up Barcelona's girls – or even visiting Americans attracted by the uniform.' I am not sure whether or not this is a recommendation.

The Moll runs beside the Passeig de Colom, a wide traffic-infested boulevard with several handsome buildings interspersed among scruffy offices and restaurants with multilingual menus and greasy food. Cervantes, the author of *Don Quixote*, is said to have lived for a while at number 33. Another monument to a great seafarer towers over the Plaça del Duc de Medinaceli. In 1331 Galceran Marquet led the Catalan fleet in battle against the Genoese. The monument – an iron column with statue and fountain – was erected in 1851. The square itself, designed by Francesc Daniel Molina, must have been lovely once, but the buildings look shabby and neglected and the pock-marked palms look as if they have been subjected to a firing squad. Two blocks north is the old 17th-century convent of **La Mercè**, hidden behind the façade erected in celebration of the 1929 International Exhibition. Since 1846 this has been occupied by the Capitania General.

The Passeig de Colum comes to an end at Plaça d'Antoni López. Set some way back, on the corner of Via Laietana, is the Correus (the Post Office), built between 1914 and 1922 to the design of Josep Goday and Jaume Torres. The Correus is excessively grand. There is a vast portico with four Ionic columns, and four statues by Manuel Fuxà, feet firmly planted on the heavy entablature, gaze out towards the sea. Four well-known *noucentista* artists helped to decorate the monumental central hall.

From here it is about five minutes' walk to the gates of Ciutadella Park along Passeig d'Isabel II and Avinguda Marques de l'Argenteria. The outstanding building here is the **Casa de la Llotja**, which has served as a trading exchange and stock market since the 14th century. To get inside you must adopt the camouflage of a stockbroker: suit and tie for men, a smart dress for women. The superb Gothic hall was begun in 1380 under the direction of Pere Llobet. Pere Arvei took over and the Saló de Contració was completed by 1392. The hall survives to this day, as does part of the Gothic Sala dels Consols, which was discovered during restoration work in 1971. The Saló de Contració consists of three naves divided by towering semi-circular arches, on which rests the wooden roof. According to Ford, in 1770 the Corporation employed a French architect 'whose improvements were so bad that even the Municipality were ashamed'. These were pulled down and the existing neo-classical building, which enveloped the Gothic hall, was begun by Joan Soler in 1772.

The Llotja overlooks the Plaça del Palau, on the far side of which is the Palace of the Civil Government, formerly the old

Customs buildings erected in 1790–92 by Count Miquel de Roncali. It is a neo-classical building which scarcely deserves Ford's admonition: 'Here is the Tuscan again, and heaviness *ad nauseam*. The vexations it entailed on the designer caused his death in 1794.' Between here and Ciutadella Park is the **Estació de Franca** (the French Station), which has recently been redeveloped.

Before heading for Barceloneta, I suggest a glass of champagne in the unnamed bar, described on page 235, halfway down Carrer Reina Cristina. With its shops selling cut-price cameras and electrical goods, this is Barcelona's equivalent to London's Tottenham Court Road. The shops are bedded into a 19th-century arcaded neo-classical building, **Les Cases i els Porxos d'en Xifré**, named after Josep Xifré, who made a fortune in the New World. Picasso lived in a flat above one of the shops when he and his family arrived in Barcelona in 1895.

During the War of the Spanish Succession (1700–13) Catalonia and Aragon joined with the English to support Archduke Charles of Austria against Philip of Bourbon, who had the support of France and Madrid. In 1707 Philip V became Spain's first Bourbon monarch, and in 1714, after a 13-month siege, Barcelona surrendered to French and Spanish troops. This was a low point in Catalan history: the university was banished, the Catalan language suppressed, and the autonomous government bodies disbanded. One of the first acts of repression involved the eviction of the inhabitants of the Barri de la Ribera, part of which was replaced by a fortress – La Ciutadella. To make way for this, 37 streets, 3 churches and over 1,200 houses were demolished.

The refugees from La Ribera were rehoused in a new development which became known as Barceloneta. Work began in 1749 under the direction of the military engineer Juan Martin de Cermeño. Initially the new suburb consisted of 15 streets of two-storey houses crossed at right angles by slightly larger avenues. Over the years new streets were built and third and fourth storeys were added to existing buildings.

Barceloneta is an intriguing quarter, quite unlike anywhere else in the city. The grid-pattern of streets reminds one of the terracing which Victorian industrialists erected to house their workers, and indeed the inhabitants of Barceloneta are predominantly working-class. Ford found the occupants last century to be 'shipbuilders, dealers in marine stores, fishermen, and washerwomen'. The population is somewhat more cosmopolitan today, but many of the men of Barceloneta have jobs related to fishing and the running of the port. Come here at nine o'clock in the morning and you will find restaurants serving fishermen meals which look more like four-course dinners than breakfasts. Often there will be plastic bags full of last night's catch on the pavement outside.

There are buses to Barceloneta – they run down the Passeig Nacional to the roundabout at the end – but it is an easy walk from Plaça del Palau (or from Barceloneta Metro). The Passeig Nacional is lined with seafood restaurants on one side and some handsome warehouses, on the Moll de la Barceloneta, on the other. There was talk of knocking these down, but good sense prevailed and at the time of writing the warehouses were about to be restored. Architecturally, there is not much to see in Barceloneta. There is a covered market in **Plaça de la Font** (if you are buying fresh fish, get it either from here or at La Boqueria), and **Plaça de la Barceloneta** is a pleasant place to relax. There is a wrought-iron fountain-cum-lamp in the centre of the square, one side of which is taken up by a baroque church dedicated to Sant Miquel. 'Built in defiance of the beautiful exemplars of better times,' wrote Ford, rather sourly. The juxtaposition of expensive restaurants (none are cheap here) and modest, overcrowded housing is typical of Barcelona.

During weekdays Barceloneta is fairly quiet, but it livens up considerably at night and during summer weekends when thousands stream out of the city to relax and swim on the Platja de la Barceloneta. To get to the beach follow any of the streets running off Passeig Nacional to their conclusion. The beach is lined with small restaurants and you can hire parasols and deck chairs. The Passeig Maritim, which runs behind the beach, has recently been tarted up. Even in winter a few hardy types – mostly dog-walkers and bronzed middle-aged men – jog up and down the beach. Now that the area further up the coast – Nova Icària – has received a face lift, the views from here are much improved. However, rather than swim at Barceloneta I would be inclined to take the train down the coast to Castelldefels or Sitges (50 minutes from Passeig de Gràcia or Sants stations, *see* page 179).

Disappointingly, the **Moll de Pescadors** (the fisherman's wharf) is closed to the public, and one cannot witness the daily fish auctions as one can at other Catalan ports, most notably at Sant Carles de la Ràpita (*see* page 200). However, it is possible to walk along the Passeig Nacional to the tall tower, Torre de Sant Sebastià, whence leaves the cable car on its long journey across the port to the hill of Montjuïc. The cable car stops midway at another tower, Torre de Jaume I. If you have the nerve for this sort of thing, you will get fabulous views of the port, and indeed of the whole city. The Transbordador Aeri was opened in 1930 and the towers certainly look their age. Lifts take prospective passengers up the towers from ground level (*see* page 226 for operating times).

CIUTADELLA PARK

Every now and then the city of Barcelona puts on a spectacular public show. In 1888 there was the Universal Exhibition; in 1929 there was the International Exhibition; and in 1992 the Olympic Games. Each of these events has had a profound effect on the city's physical geography. Ciutadella Park, the delightful oasis of green to the north-east of the medieval city, was remodelled for the 1888 Exhibition, and the slopes of Montjuïc were transformed for the Exhibition of 1929. The Olympics, too, have had an impact on Barcelona. The creation of the new Olympic Village at Nova Icària has turned Poble

Nou – once a run-down area of small factories and tenements – into a sparkling, modern development, and the demand for new sporting facilities has brought great changes to Montjuïc, Vall d'Hebron and the Diagonal.

But exhibitions and sporting occasions such as these are about much more than the mere restructuring of the city. They are about pride and kudos. In each case, we see a city reaffirming its faith in itself, and suggesting to the rest of the world that the Catalans are a people to be reckoned with. The Universal Exhibition of 1888 took place at the most propitious of times. While much of Spain remained in bondage to the feudal values of an agrarian society, Barcelona was, as Ford put it, 'the most manufacturing city of Spain'. Here was a confidently modern industrial city which believed, quite rightly, that it could rub shoulders with the great capitals of the more progressive European nations. The 19th century witnessed the birth of the Catalan Renaixença, a movement which was to affect not just local politics but all the arts, from architecture to painting and literature; and in Ciutadella Park we see the first glimmer of what *modernista* architecture was to achieve over the next forty years.

Parc de la Ciutadella (Ciutadella Park) gets its name from the citadel erected there after the War of the Spanish Succession (*see* page 16). Once Barcelona had surrendered to Philip V's forces in 1714, the victors evicted more than 10,000 people from the Ribera district and set about the building of a fortress from which to subdue the citizenry. The architect was the military engineer Prósper de Werboom and the bulk of the work, carried out between 1716 and 1727, centred on a bar-racks capable of supporting 8,000 soldiers. As it happened, there were just 20 soldiers here by 1808 when the French took over Barcelona. 'The citadel is an abomination in the eyes of the town's folk,' wrote Ford; 'it is a bridle in their mouths, and prevents the city's increasing to its full commercial growth: hence the attempts to pull it down.' Some of the buildings were destroyed in 1841 and more came down after General

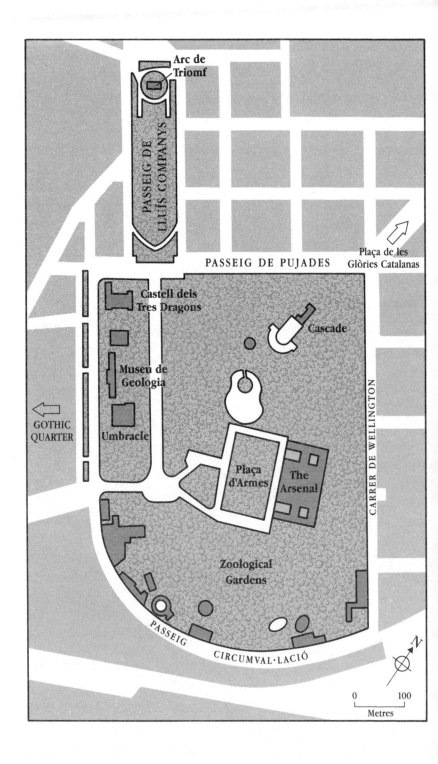

Arc de
Triomf

PASSEIG DE
LLUÍS COMPANYS

PASSEIG DE PUJADES

Plaça de les
Glòries Catalanas

Castell dels
Tres Dragons

Cascade

Museu de
Geologia

GOTHIC
QUARTER

Umbracle

Plaça
d'Armes

The
Arsenal

CARRER DE WELLINGTON

Zoological
Gardens

PASSEIG

CIRCUMVAL·LACIÓ

N

0   100

Metres

Prim handed the land to the city in 1869. However, several buildings – the Arsenal, a chapel and the Palau del Governador – have survived.

The most notable of these is the **Arsenal**, a long, sprawling building of French neo-classical bent. The Arsenal became the seat of the Catalan Parliament in 1932, but on Franco's conquest of the city in 1939 it reverted to its original function as a barracks. From 1900 to 1932 the Arsenal had been home to the collections of the Fine Art and Archaeological Museums. These were later relocated, and from 1945 the Arsenal has been the site of the Museu d'Art Modern (*see* page 117). At the time of writing the museum shared the building with the semi-autonomous Catalan Parliament (restored since Franco's death), but the art collection was destined to move to the Palau Nacional on Montjuïc.

In front of the Arsenal is the **Plaça de les Armes**, a formal garden designed in 1917 by the French landscape architect Jean-Claude-Nicolas Forestier. At the heart of the Plaça lies an oval pond, surrounded by clipped yew hedges and cypresses. In the middle of the pond is a marble statue of a naked woman, head hidden in limp despair. This is Josep Llimona's *El Desconsol*, one of the loveliest pieces of sculpture in the city (compare this, for example, with Antoni Tàpies's *Homenatge a Picasso* near the Passeig Picasso, or Miró's phallic offering behind the Plaça d'Espanya). There are some very comical bits of statuary in Ciutadella Park, none more so than the bust of the artist Joaquim Vayreda i Vila, with regulation beret and moustache, near the entrance to the Arsenal.

Ciutadella began to take on its present shape in the 1870s, when the city gave the task of landscaping the park to Josep Fontseré. His greatest contribution was the colossal **cascade** constructed between 1875 and 1881 in the northern corner, though one wonders whether he was suffering from delusions of grandeur. The centrepiece is a triumphal arch crowned with four horses pulling a chariot. This is reached by two oversized stone stairways with balustrades, between which lies the cascade itself. There are ponds on two levels separated by winged griffins spouting water, and dominating the lot is a bizarre, naturalistic grotto with seahorses and a statue of Venus rising from a scallop shell. The overall effect is splendid. Incidentally, Fontseré was helped by a young architectural student called Antoni Gaudí. Fontseré was also responsible for the wood and brick **Umbracle**, built in 1883-84, and for landscaping the gardens, which were to prove an ideal venue for the 1888 Universal Exhibition.

The idea of an international fair was by no means novel: London and Paris had already proved that such ventures could be a commercial success, and indeed a year after Barcelona held the 1888 exhibition, Paris was to hold one of the most spectacular of all times. Nothing quite on the scale of the Eiffel Tower was erected in Barcelona, but there was, none the less, some serious creative activity. The plan for an exhibition had been conceived originally by local businessmen, but their failure to bring it towards fruition led to the City Council, under the dynamic leadership of Francesc Rius i Taulet, taking matters into its own hands. At one time over thirty architects were engaged on projects within or near Ciutadella Park, and during a period of just over one year eight large buildings and many small pavilions were designed and erected. The most astonishing of the larger buildings was Lluís Domènech i Montaner's Gran Hotel International on Passeig de Colom. It was only intended to be a temporary structure and was pulled down after the exhibition closed. It is well described by Judith Rohrer in an essay on the exhibition published in *Homage to Barcelona: The City and its Art, 1888–1936*:

> The construction of the hotel – a temporary, city-run hostel intended to accommodate up to two thousand visitors a day in luxurious fashion – was characterised at the time as a veritable 'Yankee' undertaking, and was completed 'with North American speed' in an incredible fifty-three days . . . The building itself combined a light ironwork structure, visible on the interior amid the medieval tapestries and tilework, with hollow

brick walls, which served to conceal the pipes, conduits, ducts and chimneys . . .

The hotel construction site, with its army of high-spirited workers one to two thousand strong, working day and night with the aid of novel electric lighting, soon attracted an admiring public, including the fifteen-year-old Puig i Cadafalch, who later recalled that it was there that he saw his 'first vision of that great Barcelona for which we are all working'. Gothic in style, but modern in spirit and construction, the hotel represented a mixture of conservative and progressive ideals that would guide both Catalanist politics and architecture well into the 20th century.

Domènech's other contribution to the exhibition still stands. The **Castell dels Tres Dragons** looks like a parody of the medieval castle. It is a heavy-set brick building, embellished by blocks of ceramic tiling and plenty of ironwork. It is, I think, one of Domènech's least attractive ventures (*see* pages 101–105 for a full discussion of his work). The building was supposed to be a café-restaurant but wasn't ready in time for the exhibition. However in 1890-92 Domènech and fellow architect Antoni Maria Gallissà set up an arts-and-crafts workshop in the tower, and the building's unusual ceramic cladding was one of the many fruits of their collaboration. Today the Castell houses the Museu de Zoologia (Zoological Museum, *see* page 136).

The finest monument of the 1888 exhibition is Josep Vilaseca's **Arc de Triomf**, which looms magnificently above the entrance to the Passeig de Lluís Companys, the long palm-lined avenue which leads from the Arc de Triomf Metro to the main gates of Ciutadella Park. The monumentality of the brick arch is lightened by the wealth of detail, and there is a frieze by Josep Llimona, whose *El Desconsol* can be seen in Plaça de les Armes. In the summer months the Passeig de Lluís Companys is a popular meeting place, especially for elderly men, who while away their time and pensions playing *petanca* and cards.

The 1888 Exhibition was a great success. When the Queen Regent declared it open on 20 May 1888 she was accompanied by a 432-gun salute from the ships in the harbour. Today Ciutadella Park is a pleasant place to relax whatever the time of year. There is a fine collection of trees around the central lake – including palms, yuccas, casuarina, plane trees, moonseed, oleanders and cypresses – and if you keep your eyes skinned you will probably see the wild parakeets which breed in the park. Their forebears escaped from the **Jardins de Zoologia** (Zoological Gardens), which occupy the seaward end of the park and are described later (*see* page 148). At every corner of the park there is something of interest to see; for example, there is an 1899 steam engine made in Barcelona and a model of a mammoth. Among the many statues is one near the entrance of the mayor Rius i Taulet; and another of General Prim on horseback. Perhaps the best-loved statue of all is *The Lady with the Parasol* within the grounds of the zoo. This was the work of Roig y Soler.

MONTJUÏC

The hill of Montjuïc, which rises to the south-west of the old city, provides Barcelona with its most extensive area of green space. That old cliché – 'there is something here for everybody' – really does apply to Montjuïc, and to do it justice you must set aside at least one day, and preferably longer. It always comes as a great relief to climb away from the noise and fumes of the densely crowded streets, and wander through the shady woodlands and ornamental gardens which are dotted around the slopes of Montjuïc. During summer weekends thousands of people visit the amusement park below the castle, and indeed the various forms of transport – the funicular, the Transbordador Aeri (cable car) across the port – constitute a form of entertainment in their own right. There are eight museums on the hill, several of international fame. In particular, I would urge everyone to visit the **Museu d'Art de**

Catalunya (*see* page 113), which boasts one of the finest collections of Romanesque art in the world, and the **Fundació Joan Miró**. The gardens, amusement park and transport systems are described in some detail in Chapter 4; this section is largely devoted to the history and architecture of Montjuïc.

During Roman times the hill was known as Mons Jovis, the Hill of Jupiter; and during medieval times, when there was a Jewish cemetery and a Jewish community living here, it was known as Mons Judaicus. Its present name is derived from one of these sources. The oldest building on the hill is the **castle** on the summit, which was built in 1640 during the War of Reapers (*Els Segadors*), when Catalonia revolted against Philip IV of Spain and affiliated itself to the France of Louis XIII. The city of Barcelona surrendered in 1652. The castle was enlarged some 40 years later. During the War of the Spanish Succession (*see* page 16), the English sided with the Catalans in support of Archduke Charles of Austria against Philip of Bourbon (who was to become Philip V of Spain). The castle was daringly captured on 9 October 1705 by Lord Peterborough and his troops, but the English deserted the city later – 'when Marlborough was disgraced, and Bolingbroke sold England and Spain to France,' as Ford put it. A report by an anonymous English officer stationed at Montjuïc paints a vivid picture of life during the siege. Apparently, some of the troops 'laid out a great share of that time upon Ladies and Balls', and neglected to repair the fortifications or stock up on provisions. Somewhere in the region of twenty English officers were captured by the Spanish and French, and others were killed in battle, including one who had 'cut to pieces half a dozen Grenadiers'. After a while reinforcements came, but they were drunk on strong Catalan wine and killed by enemy bombs, 'for want of sense to observe and shun them'.

Barcelona fell to the French and Spanish forces in 1714, and midway through the century the castle was rebuilt in its present form by the military engineer Juan Martin de Cermeño, who was also given responsibility for designing the suburb of

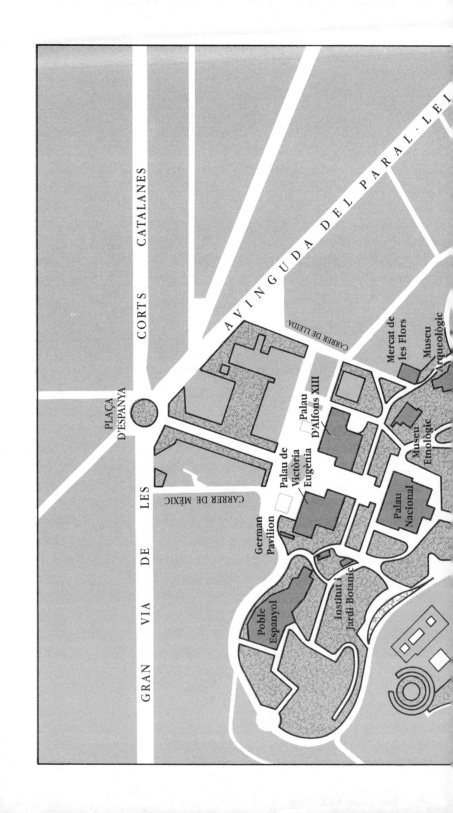

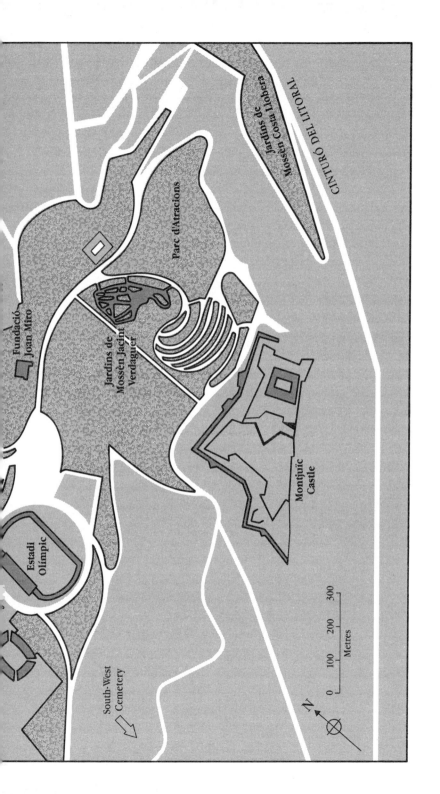

Fundació
Joan Miro

Estadi
Olímpic

South-West
Cemetery

Jardins de
Mossèn Jacint
Verdaguer

Parc d'Atracions

Montjuïc
Castle

Jardins de
Mossèn Costa Llobera

CINTURÓ DEL LITORAL

N

0   100   200   300

Metres

Barceloneta. The castle takes the form of a star-shaped pentagon; a wide moat surrounds the massive walls. With its thick cladding of ivy and its formal gardens, this is a pleasant place to visit, and it takes an effort of will to remember the nasty deeds which happened here. It was, of course, an excellent place from which to bomb the city below, and that was precisely what happened during the uprising of 1842; and with its heavy fortifications it also made a good prison, which was its function during the Civil War. Among the many people held here was Lluís Companys, the last President of the Generalitat before the Franco era. He was executed in the castle of Montjuïc on 15 October 1940.

The castle was handed over to the city in the 1960s and it contains the **Museu Militar** (the Military Museum). This is not, as they say, essential viewing, but the Museum's exhibits are well laid out and include all manner of paraphernalia relating to Barcelona's military history. There is a display of weaponry from wars going back to the Battle of Lepanto; and there is also a collection of lead soldiers, helmets, chain-mail and so forth. Several rooms deal with the history of the castle and the role it has played during the various wars which rocked the city.

The views from the castle are stupendous: to the north-east lies the old city, all pink and white from a distance like a fine-grained Seurat. The roofscape of the medieval quarters is punctuated by the spire of the cathedral, and some way beyond the remarkable gold-twinkling spires of Antoni Gaudí's Sagrada Familia rise above the grey suburbs. Wander round to the other side of the castle and you can gaze down on to the jetties and cranes of the commercial port. The best way to get here is by the *teliféric*, the small 4-seater cable cars which swing across the amusement park. Alternatively, you can drive up or walk.

Most visitors will probably approach Montjuïc from Plaça d'Espanya, and they will immediately be confronted by a series of buildings and monuments commissioned for the International Exhibition of 1929. The work carried out for the exhibition was to have a dramatic and enduring influence on the development of the city. As early as 1901 the Lliga Regionalista (the Catalan Industrial Party) put forward suggestions for an international exhibition, and from time to time new plans were mooted: one foresaw an exhibition of electrical industries; another an exhibition on furniture and interior design. None of these came to much, although some landscaping work was carried out on Montjuïc by Jean-Claude-Nicolas Forestier (who was also responsible for the Plaça de les Armes in Ciutadella Park), and some exhibition pavilions were erected under the direction of Josep Puig i Cadafalch.

Puig is one of the most significant figures in recent Catalan history. He wrote a definite work on the Romanesque architecture of Catalonia, and was himself one of the outstanding architects of the *modernista* period (*see* page 105). He was also a formidable politician, being a co-founder of the Lliga Regionalista, and president from 1917 to 1924 of the Mancommunitat, which was the closest thing Catalonia had had to its own Government since the Bourbon conquest of 1714. The inauguration in 1923 of Puig's first exhibition halls coincided with a military coup led by Primo de Rivera. Henceforth, with the Mancommunitat abolished and the country in the hands of a dictatorship, the exhibition developed along lines somewhat different from those anticipated by Puig and his friends.

However, by 1924 work had begun in earnest and the northern slopes of Montjuïc were gradually transformed; the city's Metro system also dates from those times, as does the funicular linking the Paral·lel with Montjuïc. The work helped reduce unemployment – 40,000 labourers were taken on to build the exhibition structures – but overspending left the public coffers virtually bare for some time after.

The **Plaça d'Espanya** may look impressive when seen from a car window but for pedestrians it is something of a nightmare, although a system of underpasses can help you from one side to the other. The commemorative fountain in the centre of the square was designed by Josep Jujol; the sculptures which adorn it are by Miquel Blay. Like nearly everything else associated with the 1929 exhibition, it was conceived in the grand manner; and like so many of the sculptures on Barcelona's monuments, these serve a symbolic purpose – in this case, they represent Spain's principal rivers.

The entrance to **Avinguda de la Reina Maria Cristina** is guarded by two ugly brick towers which are none the better for being of neo-Venetian design. The palaces which flank the avenue are still used as venues for fairs and exhibitions. The avenue is lined by fountains and lights and it culminates in a broad swathe of stairs leading to a higher level which is dominated by the **Fuenta Magica** (the magic fountain) built to the design of Carles Buigas. This is the centrepiece for possibly the most vulgar sound-and-light show in the world. On weekend evenings, between 21.00 and 23.00, the fountains are garishly illuminated by 5,000 lamps. All this is accompanied by music ranging from rock to classical. Highly recommended.

Further up the hill, the stone stairways are flanked by two large exhibition halls designed by Puig; the **Palau de Victòria Eugènia** and the **Palau d'Alfons XIII** (who both opened and closed the exhibition). The pagoda-like turrets and porticos give them a quasi-oriental feel. However the exhibition halls are dwarfed by the colossal and much derided **Palau Nacional**. It is derided not on account of its contents – which are magnificent – but its appearance. The building was supposed to combine several different styles of Spanish architecture, and in so far as it looks like a pastiche, its architects – Enric Catà, Pere Cendoya and Pere Domènech – have been reasonably successful. It is, in essence, a florid neo-classical building with a huge central dome and other lesser cupolas and towers scattered about its flanks. The Palau is the home of the outstanding **Museu d'Art de Catalunya** (the Catalan Museum of Art). It would be worth crossing continents just to see the displays of Romanesque art, much of it rescued from Pyrenean churches under the direction of Puig i Cadafalch earlier this century. The **Museu de Ceramica** (the Ceramics Museum) does justice to a craft in which the Spanish have always excelled. At the time of writing there was talk of removing the **Museu d'Art Modern** (the Museum of Modern Art) from

1. St George slays the dragon: detail from Josep Puig i Cadafalch's Casa Amattler.

2. Oriental dragon, Casa Bruno Quadras, the Ramblas.

3. Dragon gate by Antoni Gaudí: pavilions to Güell Estate.

5. The tree-lined Ramblas, with
Tibidabo in the distance, seen
from the Columbus Monument.

4. Iron font, the Ramblas.

6. Palau de la Generalitat.

7. Plaça Reial.

8. Plaça del Rei: arched façade of Saló del Tinell, five-storey Renaissance tower of Rei Martí, cathedral belfry and spire beyond.

9. The superb Gothic church of Santa Maria del Mar.

10. Romanesque doorway, Sant Pau del Camp.

11. Courtyard, Casa de Convalescència.

12. Antoni Gaudí's Sagrada Familia.

13, 14. Air flues and wavy balconies, Antoni Gaudí's Casa Milà.

15. Polychromed gable to one of the entrance pavilions at Park Güell, Antoni Gaudí.

16. Main entrance to the *modernista* Hospital de la Santa Creu i de Sant Pau by Lluís Domènech i Montaner; the bust is of the hospital's chief benefactor, Pau Gil.

17. Passion façade of Sagrada Familia; sculptures by Josep Subirachs.

18. *The Lady with the Parasol*, Ciutadella Park.

Ciutadella Park and installing it here. It may not stand comparison with New York's MOMA or the Tate Gallery in London, but it is not without interest. All these museums are described in detail in Chapter 3.

It does seem curious that the 1929 Exhibition produced so much reactionary architecture: after all, the Palau was begun while Gaudí was still working on the Sagrada Familia, and during the previous half-century Barcelona's architects had been among the most innovative in Europe. Not that all the buildings constructed for the exhibition were hewn from the same conservative block. Indeed, one of the pavilions, pulled down after the exhibition but re-erected later in celebration of the 100th anniversary of its architect's birth, is now considered a key work of the 20th century.

Ludwig Mies van der Rohe's **Germany Pavilion** stands alone a little way to the west of Plaça de Carles Buigas. It was virtually ignored at the time it was built, but historians since have been unequivocal in their praise. Making brilliant use of polished marble, onyx and chromium, Mies dealt with space – and the connections between the outer and inner worlds – in a manner reminiscent of the American architect Frank Lloyd Wright. Discussing the architecture of the late 1920s, the art historian Nikolaus Pevsner wrote:

> If one were compelled to choose one work as the most perfect, it ought probably to be the German Pavilion at the Barcelona Exhibition of 1929 by Ludwig Mies van der Rohe (born 1886 at Aachen), low, with a completely unmoulded travertine base, walls of glass and dark green Tinian marble, and a flat white roof. The interior was entirely open, with shiny steel shafts of cross section and divided only by screen walls of onyx, bottle-green glass, etc. In this pavilion . . . Mies van der Rohe proved, what the enemies of the new style had always denied, that monumentality was accessible to it by means not of columnar shams but of splendid materials and a noble spatial rhythm.

Pevsner described the building in the past tense, as he wrote this long before it was re-erected in 1986. I think the Pavilion is best seen under a midday sun, when it is hot and bright outside and cool within. This is the sort of building which should be felt as well as seen; like all great works of art, it has the power to move and stimulate. That famous piece of furniture, the leather and steel Barcelona chair, made its first public appearance in this Pavilion.

A little distance further along Avinguda del Marquès de Comillas is **Poble Espanyol** (Spanish Village). This is an open-air architectural museum, built for the Exhibition of 1929 to show the great wealth of architectural styles existing in Spain. Don't be put off by all the coach traffic or the Disney-like entrance (a replica of the crenellated gate of San Vicente in Avila). The whole thing is very well done indeed. There are exact reproductions of scores of buildings, ranging from Moorish churches to Gothic squares and workers' housing. It is a place of entertainment as well as education, and there are numerous arts-and-crafts studios and shops, many of which make their wares here, a dozen or so restaurants, some nightclubs, a couple of museums and a cinema. The latter puts on a 22-minute slide show throughout the day called 'The Barcelona Experience'. As a promotional exercise it could scarcely be bettered. The first thing you should do on entering Poble Espanyol is acquire a plan of the Village from the Information Kiosk.

Several other buildings around Montjuïc date from the time of the 1929 Exhibition. The **Palau Albéniz**, which overlooks the Joan Maragall gardens behind the Palau Nacional, is today used as a guest house for distinguished visitors. There is a ceiling inside painted by Salvador Dalí. At the foot of Passeig Santa Madrona, just past the open-air **Teatro Grec** (Greek Theatre, also constructed for the 1929 Exhibition) is the **Museu Arqueològic** (Archaeological Museum, *see* page 137), which is housed in a palace built in the Italian Renaissance style. The flower market opposite has been converted into a theatre which still uses the name **Mercat de les Flors**.

*

By the time of the 1929 Exhibition the artist Joan Miró was beginning to make his mark on the world. Born in the old city in 1893, Miró was to spend most of the 1920s in Paris, where he began to develop his own highly distinctive style of surrealist painting. During the summer Miró used to return to Catalonia, and in 1929 he married Pilar Juncosa of Majorca, where he was to live from 1940 till his death in 1983. Though Miró spent much of his life away from Barcelona, he never turned his back on the city. His quixotic presence lingers still, both in his public sculptures and, more significantly, in the **Fundació Joan Miró**, which was established on Montjuïc in 1974 as an exhibition space for Miró's work and to help foster the talents of young artists from across the world (*see* page 126).

The Fundació Joan Miró is housed in a building designed by Josep Lluís Sert. Born in Barcelona nine years after Miró, Sert was also beginning to make his presence felt at the time of the 1929 Exhibition. He spent much of that year working in Le Corbusier's office in Paris, but he also contributed to an exhibition of architectural projects at the Galeries Dalmau. The following year Sert and several other architects founded the GATCPAC (Grup d'Arquitectes i Tècnics Catalans per al Progrés de l'Arquitectura Contemporània – the Association of Catalan Architects and Technicians for the Improvement of Contemporary Architecture). The GATCPAC was established with the aim of creating a new rationalist architecture, and as such it was a reaction against the romanticism of the *modernista* period. With the help of Le Corbusier, the GATCPAC group produced a new urban plan for Barcelona, which Le Corbusier named after Fransesc Macià, then the leader of the Catalan Generalitat. However, the Macià Plan never got off the ground. The GATCPAC folded shortly after Sert designed the Spanish stand at the Paris Universal Exhibition in 1937. On display there were Picasso's *Guernica* and Miró's *The Reaper*. After the Civil War, Sert left for the United States, eventually succeeding Walter Gropius as Head of the Architectural Department at Harvard.

The Fundació Joan Miró is a concrete and glass structure of startling beauty. It is a building of the Mediterranean, and for the Mediterranean. From the outside the white walls, some flat, others curved, have a classical purity which sits easily among the green pines and cypresses. Inside, the building is full of light, yet utterly restrained. There is nothing about it to compete with or distract from Miró's paintings and sculptures.

The Barcelonans – or perhaps it is just the city authorities – adore slogans, which you will see slung across buildings and streets and hung from street lamps. The slogans go in and out of style as rapidly as the night spots favoured by the European smart set. 'Barcelona – more than ever' was one of the more appropriate, for during the period before the Olympic Games the city really did seem to be expanding. The most radical changes took place in Poble Nou and on the southern flanks of Montjuïc, which was transformed into one of the principal venues for the Games. During the period of construction there was much grumbling in the architectural press about 'lost opportunities', and many of the new installations – especially Ricard Bofill's neo-classical University of Sport – were castigated for being unadventurous. 'Only the Isozata-designed Indoor Sports Centre [Palau d'Esports Sant Jordi] takes its inspiration from modern technology,' mourned one magazine. Well, perhaps; but this *is* Barcelona, and one expects a mixture of the conservative (or reactionary) and the progressive (or avant-garde). I feel that at Montjuïc the complex as a whole does justice to the Catalan tradition of eclecticism.

The centrepiece is the **Estadi Olímpic**, which began life in 1929 as a temporary stadium, and was inaugurated with a football match between Catalonia and England, the latter winning easily. Like so many of the temporary structures put up then, it survived, and in 1936 the 'Free Olympic Games' (for those athletes or nations wishing to shun Hitler's not-so-free Berlin Olympics) were going to be held here. Unfortunately the Civil War began at the same time as the opening ceremony, so the athletes remained in their track suits and in some cases even joined up to fight. The stadium was used as a venue for the 1955 Mediterranean Games, but was left to rot over the following years. Periodically there was talk of knocking the stadium down, but nothing happened and it was taken over by a large gypsy encampment. The stadium was revamped for the 1992 Olympics by the Italian architect Vittoria Gregotti. He left the main façade intact, and created more seating by lowering the surface of the arena. Lluís Companys (the former President of the Generalitat who was executed in 1940 in Montjuïc Castle) and the organizers of the 1936 Free Olympic Games are commemorated by a plaque at one of the entrances.

The stadium was re-inaugurated in September 1989 for the World Athletics Cup. To the delight of non-Catalan Spain – there was much resentment that Spain's first Olympics should be held in one of her most troublesome provinces – the stadium flooded a few days before the games began. However, the teething problems were soon put right and the city is justifiably proud of its stadium. Arata Isozata's smaller **Palau d'Esports Sant Jordi** was by far the most modern of the structures erected for the Olympics. From a distance – you can see it from the road which links the city with the airport – it looks like a flying saucer. The roof was constructed on the ground and raised 150 feet by hydraulic lifts.

THE EIXAMPLE AND THE *MODERNISTES*

Midway through the last century Barcelona was finally released from its medieval strait-jacket, and the pulling down of the old walls presaged the beginning of a new era. In 1859 a Royal Decree approved a plan by the engineer Ildefons Cerdà to create a modern city beyond the confines of the old (*see* page 17). The Eixample (or extension) was to link the old city with the ancient townships of Sants, Sarrià, Gràcia and Sant

Gervasi. (A further eight surrounding towns were incorporated into the municipality between 1897 and 1921.)

Cerdà's plan was simple: he envisaged a series of streets running parallel to one another and to the sea, to be crossed by others, again equidistant from each other, and running at right angles to the sea. This made for an extensive grid-pattern of streets, which was to be diagonally intersected by two broad avenues, the Diagonal and La Meridiana, which today meet the other major avenue, Gran Via de les Corts Catalanes, at the Plaça de les Glòries Catalanes.

As an exercise in town planning, the Eixample is comparable to Haussman's 19th-century restructuring of Paris. Though many find the grid-pattern of streets somewhat dull – and it is certainly unusual for a European city – its main faults stem from the fact that some of Cerdà's stipulations were wilfully ignored. The Eixample is depressingly lacking in gardens and parks, yet Cerdà had seen it in terms of the garden city. He had intended that only two sides of each block would be built up, and that the other two sides, left open, would give access to a channel of greenery and gardens. For an idea of what the Eixample might have been like, it is worth visiting the Passatge Permanyer, one of the few places where this has happened. You will notice too that the corners of all the blocks have been chamfered. Cerdà intended the triangles between the streets and the corner buildings to be left open or planted with trees and shrubs. Nowadays most provide parking space, and indeed one of the worst things about the Eixample is the traffic.

The Eixample's early development coincided with the flowering of *modernisme*, and most of Barcelona's outstanding buildings of this period are to be found dotted along these broad streets. The Eixample is divided into two halves: La Dreta (the right) lies to the north-east of Rambla de Catalunya; L'Esquerra (the left) to the south-west. Most of the great *modernista* buildings are to be found in La Dreta. The ideal introduction to this section of the Eixample, and indeed to the development of the modern city, comes in the form of the

Passeig de Gràcia, which runs from the northern corner of Plaça de Catalunya up towards the smart suburb of Gràcia.

Passeig de Gràcia is lined by expensive shops and large offices. The airline companies are here and so are the big banks, together with some of the city's plushest hotels. One's first impression, heading away from the Plaça de Catalunya, is that this is Barcelona's version of the Champs-Élysées, a commercial artery lined by handsome, if not particularly exciting, buildings. But soon one notices the little touches: the beautiful wrought-iron lamps with bat motifs above the lights; the octagonal paving stones; the benches covered with ceramic tiles.

The first intersection – with Gran Via – is guarded by two 'Chicago-style' buildings: classical in design, and gradually tapering in a stepped manner towards their summits. Observe the sculptures around their main entrances. The **Banco Vitalicio** (1942-50, by Lluís Bonet) boasts some firm-bosomed girls holding fruit, sheaves of corn and so forth; note too the brass door with its iconography of chalice, book, crucifix, dove and balance. These may not be outstanding works of art but they are certainly superior to the sculptures of the socialist-realism school favoured by some of the other institutions along the street, and no less interesting than the works by Josep Subirachs (Barcelona's best-known modern sculptor) outside the Banc de Sabadell further up on the right hand side.

Higher up, lining the roofscape, there appears to be a veritable conversation going on among the statuary that adorns the buildings. Classical figures gaze out from the upper tiers of the Banco Vitalicio, and dotted along the skyline are other statues of both human and animal form. A huge phoenix hovers over the roof of one building, and further up on the right hand side the undulating roofs of Gaudí's Casa Milà are populated by clumps of air flues and chimneys which look like little armies of vizored invaders. But long before you reach there you will arrive at one of the most unusual street fronts in Europe.

Within a 100-yard (30-metre) stretch along the left-hand side of Passeig de Gràcia between Carrer de Consell de Cent and Carrer d'Aragó, are three buildings by the three outstanding architects of the *modernista* period. Antoni Gaudí's curvaceous Casa Batlló (1904) rubs shoulders with Josep Puig i Cadafalch's angular Casa Amatller (1900), while at the other end of the block Lluís Domènech i Montaner's Casa Lléo-Morera (1902-06) stands in splendid and eccentric isolation. It says much about the nature of *modernista* architecture – and the problems of defining it – that its three leading practitioners should create not a picture of stylistic unity, but one of visual chaos. And indeed this is known as the *Manzana de Discòrdia* (the Block of Discord).

Modernisme must be seen within the context of Catalan history. The 18th century had begun badly for Barcelona with the Bourbon conquest of 1714 (*see* page 16): the Catalan language was suppressed, the university was closed down and the autonomous government institutions abolished. Some would say that Barcelona's decline began even earlier, with the opening up of the New World and the waning of Catalonia's naval power. The 19th century also opened inauspiciously for the Catalans, with the French invasion during the Peninsular War and great loss of life. However, the Catalans have always been an irrepressible race and before long they were agitating for self-government. As it happened they didn't get it, but such political setbacks failed to stem the rising tide of Catalan nationalism. Rapid industrialization brought greater prosperity to the region, and the revival of Catalonia's self-esteem was expressed through the *Renaixença* (a cultural Renaissance) which eventually paved the way for the emergence of *modernisme*.

Modernisme is sometimes thought of as a Catalan form of art nouveau; and it is true that there is much in common between the two, as indeed there is between *modernisme* and the other *fin-de-siècle* movements such as *Sezessionstil* in Austria, *Jugendstil* in Germany and Hungary, and the Modern Style in Britain. But Catalan *modernisme* stands apart from all of these, not least because it was much more than an aesthetic movement; *modernisme* was, if not exactly an ideology, a multi-faceted expression of Catalonia's regional identity. It sought – whether through architecture, art or literature – to reflect the region's progressive aspirations without forsaking the achievements of the past. The growing industrial bourgeoisie, eager to leave its mark on the world, proved more than willing to promote and sponsor this peculiarly original movement.

In 1878 Domènech called upon his compatriots to search for a 'national architecture'. He reminded the Catalans of their strong affinity with the Romanesque and the Gothic (classical architecture, rightly or wrongly, was perceived to be rigid, unwelcoming, even undemocratic), and he urged architects to create a style which would be thoroughly modern, yet capable of reflecting the region's history without degenerating into eclectic pastiche. Domènech lived by what he taught and his creations are always dazzlingly original. Others drank more deeply and less imaginatively from the waters of the past and many *modernista* buildings are little more than eccentric cocktails. Neo-Gothic and Moorish designs are among the most powerful elements of the early *modernista* period; but to this one must add dollops of baroque, Catalan vernacular and art nouveau.

Written across the Block of Discord are the basic tenets of *modernista* architecture. One common thread is the obsession with detail. Gaudí designed his own furniture for his buildings, while Puig and Domènech clothed their creations with the most elaborate sculptural details. Frequently these reflected Catalan themes: inside Domènech's house on the Block of Discord an entire Catalan nursery rhyme (with princes, hunting scenes, Virgin and child) is sculpted in bas-relief around the central hall; and beside the doorway of Puig's Casa Amatller there is a magnificent representation of St George, the patron saint of Catalonia, slaying the dragon. This theme is dealt with even more dramatically by Gaudí's Casa Batlló. The rucked roof of glazed green and blue tiles is said to represent the dragon's back, impaled by the cross of St George, while the slatted balconies and iron window mullions represent the skulls and bones of the dragon's victims. Whether or not this interpretation holds true, Casa Batlló exemplified the way in which the *modernistes* conceived of their buildings as works of art, as pieces of sculpture even. They would all have agreed with John Ruskin that 'the architect who was not a sculptor, or a painter, was nothing better than a frame-maker on a large scale'. All these buildings on the Block of Discord are testimony to the revival of the native arts and crafts which occurred during the *modernista* period. Once again the Catalans began to make and use beautiful ceramics, stained glass, elaborate ironwork, finely crafted woodwork. And at the same time the *modernistes* showed a distinct preference for the use of local materials, especially during the early years of the movement, when red brick was preferred to dressed stone.

If anyone deserves to be known as the father of *modernista* architecture it is Domènech, whose Hospital de la Santa Creu i de Sant Pau and Palau de la Música Catalana are two of the movement's greatest achievements. His concern with the rational use of space, his cheerful use of decoration, his complete lack of interest in notions of 'good taste' – all these elements are to be seen in Casa Lléo-Morera in the Block of Discord. Puig was a pupil of Domènech and he carried the same rationalist torch. Though his work paid greater homage to medieval architecture – the foyer of Casa Amatller reminds one of the Gothic courtyards in Carrer Montcada, and the façade has a Nordic/medieval influence – Puig's buildings are constrained and tasteful; it comes as no surprise that he abandoned *modernisme* later in life and became an exponent of *noucentisme*, a sober, Catalan interpretation of neo-classical architecture. Gaudí's Casa Batlló is the odd man out in the Block of Discord; indeed, Gaudí himself was the odd man out in the *modernista* movement. Domènech and Puig were both prominent politicians and their architectural work was primarily concerned with the secular aspects of Catalan life. Though a fervent supporter of Catalanism – he hardly ever spoke Spanish – Gaudí would have been appalled to find historians pushing him under the *modernista* umbrella together with others whose philosophical views were at such variance with his own. Gaudí was a fervent Catholic whose life – and architecture – was devoted first and foremost to God.

Gaudí: The Sagrada Familia and Other Work

George Orwell called the Sagrada Familia, Barcelona's modern cathedral, 'one of the most hideous buildings in the world' and berated the anarchists for not blowing it up when they had the chance during the Civil War. Salvador Dalí, in contrast, praised Gaudí's 'supremely creative bad taste' and suggested that the building was unfinishable, 'at least until a new genius appears'. The Sagrada Familia (the Expiatory Temple of the Holy Family) has become a place of pilgrimage for students of architecture and one of the main attractions for visitors to Barcelona. Not to see it would be like missing the Pyramids when in Cairo or the Sistine Chapel in Rome. The cathedral has its own Metro stop (Sagrada Familia, Línia 5) and is open every day of the year (October to June: 09.00–19.00; July to September: 09.00–20.00). I suggest you buy a guide on arrival; and later you may wish to make your way along Avinguda de Gaudí to Domènech's *modernista* Hospital.

Antoni Gaudí i Cornet was born in 1852 in the town of Reus, the son of a Catalan coppersmith. He began his studies in Barcelona at the age of twenty, and his early works were sufficiently impressive to prompt the Spiritual Association of Saint Joseph to invite him to build the Sagrada Familia. The preliminary plans for the cathedral had been drawn up in the neo-Gothic style by Francisco de P. Villa and the first stone was laid while he was still in charge in 1882. Gaudí's early work – both at the cathedral and elsewhere – bears the unmistakable stamp of Gothic revival, but before long he was to develop his own highly idiosyncratic style. From the outset Gaudí intended the cathedral to be the work of generations, and its construction has followed the fitful fortunes of fundraising by the association. Since his death – he was hit by a tram on the Gran Via in 1926 – the financial problems have been compounded by the difficulties, for those who have inherited his task, in deciding exactly how to proceed with the building.

In his early days Gaudí appears to have been a dandy and a socialite but later he retreated more and more into himself and his work, concentrating above all on the Sagrada Familia. For the last twelve years of his life he worked, ate and often slept on the site of the cathedral, his daily routine virtually that of an ascetic. He would frequently go on fasts, and at least once this nearly led to his death. He always wore the same scruffy suit and was sometimes offered alms by those who mistook him for a beggar. During the later years of his life he refused all payment for his work on the cathedral and when funds ran too low to continue building he himself would go out and solicit money.

Gaudí left little in the way of drawings and instructions. He constantly modified his plans for the cathedral and worked mostly from models (see the exhibits in the excellent museum in the crypt below the Passion Façade). His writings, though few and disorganized, are none the less revealing. Above all, they show the intense importance which he attached to the Mediterranean countryside in which he lived. The brilliant blue skies and the bright light of his native Catalonia, the red earth of the scorched mountains, the dark green foliage of the carob and the gnarled vine, all were translated through the artist's eye into the structures and colours of his buildings. 'Let us think,' he would say, 'what it means to be Mediterranean. It means we are equidistant from the blinding light of the tropics and the northern lack of light which creates ghosts. We are brothers of the Italians and this makes us more apt for creative work.'

Gaudí looked to the shapes and colours in nature to help him solve structural problems and to provide inspiration for the design of all the visible aspects of his buildings. The great bell towers of the cathedral – hock bottles, according to

Orwell – mirror the spiral cones of slender sea snails. In characteristically flamboyant style Dalí described his architecture as 'a tactile erogenous zone which bristles like a sea urchin'. Indeed, there seems to be scarcely a single plant or animal which does not appear in some form on the cathedral. Serpents, whelks and clams double as gargoyles; and Nile turtles, pelicans, chameleons and a wealth of other plants and animals adorn the intricate sculptured scenes from the Bible on the Nativity Façade.

Gaudí's use of colour was as adventurous as his structural design. He wanted the cathedral to sparkle with coloured glass, and the bell towers have been clothed in dazzling ceramic mosaics. It is doubtful, however, whether the unborn architects whose task it may be to complete the cathedral will have the courage to polychrome the entire eastern façade in the brilliant colours that Gaudí had originally foreseen.

The power of the Sagrada Familia was well described by Federico García Lorca, the poet murdered by Franco's Falangists. He told Dalí how he heard 'a veritable din of sonorous cries of such loudness that they became increasingly more and more strident in proportion to the façade's heavenward climb, to the point of blending with the angels' trumpets into a glorious hullabaloo which he could not put up with for more than a few seconds'. One can only guess how Lorca would have reacted had Gaudí, as he at one time intended, surmounted the bell towers with angels whose flexible wings would flap with the wind.

Though the Sagrada Familia already dominates the city's skyline, it is scarcely half complete. The central tower, which is yet to be built, will be 580 feet (177 metres) high. Gaudí dreamed that it would reach so high towards the heavens that clouds and the fowls of the air would pass beneath its roof. And one day 13,000 people may worship in the cathedral, though it is unlikely that they will have to sit in stone pews of the type designed by Gaudí to thwart the profane habit of crossing legs. Gaudí conceived of the Sagrada Familia as a 'cathedral of the poor', its symbolism simple enough to be accessible to the illiterate; its beauty and power capable of inspiring faith through times of hardship.

When Gaudí died only one of the four towers which soar above the Nativity Façade was complete; the others were clothed in scaffolding and still climbing. Since then the Passion Façade, which also has four hock-bottle spires, has taken shape, and gradually, decade by decade, the cathedral has begun to look less like an abandoned ruin and more like a place of worship. (The crypt functions as a parish church and is open during services. Gaudí's tomb – which, like much else in the cathedral, was abused by anarchists during the Civil War – lies in the crypt.) Inevitably there has been plenty of controversy about what to do with the cathedral: Le Corbusier and others have argued that it should be left unfinished; rather more have urged its completion. However, there are some among the latter category who are not entirely happy with recent developments, and the sculptures done for the Passion Façade by Josep Subirachs have met with plenty of criticism.

These depict events in the final moments of Christ's life, from the Last Supper to the Crucifixion and the burial in Gethsemane. The sculptures are harsh, angular and entirely lacking in the organic softness which informs the sculptures on the Nativity Façade. And this, I think, is precisely as they should be. Those who dismiss Subirachs' work on the grounds that it is inappropriately avant-garde ignore the fact that the Passion Façade now tells its story – of betrayal, death, resurrection – with great power and an admirable lack of sentimentality. Subirachs' sculptures must rate among the best religious art of this century.

Though Gaudí spent most of his working life on the Sagrada Familia, the development of his ideas can more easily be traced by looking at his other ten works in and around Barcelona. He began his first major building in 1883, the year he took on the commission for the Sagrada Familia. **Casa Vicens** (Carrer de los Carolines 18–24; Metro: Lesseps or Fontana) already hints at the presence of an extraordinary and unorthodox talent. This brick house, built for a tile manufacturer, looks like a cross between a public lavatory and an Arab harem; it is compelling yet grotesque, its myriad surfaces studded with a patchwork of blue, green and white tiles (*azulejos*). There is a strong Gothic and Moorish influence to Gaudí's early works, readily apparent in Casa Vicens, at Palau Güell (*see* page 60) and at the pavilions and stables on the Güell Estate at Pedralbes. 'The design of these buildings,' suggests Ignasi de Solà-Morales, 'with all the diversity of the "pieces" which form them – rooms, towers, galleries, arcades, domed spaces, all with profuse and varied ornamentation – tends to produce an effect of something like the sensation of chaos, of a kaleidoscopic world which has no beginning or end; but also a sensation of hard aggression . . .'

The aggression derives from both the harsh lines of these early works and from the fearsome use of ironwork. Casa Vicens is guarded by a gate and fence whose panels are life-size representations of the fronds of the dwarf fan palm. The ironwork around the entrance of Palau Güell has already been mentioned, but above all I urge visitors to make their way to the pavilions of the **Güell Estate** (Avinguda de Pedralbes 7; Metro: Palau Reial or Maria Cristina). Hung between the two pavilions – one has a minaret-like tower – is a superbly crafted wrought-iron gate in the form of a dragon, whose tongue, which slithers out of a gaping mouth, is attached to the opening mechanism.

Gaudí first met Count Eusebi Güell, who was to be his lifelong patron, in 1882. Güell was a wealthy textile manufacturer with a keen interest in the arts. He travelled widely and it seems that Gaudí became acquainted with the writings of people like John Ruskin and William Morris (the founder of the English Arts and Crafts Movement) through Güell's large library. The pavilions and stable mentioned above were the first commissions Gaudí received from Güell. Then came Palau Güell (1886–90), the church for the Colonia Güell (1898–1915) and Park Güell (1900–14). 'Gaudí achieved full liberation in 1898,' suggests Nikolaus Pevsner, 'and his first completely mature masterpieces were begun in that year and in 1900, both for Güell. It is in the Colonia Güell and its amazing, fascinating, horrible, and inimitable church, Santa Coloma de Cervelló, that walls are first set in motion, windows appear in the seemingly most arbitrary positions and the seemingly most arbitrary forms, that columns bend or stand out of plumb, and that the craftsman is encouraged to leave work rough.' **Colonia Güell** (Güell Colony) is situated in an industrial suburb south of Barcelona; you must set aside half a day to get there and back, and leave enough time to visit the church and other buildings. Regular trains (Ferrocarrils de la Generalitat) connect Barcelona's Metro system (at Espanya and L'Hospitalet) with Santa Coloma de Cervelló.

When Pevsner says that the church was begun in 1898, what he really means is that Gaudí began thinking about it then. He actually spent ten years on the design of the church, and the first stone was not laid until 4 October 1908. The finished product was blessed by the Bishop of Barcelona on 3 November 1915. And yes, it is a fascinating and inimitable building, though to judge it horrible strikes me as being very unfair. It was here that Gaudí first experimented fully with tilted columns; these were able to absorb stress in a manner which could not be achieved by vertical columns or unbuttressed walls. In a sense, they are Gaudí's version of flying buttresses (he called them crutches) and they are even more pronounced in the viaducts of Park Güell. Gaudí chose as a location for the church a small knoll covered with pine trees, and the building blends beautifully with the landscape. Many of the columns and crutches – some made of grey basalt, others of sandstone and brick – seem to mirror the rough trunks of the trees outside, and indeed walking around inside the church is not unlike a journey through a densely canopied forest. The quality of light which enters in a mesh of dapples and rays through the oval windows and parabolic doorways seems appropriately sylvan. An elderly gentleman is often to be found in the church (he speaks some English) and he takes pleasure in showing the visitor the sorts of details they might otherwise miss: the curious way in which the windows open; the six original pews designed by Gaudí; an altar by one of Gaudí's great collaborators, Josep Jujol. He will also sell you a useful little guide to the church. It is well worth looking at the rest of Güell Colony, which was set up as a factory-cum-workers' estate in the 1890s. There are several streets of neat brick terraced housing, a school designed by Fransesc Berenguer, some good *modernista* villas, a little square with a statue of Güell, and a couple of cafés, in one of which you should take refreshment.

Getting to **Park Güell** is a good deal easier, and its virtues as a place for relaxation are described later (*see* page 148). Several buses pass near the park, but I recommend the Metro to Vallcarca (L3), from where it is a short walk down Avinguda de L'Hospital to the foot of a great cascade of elevators – Escales de la Baixada de la Glòria. Park Güell confirms Gaudí's talent not just as a designer of buildings but as a landscape architect. Like so many of his works Park Güell is unfinished, and indeed when judged by its original objectives – the intention was to create a garden city – it is a failure. The land was divided up into sixty plots, only two of which were sold, one to Gaudí and another to a friend of his. In 1922 it was handed over to the city to be run as a public park.

The main entrance is on Carrer d'Olot. Two extraordinary, Disneyesque pavilions guard the entry to the park. Both have polychromed roofs, rucked like meringues and sporting phallic protuberances and bizarre crenellations. Their playfulness contrasts with the elaborate austerity of the iron gate hung between them. From here stairways lead either side of two fountains – one a spectacularly colourful representation of a large lizard – to a market hall whose roof is supported by 86 Doric columns. The outer columns are tilted to take the stress of the roof, whose underside is decorated by a rich mosaic of broken tiles, bits of bottle, discarded toys and so forth. A sinuous bench by Josep Jujol, clothed in abstract patterns of ceramic tiling, wriggles around the crinkled edge of the roof. The space here, originally conceived as a Greek orchestra, is now a popular playground. According to one assessment of *modernisme*, this bench was 'the first great abstract work in the history of art'. This is a rather ambitious claim, though the park was much revered by the surrealist painters, who were particularly struck by the weird viaducts, supported by tilting columns, which snake across the hillside. 'The open spaces between the artificial trees gave me a sensation of unforgettable anguish,' wrote Salvador Dalí.

At the heart of the park is the house where Gaudí lived, on and off, from 1906 to 1926. In 1963 this was converted into a museum (open every day except Saturdays, 10.00–14.00 and 16.00–18.00). The house was designed by Fransesc Berenguer. If you happen to be in the park when the museum is open you may feel it merits a visit; I found it rather disappointing. There is some furniture designed by Gaudí (including benches and cupboards intended for the entrance of Casa Milà, and some lovely chairs); there is also a fair amount of excruciatingly vulgar stuff, including some heavily gilded sofas and chairs. Gaudí's real genius is to be seen outside – in the viaducts, the pathways, and, most significantly of all, the market hall/theatre.

Gaudí's last two secular works, **Casa Batlló** (1904–6) and **Casa Milà** (1906–10), are both to be found in Passeig de Gràcia. Entirely gone is the harsh angularity of his early works; gone too are virtually all traces of Gothic and Moorish influence. The façade and roof of Casa Batlló (*see* page 90) have been interpreted by some as a representation of St George slaying the dragon. Others see it as a piece of marine theatre; or, as Dalí put it, 'an immense, senseless multicolour mosaic shimmering with scintillating light from which various forms of water emerge'. What no one disputes is that both these buildings owe much to Gaudí's desire to incorporate, both in the structure of his works and in their sculptural cladding, the sinuous and organic qualities of the natural world.

The seven-storey Casa Milà, at Passeig de Gràcia 92, is known as La Pedrera (the quarry). This, the largest of Gaudí's residential works, was commissioned by Pere Milà and his wife, who claimed that Gaudí's extravagance ruined them. Quite possibly, but they should be posthumously proud of their patronage. The main façade undulates in a series of waves around the chamfered corner where Passeig de Gràcia is intersected by Carrer de Provença. The impression of fluidity and motion is enhanced by wrought-iron balconies fashioned in the shape of seaweed (and designed by Jujol) and by the grotto-like entrances and windows from which, at any moment, one expects some weird sea-creatures to appear. The building is best explored from its rooftop, which can be visited on the regular guided tours (on the hour: 10.00–13.00 and 16.00–18.00, Mondays to Friday; 10.00–13.00, Saturday; 11.00–13.00, Sunday). The roof rises and falls like a rough sea frozen in time, but there is reason behind this apparent madness: the roof is simply reflecting the different heights of the parabolic arches of the garrets below. Dotted about the roof are clumps of air flues, which look like gangs of helmeted invaders, and six ceramic-tiled sculptures which are the outer manifestations of the internal stairwells. Gaudí had originally planned to build on the roof a huge statue of the Virgin, but after the anti-church rioting of 1909 Pere Milà vetoed the idea.

Other works by Gaudí in Barcelona include: Col·legi de les Teresianes (1888–90), Carrer de Ganduxer 95-105; Casa Calvet (1889–1904), Carrer de Casp 48; Torre Bellesguard (1900–04), Carrer Bellesguard. Gaudí collaborated with Fransesc Berenguer on the Bodegas Güell (1888–90), the wine vaults built for Eusabi Güell on the coast road between Castelldefels and Sitges.

Lluís Domènech i Montaner (1850–1923)

Domènech is one of the great figures in Catalan history. Not only was he an outstanding architect, but he also distinguished himself as a politician and academic. At the age of thirty-eight he became President of the Lliga de Catalunya and four years later, in 1892, he was made President of the Unió Catalanista. In 1901 and 1903 he was elected to the Cortes (National

Parliament) in Madrid. In 1901 he also became Director of the Barcelona Escola Superior d'Arquitectura (where he had begun teaching in 1877). Some years earlier he had co-authored a general history of art with Puig i Cadafalch.

Domènech's first significant building was the Editorial Montaner i Simon (1881–86) at Carrer d'Aragó 255. This has recently been turned into a museum exhibiting the work of Antoni Tàpies (*see* page 130). For the 1888 Exhibition Domènech contributed the Gran Hotel International (dismantled soon after) and the Café-Restaurant, which now houses the Zoological Museum (*see* pages 74 and 75). Then came Palau Montaner (1889–96) at Carrer de Mallorca 278 (this is now the headquarters of the Government Delegation of Catalonia); Casa Thomas (1895–98), at 291–297 on the same street; and the splendid restaurant for Hotel España at Carrer de Sant Pau 9–11. However his greatest works – and arguably the purest and most mature *modernista* creations – were reserved for the early years of this century.

The **Palau de la Música Catalana** (1905–08) is tucked away down a narrow side street off the upper end of Via Laietana. As Alastair Boyd suggests, it 'trembles on the brink of vulgarity but is saved from this by the architect's powerful vision, through which all the potentially warring elements are made to serve the functional and symbolic purposes of the whole'. The Palau is a building of such richness and complexity that it must be savoured slowly, ideally during a concert.

Both inside and out Domènech has made remarkable use of every possible form of decoration: brick columns are surmounted with floral capitals of ceramic tiles; a rich mosaic clothes the upper reaches of the main façade; a fantastic stained glass bowl hangs from the ceiling of the auditorium; balustrades are constructed of amber glass, iron, marble and ceramic tiling. In short, this building is a monument to the arts and crafts movement, heavily reliant on art nouveau motifs – such as flowers and snaking lines – and at times utterly tasteless. One wonders what the audience thought when the first concert was held in 1908. It is hard to keep one's eyes on the orchestra, or choir, when there is so much else to observe. On the left of the stage is an allegorical representation of Catalan folk music, sculpted in stone by Pau Gargallo; on the right a billow of smoke rises from beside a bust of Beethoven to become the cavalcade of Wagner's Valkyrie. Even more bizarre is the scene behind the stage: porcelain bas-reliefs of soppy-looking maidens gaze like pre-Raphaelite prima donnas from a mosaic mural. The same technique – porcelain bas-reliefs implanted in mosaic depictions of clothes and landscapes – was also used in Casa Lléo-Morera, on the Block of Discord. Domènech employed many of the outstanding craftsmen of his day – Gaspar Homar, Eusebi Arau, Joan Carreras, Mario Maragliano and Josep Pey among others; and with Antoni Maria Gallissà he founded a studio to train craftsmen in his café-restaurant in Ciutadella Park (*see* page 75).

There is something whimsical – indeed, almost mad – about Domènech's desire to coat every surface of the Palau with decoration, yet (unlike Gaudí) he belongs very much to the rational school of *modernisme*. Domènech was adventurous in his deployment of modern materials and systems of construction (making good use, for example, of large metal frames) and he showed greater concern for the spatial properties of his buildings than did Gaudí. One can exist *comfortably* within a building by Domènech, whereas Gaudí's creations possess a warped, surrealistic quality, much as one experiences in a bad dream.

Domènech's sensitive attitude to space is more clearly seen in the **Hospital de la Santa Creu i de Sant Pau**. The best way to approach it is along Avinguda de Gaudí, a pleasant tree-lined, largely pedestrianized street which runs diagonally (as though in protest against Cerdà's grid-pattern) from the Sagrada Familia up to the hospital. Ignore the Pizza Hut and Kentucky Fried Chicken restaurants guarding the entrance to the street, and drop in instead at one of the small *tapas* bars: Granja Gaudí, a forcep's throw from the hospital entrance, is as good as any. The hospital complex, like Avinguda de Gaudí, is also at odds with Cerdà's street system, with the main building facing south and a series of smaller pavilions following suit behind. Domènech worked on the hospital from 1902 until 1912, after which his son, Pere Domènech i Roure, took over. The hospital, which consists of over twenty buildings, replaced the medieval one (described on page 61). Money to build it came in 1892 in the form of a legacy from a Tarragonese banker, Pau Gil, on condition that it carried the name of his patron saint, Sant Pau. The legacy ran dry in 1911, but work continued in 1914 and the hospital was effectively completed by 1926. It is one of Domènech's more subdued works, and arguably the most beautiful. In fact, just looking at the buildings would be enough to revive an ailing aesthete.

A slender clock tower rises high above the pantiled roof of the large entrance building, whose brickwork supports mosaics depicting various historical scenes. The horseshoe-arch entrances are among the many Moorish (*mudéjar*) features of the hospital. The arches themselves rest on floral (art nouveau) capitals and the benefactor's initials appear in ceramic around their periphery. In front is a bust of Gil presiding over a sentimental scene where a nurse gives comfort to a sick child and an old man. The large vaulted foyer also shows strong Moorish influence. Especially lovely are the domed pavilions behind, with their exotic tiling and wealth of statuary. Each is devoted to a particular function (the gynaecology pavilion has an ominous sign which simply reads 'PARTS') and all are linked by a complex system of subterranean passageways. As always, Domènech has made extensive use of the city's craftsmen. Much of the iconography is religious in character; appropriately enough, scores of angels hover above the buildings and balconies. Moving further north, or away from the sea, the buildings become larger and less ornate. The hospital café lies behind the baroque façade of the church of Santa Maria, constructed in 1747 and transplanted here from the old city. Patients (and visitors) can relax in the delightful gardens.

Other works by Domènech in Barcelona, not mentioned so

far, include: Casa Lamadrid (1902), Carrer de Girona 13; and Casa Fuster (1908–11), Passeig de Gràcia 132. Domènech also collaborated on La Rotunda (1906), which stands near the Tibidabo Tram Terminus, on the corner of Passeig de Sant Gervasi and Avinguda de Tibidabo.

Josep Puig i Cadafalch (1867–1957)

Josep Puig i Cadafalch was the leading light of the second generation of *modernista* architects. Like Domènech, he was a man of many parts, making a name for himself both as a historian and archaeologist, and as a politician. He was a co-founder of the Lliga Regionalista in 1901; he was elected to the Cortes in 1907; and he held the Presidency of the Mancom-munitat from 1917 until its dissolution in 1924. In 1936 he went into exile in France.

The architect Xavier Güell i Guix has pointed out that all Puig's *modernista* works are examples 'of good sense, good construction and good taste'. When compared to Gaudí and Domènech, Puig seems distinctly unadventurous, and his build-ings lack the eccentricity and the Mediterranean warmth of, for example, Domènech's Palau de la Música Catalana or Gaudí's Casa Batlló. Nevertheless Puig was a significant figure in the *modernista* movement. Two of his buildings have already been mentioned: Casa Martí, at Carrer de Montsió 3, was an apartment block whose ground floor became the famous Els Quatre Gats café; shortly after completing that, in 1898, Puig rebuilt Casa Amattler on the Block of Discord, Passeig de Gràcia 41. Puig's strong attachment to the medieval-ism of northern Europe, as well as to Catalan vernacular, is apparent in all his early works. **Casa de les Punxes** (1903–5) – a large five-storey apartment block occupying a triangle of land between the Diagonal and Carrer del Rosselló – has mullioned windows, prominent triangular gables and conical spires at each corner: all of which remind one of the Nordic north. The *modernista* features include the mosaics beneath the roof line, and the columns and floral capitals supporting the horseshoe-arch entrances.

The smaller **Casa Serra** at Rambla de Catalunya 126 was begun in the same year as the Casa de les Punxes; architecturally the two have much in common, though in Casa Serra Renaissance features have replaced the Gothic previously favoured by Puig. His largest building was the **Fabrica Casarramona** (1911), a spinning mill on Carrer de Mèxic, and now a shabby police barracks. Its most eye-catching features are the two minaret-like towers. Soon afterwards Puig forsook the tenets of *modernisme* and adopted the more staid neo-classical style of *noucentisme*.

Other buildings dating from Puig's *modernista* period, and not mentioned so far, include: Casa Macaya (1901) at Passeig de Sant Joan, 108; Casa Muntadas (1901) at Avinguda del Doctor Andreu 48; Casa Quadras (1904) at Avinguda Diagonal 373, now the Museu de la Música; and Casa Company (1911) at Carrer de Casanova 203.

Modernisme - A Further Selection

It is curious to think that for much of this century – from, say, 1910 to around 1960 – *modernisme* was derided and frowned upon by the academics and chattering classes. For them a wander around the Eixample must have been a painful experience, for there is scarcely a street which doesn't possess at least one building exhibiting a strong *modernista* influence. Visitors who enjoy the casual experience of discovery will doubtless wander where the fancy takes them. Others may wish to adopt a more organized approach and take themselves on a guided tour of *modernista* architecture. (One city map, published by the Patrionat de Turisme, includes recommended walks, one of which takes in many of the best *modernista* buildings.)

There are hundreds of *modernista* buildings in Barcelona, and it would be impractical (and indeed silly, for many are of little architectural merit) to mention anything but a handful here. Two buildings in the vicinity of Ciutadella Park deserve a mention. Pere Falqués – who was also responsible for the street lamps on Avinguda de Gaudí, and for the bench-lights on Passeig de Gràcia – was the architect of **Hidroelèctrica de Catalunya**, a power station built on Avinguda de Vilanova in 1897, and now the offices of an electricity company. This is a large iron and brick structure with a superb portico with tiled columns, ornate iron balconies and grilles, and elaborate brickwork. Not far from here is the **Palau de Justicia** (1887–1908) on Passeig de Lluís Companys, whose architects were Enric Sagnier and Josep Domènech i Estapa. Its principal *modernista* feature is the large entrance.

Back at the heart of *modernista* territory, at Avinguda Diagonal 442, is Salvador Valeri's remarkable **Casa Comalat** (1909–11). The front of this apartment block is topped by an extravagantly curly green tiled roof (reminiscent of Gaudí's Casa Batlló); the back of the building on Carrer de Còrsega looks like the bulging stern of a medieval galleon. There are two bull-rings in Barcelona, the one at Gran Via 749 – Plaça de Toros Monumental – being in the *modernista* style: Ignasi Mas was obviously much influenced by Moorish architecture.

There are dozens of shop fronts whose art nouveau façades have survived both the depredations of time and mid-century obloquy. For some reason this style was especially favoured by pharmacies and bakeries. An art nouveau pilgrimage though Barcelona would be incomplete without a visit to the following:

- Fruites i Verdures (stand 435-6), La Boqueria Market.
- Farmacia J. de Bolós, Rambla de Catalunya 77.
- Antigua Casa Figueras, La Rambla 83.
- Panaderia y Pasteleria Sarret, Carrer de Girona 372.
- Confiteria y Bomboneria, Carrer de Consell de Cent 362.
- Farmacia Robert, Carrer de Roger de Llúria 74.
- El Indio, Carrer de Carme 24.

FROM PEDRALBES TO THE DIAGONAL

Visitors to Barcelona will probably spend most of their time in the areas already described: the medieval city, the Eixample, Montjuïc and Ciutadella Park. However, those with time on their hands may wish to go further afield and explore the outerlying suburbs. Park Güell and Colonia Güell have been included in the section on *modernisme*; and Horta and Tibidabo are dealt with in Chapter 4 (*see* page 141). From an architectural point of view, one of the most fascinating areas in the outskirts of Barcelona is Pedralbes, and this section takes the reader from the superb Gothic monastery of Santa Maria de Pedralbes down the Avinguda de Pedralbes (past Gaudí's pavilions for the Güell Estate) to the Diagonal, where there is a Royal Palace and several towering monuments to the Modern Movement (not to be confused with *modernisme*].

The **monastery of Santa Maria de Pedralbes** is best reached by bus (number 22 goes from Plaça de Catalunya via Passeig de Gràcia; number 64 from Passeig de Colom via Avinguda del Para·lel), and if you are in need of sustenance on arrival, a flight of steps at the lower end of Plaça de Pedralbes leads to a delightful garden-café, popular with local workmen and surrounded by palms and flowering shrubs. From here head west past one of the worst examples of *modernisme* – the Banco de Santander looks like a cream bun covered with coloured Smarties – and the monastery is to your right. It was founded in 1325 by Elisenda de Montcada, the wife of Jaume II. A community of Clarist nuns still lives here, although their number is a fraction of what it used to be. The church is simple and elegant, with a tall nave, a semi-circular apse, six side chapels and an octagonal bell tower. There are tall lancet windows in the nave and apse and a rose window at the rear of the nave, just visible above the screen which divides the nuns' choir from the rest of the church. The stained glass is original. To the right of the altar is Queen Elisenda's regal tomb carved in alabaster. The church is open every day of the

week, and if you are fortunate you may hear some beautiful
organ music.

Beside the church are the Gothic cloisters and associated
buildings. The clustered columns with leaf-motif capitals support twenty-six ogival arches along each side of the lower two
storeys of the three-storey cloister, at the heart of which is a
garden with cypresses and orange trees. The walls of the small
chapel dedicated to Sant Miquel are covered with paintings by
Ferrer Bassa dating from 1346. Bassa was influenced by the
Sienna school and by Giotto, and his paintings provide a
wonderfully expressive interpretation of such events as the
Annunciation, the birth of Christ and the Passion. Of the
twenty-nine wood panels the loveliest, I think, depicts Saint
Francis and Saint Claire.

In contrast to the opulence of Sant Miquel's chapel are
other cells of great simplicity: one, for example, has
whitewashed walls, a wooden chair, a table and a small *pietà*;
another, a tiny piano. The Chapter House, completed in 1419,
has been turned into a small monastic museum, but more
interesting in many ways are the refectory, kitchens and
bedrooms. The large refectory has 'Silentium' written on the
walls, though evidently not everyone had to hold their tongue:
there is a pulpit on one wall. The kitchens are vast and there is
some good ceramic tiling – depicting peasants, troubadours,
monks, etc. – above a huge sink; it is a shame that the
vegetable garden outside has been left to go wild. From here
the visitor passes into the sick bay, with a jerry beneath each
bed, and then to the main dormitory.

There are no buses running down Avinguda de Pedralbes to
the Diagonal, so you must go by foot or taxi. It is a pleasant
stroll through one of the city's smarter districts and takes
about 20 minutes. Gaudí's pavilions for the Güell Estate (*see*
page 97) are on the right-hand side, some two-thirds of the
way down. Turn right when you reach the Diagonal and head
for the **Parc de Palau Reial de Pedralbes**. The palace itself was
built in 1915 as a residence for the Spanish Royal Family. The
palace is frequently closed to the public, but the semi-formal

gardens are worth visiting: there are some avenues of pollarded limes; stands of palms, pines and bamboo; numerous flower beds (some rimmed with ornamental cabbages); a small fountain designed by Gaudí; and plenty of statuary. (The gardens are open: 10.00–18.00, November to February; 10.00–20.00, March and April; 10.00–21.00, May to August; and 10.00–19.00, September and October.)

This part of the Diagonal is liberally sprinkled with giant office blocks, department stores and hotels. Some, like El Corte Inglés, are plain ugly, but there are others which deserve more than a passing glance. The **Torres de Oficinas** (1966–9) is a monumental complex of curvaceous black-glass towers and one of the best works by the Barcelonan architect Josep Antoni Coderch. Less celebrated – though more to my taste – is the **Edifici Banca** at Diagonal 662–664. The academics evidently don't think much of it: it does not even get a mention in the comprehensive *Guía de Arquitectura de Barcelona*, whereas such modern monstrosities as the nearby Faculty of Law and the Architects' College opposite the cathedral do. The Edifici Banca is almost embarrassingly good when compared to these two. It is a glass and concrete structure consisting of three interlocking octagonal wings some nine storeys high. The glass walls of each floor slope inward, like eels' teeth, and the mirror glass reflects the profusion of plants which tumble, sprout, bloom and twist from the boxes which run round the balconies. All a far cry from the sterile curtains of glass and concrete which characterize so may buildings of the Modern Movement.

3:
MUSEUMS AND GALLERIES

For a city of its size, Barcelona has an astonishing number of museums and art galleries. A guide to the museums, published by the Caixa de Pensions in 1978, listed 55. There are rather fewer today: the tourist board lists 47. They range from the world-famous Museu d'Art de Catalunya to the tiny Museu del Perfum (Perfume Museum). Virtually every specialist interest is catered for, from stamp-collecting to firemen's clothes, antique footwear to bullfighting.

This chapter is divided into three sections: the first describes the museums and galleries devoted to painting and the arts; the second looks at the more important collections covering the sciences; and the third deals with subjects of a miscellaneous nature. Eight museums have already been described in Chapter 2, 'A City Guide', as their contents form an integral part of the architectural fabric in which they find themselves (for the Museu Catedral, *see* page 30; for the Museu d'Història de la Ciutat, *see* page 31; for the Museu Marès, *see* page 33; for the Museu Textil i de la Indumentària, *see* page 48; for the Museu Maritim, *see* page 58; for the Museu Militar, *see* page 80; for the Museu Sagrada Familia, *see* page 94; and for Gaudí's Home Museum, *see* page 100).

A word of warning: the Barcelonans are fond of playing musical chairs with their museums. Collections are shifted, opening times are changed, rooms are closed for refurbishment and new displays are set up with a rapidity designed to frustrate the best intentions of the guide-book writer. Back in 1949 Rose Macaulay noted 'that many museums that house pictures, sculpture, archaeological finds, historical exhibits, and so on seem to be moved in Barcelona, as elsewhere in Spain, from one habitation to another every few years'. *Plus ça change, plus c'est la même chose.* The period leading up to the 1992 Olympics was especially traumatic and if things are not what they seem – or where this book suggests they should be – the local tourist offices will provide visitors with the latest information. In any case, it is worth visiting the tourist offices to get details of the many temporary exhibitions which make Barcelona such a joy to visit, even for those who know its museums well.

THE ARTISTIC HERITAGE

Represented, albeit patchily, in the museums and galleries of Barcelona is virtually the whole spectrum of Western European art from the 11th century onwards. The Museu d'Art de Catalunya possesses what is possibly the best collection of Romanesque art in the world, as well as an admirable selection of works from the Gothic, Renaissance and baroque periods. Housed in the same building – the Palau Nacional – is the excellent Museu de Ceràmica, with a large collection of Spanish ceramic pieces from the 13th century to the present day. For those familiar with the Tate Gallery in London or the Museum of Modern Art in New York, Barcelona's Museu d'Art Modern (at the time of writing in Ciutadella Park, but destined for Montjuïc's Palau Nacional) is somewhat disappointing. Most of the paintings and sculptures are from the second half of the last century and the early years of this; Catalan artists such as Fortuny, Casas, Rusiñol and Nonell are well represented, but for more contemporary painters – Picasso, Miró, Tàpies – you must look elsewhere. Indeed, each of these artists has a museum, or a *fundació*, to himself; those devoted to the works of Picasso and Miró are particularly recommended.

Museu d'Art de Catalunya (Catalan Museum of Art)

(Palau Nacional, Montjuïc. Closed on Monday; 09.00–14.00, Tuesday to Saturday. Metro: L1 or L3 to Espanya; bus: 61.)

The museum is divided into three sections: Romanesque (to the right of the foyer); Gothic; and Renaissance, baroque and neo-classical (all to the left of the foyer). There is a bookshop in the foyer, but no guide to the museum. The exhibits are well labelled, but only in Catalan and Spanish.

There are roughly 2,000 Romanesque buildings – 1,800 churches and 200 castles – in Catalonia, some of which are described in Chapter 7. The Romanesque style endured from the early years of the 11th century to the beginning of the 13th. The architect and historian Josep Puig i Cadafalch, who rescued many of the museum's frescoes from the crumbling churches of the Pyrenees, recognized two distinct phases in the Romanesque period. Primary Romanesque arrived from Lombardy and spread across northern Catalonia during the 11th century. During the second phase, which occupied the 12th century and saw the style spread to all corners of Catalonia, Romanesque architecture reached full maturity and was characterized by a great degree of structural complexity and a remarkable attention to sculptural detail. Romanesque art is to be found in two forms: as frescoes (in Romanesque churches the walls were often considered as scaffold for murals) and as paintings on wood panels. The following is a selective guide to the Romanesque treasures of the Museu d'Art de Catalunya. Many of the exhibits are accompanied by photographs showing the churches from which they came.

Room 2: Apse from the chapel in Marmellar castle (12th century). **Room 3**: An exceptionally beautiful – and harrowing – fresco from the Church of Sant Joan de Boí depicting, in earthy greys, ochres, reds and blues, the stoning of St Stephen (11th century). **Room 4**: Wall paintings from Sant Joan de Boí; fresco from the apse from Sant Pere, La Seu d'Urgell; a polychromed Christ in Majesty. **Room 5**: The frontals from the tiny church of Sant Quirc, which is perched high up in the hills of the Vall de Boí above the village of Durro (*see* page 207). **Room 6**: Frescoes from the apse from Ginestarre. The serenity of Christ and the other figures depicted in this and most other murals contrasts with the gruesome acts of torture in the frontal dedicated to Sant Quirc of Durro. **Room 10**: The apse fresco from Argolell, and another with a droll depiction of the wise and foolish virgins. **Rooms 11–13**: A series of wood carvings (including the magnificent Battló Majesty, and several of the Virgin and the Apostles), mostly from the 12th century. Note also the painted wood frontal from Sant Saturnino de Tabernoles. **Room 14**: One of the most celebrated works of Romanesque art, the *Pantocrator* (God the Majesty), a fresco from the apse of Sant Climent de Taüll, possibly the loveliest of all the churches in the Vall de Boí (*see* page 205). A wonderfully doleful Pantocrator, robed in a rich greeny-blue with dexter hand raised, is surrounded by the symbols of the Evangelists and a group of Apostles. Above, in the dome, is an image of the right hand of God (similar to the one carved over the portal of the church of Sant Pau del Camp, at the foot of Montjuïc). This is a work of great sophistication and beauty. **Room 15**: The apse painting from the nearby Santa Maria de Taüll, which was consecrated on the day after Sant Climent, on 11 December 1123. **Room 16**: Paintings from the aisle of Santa Maria and a fine wooden grouping (12th century) depicting the Descent from the Cross. (Another moving Romanesque portrayal of the Descent can be seen in the monastery of Sant Joan de les Abadesses, *see* page 213.) There is also a 12th-century crucifixion in this room. **Rooms 19–20**: More wooden figures, of the Virgin and of the crucifixion. **Room 21**: Exquisite 12th-century altar frontals from various churches in the Pyrenees. Between **Rooms 21** and **22** are four columns with capitals rescued from the cloister of Sant Pere de Les Puelles (*see* page 48), one of the few Romanesque churches in Barcelona. **Rooms 23–24**: The remaining rooms exhibiting Romanesque art contain stone sculptures, crucifixes, censers, chests, etc., mostly from the 12th and 13th centuries.

On the other side of the main foyer are a further twenty rooms devoted to Gothic art. This section is also worthy of a thorough visit, although Gothic art may strike some visitors as agonized and indigestible when compared to the simplicity and purity of the Romanesque. It is best, I think, to visit the two sections on different days.

There are two distinct strands in early Gothic painting, both well represented here. The linear style, also known as Franco-Gothic, was superseded by the Italo-Gothic style in the second quarter of the 14th century. **Room 52**: Outstanding among the latter school are the works of Arnau Bassa (the Annunciation and Epiphany), and the Serra brothers (several retables). The Italo-Gothic style gave way to international Gothic, and of particular note among Catalan artists of this later period were Lluis Dalmau and Jaume Huguet. **Room 59**: Bartolomé Bermejo's *Christ descending into Hell* (his magnificent *Pietat* of 1490 is in the Museum Cathedral). **Room 60**: Dalmau's *Virgin of the Councillors* (1445), and some superb retables by Huguet (you may already have seen his Epiphany retable in the chapel of Santa Agata, *see* page 31).

Eventually one emerges from the Gothic rooms into a rather different world of Renaissance, baroque and neo-classical art. It is a great shame there is not more of it. Outstanding among the paintings here are El Greco's *Saints Peter and Paul*, and Velásquez's *St Peter*.

Museu de Ceràmica (Ceramics Museum)

(Location and openings hours: as for Museu d'Art de Catalunya. The Museu de Ceràmica is on the second floor of the Palau Nacional; entry through **Room 20** of Museu d'Art de Catalunya (on the same ticket). The Museum may have moved to Palau de Pedralbes by the time you read this. Metro: L3 to Palau Reial; bus: 7, 75.)

Most visitors to Barcelona are immediately struck by the adventurous use of ceramic tiling as a means of decorating buildings. Such tiling is as prominent as the malevolent

ironwork for which the Spanish have such a passion; aesthetically, it is much more pleasing. Wander round the medieval
quarters and you will come across several drinking fountains
clad with ceramic tiles depicting mythical or historical events,
or scenes and objects from everyday life: peasants ploughing,
women fetching water, huntsmen, musicians, soldiers, washerwomen, vegetables, monsters, fish, demons, saints. The
favoured colours are golds, yellows and blues on a white
background. Some of the tiling is modern – for example, the
scenes by the ceramic artist Josep Aragay surrounding the
fountain at Portal de l'Angel date from 1918 – but many of the
decorated fountains are much older. The Catalans have long
used ceramic tiling inside their buildings: such work ranges
from the superb murals depicting the life of Saint Paul in the
entrance to the Casa de Convalescència (by Llorenç Passoles in
the 17th century) to the cheerful tiling lining the walls of many
cafés and restaurants (see, for example, Los Caracoles at
Carrer dels Escudellers 14).

The use of ceramic tiling is seen at its most flamboyant in
the *modernista* buildings of the city, and indeed the
modernistes did much to rescue the craft of making ceramics
by hand from extinction. The façades of Gaudí's Casa Batlló
and Puig's Casa Amattler are clothed in tiles, while Domènech
used ceramic tiles to clad the walls and ceilings of buildings
such as the Palau de la Música Catalana. With the help of
Antoni Maria Gallissà, Domènech set up a workshop to train
craftsmen in the decorative arts (see page 75). Domènech and
Gaudí, in their quest to seek out the few who still practised
traditional ceramic techniques at the turn of the century, set
off together on an expedition to Manises in Valencia. Here
they found a master of the art called Casany, who joined
Domènech's workshop to share his knowledge with a new
generation of craftsmen.

The Museu Ceràmica has an extensive collection of ceramic
art – bowls, plates, jugs, tiles – most of it originating from the
great centres of production: Manises, Muel, Reus, Palma,
Paterna and Teruel. **Room 1**: Early Catalan ware dating from

the 15th to 18th centuries: 23 pieces found in Palma in 1937 are on display here. There are also Arab ceramic objects from the 12th and 13th centuries. **Room 2**: An outstanding range of ceramics, most from Paterna (near Manises) and Teruel, which lies inland from Paterna. There are some gorgeous platters and bowls from the 13th and 14th centuries, predominantly green and white, many depicting wild animals, domestic stock, birds, fish and snakes. These look so 'modern' that one half expects them to be attributed to Picasso (who may well have been influenced by the Paterna pottery). Also on display here are tiles, most painted with cobalt blue, from Paterna and Teruel. Note the curious representations of animals like rabbit, deer and flea. **Room 3** covers the period from the 15th to 18th centuries, and includes ceramic pots, jugs, plates and tiles from Manises, Reus, Paterna and Muel. **Room 9** brings the history of ceramic art in Northern Spain almost up to date, with a collection of 19th-century plates and tiles from Manises. The kitchen scenes – housewife bartering with game seller; thrushes, mallard and partridge slung from butcher's hooks; cat looking ill – are typical of the period.

Museu d'Art Modern (The Museum of Modern Art)

(Plaça de les Armes, Ciutadella Park. 15.00–19.30, Monday; 0900–19.30, Tuesday to Saturday; 09.00–14.00, Sunday and holidays. This museum may have moved to the Palau Nacional by the time this guide is published. The museum catalogue is exhaustive, but costs 10,000 pesetas (about £60). Metro: L1 to Arc de Triomf; bus: 14, 16, 17, 36, 39, 40, 45, 51, 57, 59, 64.)

The historian Alastair Boyd suggests that the Museu d'Art Modern 'is strictly for Hispanophiles with a strong Catalanophile streak'. It is true that much of the work on display is of poor quality, but there is enough good art to justify a visit, although this is the sort of museum one wishes to see at a canter, pausing from time to time to study a few choice paintings and hastily bypassing the rest. The museum is largely devoted to Catalan painting, drawing and sculpture from around 1870 to 1920. (The paintings are arranged in chronological order; in view of the impending move, room numbers are not given here.)

One of the father figures of 19th-century Catalan painting was Ramon Martí i Alsina (1826–94), and the museum possesses several fine canvasses by him, including the dramatic *La Companyia de Santa Bàrbara* with women tending wounded soldiers. A teacher at Barcelona's Llotja (the school of Fine Arts), he and his pupils were strongly influenced by the realist ideas of Gustav Courbet. Among those who were indebted to Martí's teaching were the landscape artist Joaquim Vayreda and two of the great names in *modernista* painting, Santiago Rusiñol and Ramon Casas. Another key figure of the pre-*modernista* period was Marià Fortuny i Marsal (1838–74), whose *Battle of Tetuan* provides a magnificently energetic portrayal of war.

Fortuny's preoccupation with the brilliant light of the Mediterranean – for many years he lived in Rome – was shared by a group of young artists known as the Sitges Luminists. One of their members, Arcadi Mas i Fontdevila (1852–1934), organized an exhibition at the seaside town of Sitges in 1892; this was the first of a series which became known as *Festes modernistes*, or *modernista* festivals. The Luminists were joined at the first *Festa* by painters from the Olot School of Landscape Artists, which was led by Joaquim Vayreda i Vila (1843–94), a bust of whom, with beret and moustache, can be seen in the Plaça d'Armes. Vayreda's landscape paintings are among the most pleasing and restful in the museum.

'For the Olot painter,' wrote Marilyn McCully in her introductory essay to *Homage to Barcelona: The City and its Art 1888–1936*, 'effects of mood and atmosphere depended primarily upon the quality of brushstroke; for example, a variety of strokes was used to suggest the motion of leaves or grasses and to establish compositional planes. Vayreda then generally unified his compositions with an overall thin application of paint – usually tones ranging from cool browns to dark greens – as if the landscape were filled with mist or late afternoon light.'

During the 1890s Sitges became known as the *modernistas'* Mecca. Its significance as a meeting place for the first generation of *modernista* artists was largely due to the presence there of Santiago Rusiñol (1861–1931), who arrived in Sitges in 1891, participated in the *Festa modernista* of 1892, and converted two rundown fishermen's cottages on the sea-cliffs into a studio/museum. He immediately filled the building with his large collection of Spanish ironwork, hence its name – Cau Ferrat. In 1894, at the time of the third *Festa*, Rusiñol returned from a trip to Paris with two paintings by El Greco and a solemn procession carried them through the streets from the railway station to his home. Something of the Bohemian flavour of those days lingers still in the Museu Cau Ferrat, and I urge anyone remotely interested in Catalonia's *modernista* period to take the train down to Sitges and combine a visit to the museum with a *paella* and a swim (*see* page 181).

If anyone can be said to have given organizational strength to the *modernista* movement it was Rusiñol, who by the time of his arrival in Sitges was already recognized as an artist and writer of unusual talent. The year before, in 1890, Rusiñol had visited Paris with Ramon Casas (1866–1932), who was undoubtedly the greatest painter of the *modernista* period, and the critic and historian Miquel Utrillo (1862–1934). Together they lived above the famous Moulin de la Galette. Rusiñol and Casas were both influenced by French Impressionism, not so much in technique as choice of subject – their café and street scenes of the late 1880s and early 1990s were something quite new to Catalan painting. There were regular *Festes modernistes* through the 1890s, but Sitges's significance as the *modernistas'* Mecca diminished somewhat after the opening of Els Quatre Gats café in 1897. The café, which occupied the lower floor of Puig i Cadafalch's Casa Martí (Carrer de Montsio 3), became an important *modernista* venue. Its founders were Rusiñol, Casas, Utrillo and Pere Romeu. Casas's huge oil (1897) of himself and Romeu riding a tandem through Barcelona was one of the many *modernista* paintings hung in the café. It is now in the Museu d'Art Modern. The café attracted a wealth of creative talent: Isaac Albéniz gave a concert here; Joan Maragall read some of his poems; and a new generation of artists – among them Joaquim Mir, Isidre Nonell and Pablo Picasso (*see* page 122) – saw the café as an agreeable place in which to meet and hang their sketches and paintings.

The Museu d'Art Modern houses a good collection of paintings, posters and drawings by both Rusiñol and Casas. There are strong similarities between their works of the early 1890s, but midway through the decade they followed different artistic paths. Rusiñol veered towards Symbolism and produced a series of paintings which were reminiscent of the syrupy pre-Raphaelites at their worst, and far inferior to his bold portraits and café scenes of a few years earlier. From the end of the century until his death in 1931, Rusiñol devoted the bulk of his artistic energies to painting the great gardens of Spain. A great shame. The Museu d'Art Modern contains a representative selection of his work (including some posters), although I think Rusiñol's talent is more readily – and perhaps fairly – assessed in the warmer and more sympathetic surroundings of Cau Ferrat.

Ramon Casas was the outstanding Catalan artist of his generation. At around the time that Rusiñol turned to Symbolism, Casas produced a number of exciting paintings reflecting the political turbulence of the day. The most famous of these was *Garrot vil* (1894), which portrayed a large crowd waiting to witness an execution. Unfortunately, Casas's *Garrot vil* is in Madrid, and another famous political painting – *La Carga* (*The Charge*, 1899) – is in the Museu d'Art Modern at Olot. However, Casas's celebrated crowd scene – *Corpus Christi procession leaving the church of Santa Maria del Mar* (1898) – can be seen in Barcelona's Museu d'Art Modern. In 1896 a bomb had exploded during the annual Corpus Christi procession, killing 12 people and leading to a wave of persecution directed against anarchists and workers. 'One of the paradoxes of Casas,' as Marilyn McCully points out, ' is that he should have been doing these almost propagandistic paintings at the same time as he was doing portraits of so many of his bourgeois friends, members of his own social class.' In 1909 Casas donated a collection of over 200 charcoal portraits to the city and these are among the prize possessions of the museum.

Casas's marvellous portraits – of politicians, architects, artists – evoke the very spirit of the age. There is one of Casas himself, wry, behatted and corpulent. The poet Joan Maragall looks world-weary, while the young Picasso, in baggy suit and broad-brimmed hat, possesses none of the pop-eyed insolence one associates with his later years. The dashingly handsome Rusiñol, with flowing hair and bushy beard, is precisely as one would have hoped, while Domènech i Montaner looks, unlike his buildings, positively unappealing. Miquel Utrillo in top-hat and long coat is every inch the dandy, and Fransesc Macià, later to become President of the Generalitat, looks astute and sagacious. There are many more portraits in the museum beside these – some in charcoal, others in oil – and there are several fine posters by Casas, too. One titled *Sifilis*, and done for the Sanatorium of Doctor Abreu, is chillingly good. A young woman with half-naked breast holds a bunch of flowers in one hand and, behind her back, a serpent in the other. A book of Casas's portraits – *Retrats al Carbo de 25 Personalitats Catalanes* – is on sale at the museum.

Other artists whose work is worth pondering here include Isidre Nonell (1876–1911) and Joaquim Sunyer (1874–1956). There is little in the way of contemporary art in the museum, with just a single work each from Picasso, Miró and Tàpies. The museum has a modest collection of sculpture; note, in particular, the works of Pau Gargallo and Josep Llimona, whose *El Desconsol* is outstanding. There is also a collection of late 19th- and early 20th-century furniture. Some of the more hideous pieces are those designed by Gaspar Homar (1870–1953) for Domènech's Casa Lleó-Morera. He commands greater respect for his porcelain-cum-mosaic murals.

Museu Picasso (Picasso Museum)

(Carrer de Montcada 15-19. Closed Monday; 10.00–19.30, Tuesday to Sunday. The museum library is open 09.00–13.30 (for more information, Tel: 319 63 10). There is a good bookshop in the foyer, selling works on Picasso, posters and postcards. The Picasso Museum occupies two handsome Gothic palaces on one of Barcelona's most celebrated medieval streets (for a full description, *see* page 47). This is a rather sombre setting for the works of one of the greatest artists of modern times, although the old city and the area round the port were very much Picasso's stamping ground during his formative years in Barcelona. Metro L4 to Jaume I; bus: 16, 17, 22, 45.)

Picasso was born in the Andalusian town of Malaga in 1881. When he was 14 years old his family moved to Barcelona, where his father took up a teaching post at the School of Fine Arts, in the same building as La Llotja (the Stock Exchange). The family rented a number of apartments in what are now the city's least salubrious quarters. They began in Les Cases i els Porxos d'en Xifré (*see* page 68), moved round the corner to Carrer Reina Cristina, and later to Carrer de la Mercè and Carrer de la Plata. Soon after the family's arrival Picasso enrolled in the advanced course at the Llotja; by his mid-teens he was already producing work of remarkable brilliance and maturity. In 1897 Picasso went to Madrid to study at the Royal Academy of Fine Arts. He spent more time painting outdoors (and visiting the Prado) than at his studies. Sickness drove him prematurely back to Catalonia, and he convalesced in the village of Horta de Sant Joan, near Tarragona, before returning to Barcelona in 1899.

By now he was leading a life fully independent of his family, and he became a regular frequenter of Els Quatre Gats café (described in the section on the Museu d'Art Modern, page 119). There he met Rusiñol, Casas and others belonging to the older generation of *modernista* artists; but just as importantly he kept company with his younger (and less bourgeois) contemporaries, among them Isidre Nonell and Carles Casagemas. Like many of the *modernistes*, he took to painting life in the streets and cafés; and like many, he was gripped by a desire to visit Paris. Rusiñol, Casas and Romeu were already *habitués* of Parisian art circles, and they had founded Els Quatre Gats as a Catalan equivalent of Montmartre's Le Chat Noir. Picasso held his first exhibition at Els Quatre Gats in February 1900, and he paid his first visit to Paris that October. With his friend Casagemas, he took over a flat previously occupied by Nonell, and he spent much of his time there in the company of Catalan artists like Casas.

At the end of the year Picasso returned to Spain, but Casagemas stayed on in Paris. In February the latter attempted to shoot his lover in a Parisian café, missed, then shot himself. Picasso was deeply traumatized by his friend's death, and Casagemas was to appear in many of his paintings over the next few years. Picasso spent much of 1901 in Paris, but came back to live in Barcelona from 1902 to 1904; this was the time of his 'Blue Period'. In 1904 he went back to Paris. From time to time Picasso paid short visits to his family in Barcelona, and in 1917 he returned with Diaghilev's Russian Ballet Company, having designed the set and costumes for Jean Cocteau's and Eric Satie's *Parade*. Picasso last visited Spain – and Barcelona – in 1936, the Civil War and Franco's victory driving him into permanent exile in France.

The Museu Picasso, which opened in 1963, was the inspiration of Jaume Sabartés, who knew Picasso during his early years in Barcelona and later became his secretary. Sabartés donated many works by Picasso to the museum, which also inherited the paintings and drawings by the artist which hitherto had belonged to the Museu d'Art Modern. Gradually the collection swelled, with donations from private individuals like Salvador and Gala Dalí, and from other galleries. In 1968 Picasso donated over 50 paintings from his 'Blue Period', as well as the *Las Meninas* series based on Velásquez's famous study. Two years later Picasso gave a further 900 paintings, etchings, drawings and other objects to the museum. The bulk of the museum is taken up by the paintings, certain periods of the artist's life being particularly well represented (for example, the early years in Barcelona and the 'Blue Period'); further sections are devoted to engravings, lithographs and lino-cuts, and there is a small collection of Picasso's ceramic work. The Museu Picasso receives more visitors than any other museum in Barcelona, almost three times as many as the Museu d'Art Modern and the Fundació Joan Miró, and four times as many as the Museu d'Art de Catalunya. Picasso's paintings are organized in chronological order, and the intention here is not to give a comprehensive resumé of the museum's collection (catalogues are available in the shop) but to indicate some of the key works on display. **Rooms 5, 7, 8** and **9** contains evidence of the teenage Picasso's precocious talent. There are some sensitive portraits of his father in watercolour and aquatint and pen, and several oil studies of male nudes done while at the Llotja. At an early age Picasso took to painting out of doors: there is an exquisite little oil of Barceloneta beach (1896); another in soft colours of the houses on the seafront at Barceloneta; and several studies from the old city itself, including one of the cloister of Sant Pau del Camp (1896). **Room 10** contains a fine oil – *Science and Charity* (1897) – which depicts doctor and nurse at the bedside of an ailing woman; beside it are sketches for the painting, which received an honourable mention when submitted to the National Exhibition of Fine Arts in Madrid.

A variety of influences can be discerned in Picasso's work during the closing years of the last century and the early years of this. While his drawing shows the influence of Ramon Casas, there is more than a hint of Van Gogh and Toulouse Lautrec in the paintings. Lautrec's influence seems particularly potent in the series of brilliant pastel sketches dating from 1900, the year he first visited Paris. Note, for example, the wonderfully tender *El Abrazo* (*The Embrace*) in **Room 16** and others depicting theatrical scenes of the sort favoured by Lautrec (such as *El Final del Número, The end of the Number*, painted in 1901 in Paris). Before returning to Barcelona, Picasso executed several canvasses of an Impressionistic bent. Outstanding among these is his painting of *La Nana*, the dwarf, with oversized head and red dress. From the same period (autumn 1901), and also in **Room 16**, is a luscious still life with a plate of oysters, bowl of oranges and jug of flowers set against a blue background. Note, too, the series of delightful crayon and ink cartoons portraying Picasso's journey to Paris by 3rd-class train with Sebastian Junyer. **Room 18** is devoted to Picasso's 'Blue Period'. An air of introspection, pity and at times despair touches many of the paintings of this period. Picasso often took as his subject matter the poor and the dispossessed and portrayed their suffering in shades of chilly blue. *Desemperats* (*Forsaken*, 1903), a tragic pastel and crayon portrait of a mother and child, is especially poignant. From this period too came *El Loco* (*The Madman*, 1904), a study in pen and watercolour, as well as several portraits, landscapes and still-lifes.

Picasso moved permanently to Paris in April 1904, and his 'Pink Period', which began that year and finished the next, is represented in the museum by an elegant portrait of Señora Canals. **Room 19** contains work from the brief period in 1917 when Picasso returned to Barcelona. *The Harlequin* (1917) is a fine study of sadness dressed in comic's apparel. *Mujer con Mantilla* is an unfinished portrait of a woman in veil painted in the pointillist style. The sketch of a disembowelled horse appears to presage *Guernica*, Picasso's agonized reflection on the Spanish Civil War, while in the cubist-influenced *Paseo de Colón* Picasso pays homage to Barcelona's seafront. **Room 20** contains most of Picasso's *Las Meninas* series of paintings of 1957. The 58 oils were based on Velásquez's painting in the Prado Museum in Madrid (Picasso had already done his own interpretations of paintings by Courbet, Delacroix and Manet) and they were donated to the museum by the artist in 1968. Midway through this extraordinary exercise, Picasso briefly turned away from Velásquez's painting to embark on nine studies depicting doves, dovecotes and trees framing the blue sea of the Bay of Cannes. *Los Pichones*, as these paintings are known, make **Room 22** one of the most enchanting in the museum. **Room 23** has several charming oils of the countryside round Cannes, also dating from 1957. The founder of the museum, Jaume Sabartés, frequently sat for Picasso. **Room 24** has a drawing (1938) of Sabartés dressed as a gentleman in the time of Philip II.

The remaining rooms are taken up with Picasso's drawings, lithographs and lino-cuts (note in particular the ink on paper and copperplate bullfighting series of 1957; *The Frugal Meal* (1904); and the lithograph of a dove (1947)). There is also a small collection of Picasso's ceramic work.

Fundació Joan Miró (The Joan Miró Foundation)

(Plaça Neptú, Montjuïc Park. Closed Monday; 11.00–19.00, Tuesday to Saturday (except Thursday, 11.00–21.30); 10.30–14.30, Sunday and holidays. The Foundation also has a library (opening times as above). Those wishing to inspect the archive containing a large collection of Miró's drawings and engravings must obtain permission from the director (Tel: 329 19 08). There is an excellent bookshop with many works on Miró and modern art. Bus: 61. There is also a funicular from Paral·lel Metro to Passeig de Miramar, every day during summer, otherwise only Sundays and holidays.)

The Joan Miró Foundation was created by the artist in 1971 as a private cultural institution. Miró asked his old friend Josep Lluís Sert, by then the director of architectural studies at Harvard, to design a purpose-built centre. The city council donated a site on the flanks of Montjuïc and helped to fund the enterprise. Sert's startlingly beautiful building (*see* page 85) was opened to the public in 1975. The Foundation has two aims. First, it is a repository for a large body of Miró's work. There are 217 paintings, 153 sculptures, 9 tapestries, and a vast collection of drawings, engravings and notes, nearly all of which were donated by Miró himself. However, Miró was also keen that the Foundation should help foster modern art, and many of the city's best temporary exhibitions are to be seen here. The Foundation has brought Barcelona the works of such celebrated individuals as Henry Moore, Max Ernst, Francis Bacon and Paul Klee, but equally important has been the encouragement given to young artists. Among those whose careers were helped by exhibitions here is the sculptress Susana Solano. The foundation also hosts conferences, seminars, film shows and concerts.

The love affair between Miró and the people of Barcelona is instantly apparent to all but the most ardent philistine. His public works are large and prominently displayed: the visitor arrives at the airport to be greeted by his vast mural; driving into the city by taxi, he or she will glimpse Miró's huge phallic sculpture in the Parc de l'Escorxador (behind the bullring in Plaça d'Espanya); and strolling down the Ramblas, Miró's pavement design near the Opera House is unmissable. Even the tourist brochures carry Miró's squiggly graphics. History will probably judge Miró to have been one of the 20th century's outstanding minor artists; the label of 'great' will be reserved for a select few, Picasso being one of them. Of course, the Barcelonans recognize this, but while they view Picasso with admiration and awe, their affection is reserved for Miró: he is a Catalan, he has breathed the same air, walked the same rugged mountains and espoused the same political causes.

Joan Miró was born in 1893 in his family's apartment in Passeig del Crèdit, an alley which runs off Carrer de Ferran, just a stone's throw from Plaça de Sant Jaume (where his body was to lie in state in the Palau de la Generalitat ninety years later). Miró came from a family of artisans: his father was a goldsmith, his paternal grandfather a blacksmith, and his maternal grandfather a cabinet-maker. Miró studied for a brief period at the Llotja (the School of Fine Arts), but he showed none of the artistic promise which had marked out Picasso a decade earlier. At the age of seventeen Miró reluctantly began work as an office clerk; depression and illness followed. To hasten his recovery his father despatched him to the family's farmhouse near the village of Mont-roig, near Tarragona. Here he developed an enduring love for the Catalan countryside. Miró painted prodigiously while at the farm, and he returned to it frequently over the coming years. Back in Barcelona he attended the art classes run by Fransesc

Galí, who noticed that while Miró had an extraordinary sense of colour, his drawing abilities were feeble. 'It was his teaching of drawing that impressed Miró most deeply,' wrote the critic Roland Penrose. 'Placing an object in the hands of a blind-folded pupil, Galí told him to become so well acquainted with it by touch that he could afterwards draw what he had felt without seeing it. Under Galí's tuition Miró found that his perception of form and his ability to interpret it developed rapidly.' Miró also went to drawing classes at the Cercle Artístic de Sant Lluc, one of whose pupils was the elderly Antoni Gaudí. Miró was a great admirer of the architect, and indeed both drew inspiration from many of the same things, especially the shapes and forms in nature.

Paris began to exert a strong pull on Miró, just as it had on Casas, Rusiñol, Picasso and others before him. Miró visited the various exhibitions of French painting which came to Barcelona. One, organized by Josep Dalmau in 1917, had a lasting influence on Miró; gathered together here were works ranging from impressionism through to fauvism and cubism. In the same year Miró attended performances of Diaghilev's Russian Ballet company. Picasso had designed the set for *Parade* and he returned to Barcelona for a short period, but Miró was not to meet him until he visited Paris in 1919. By then he had had his first one-man exhibition, held at the Galeries Dalmau a year earlier. There was nothing remarkable about the subject matter – landscapes, portraits, still lifes – but his youthful work was stamped with unmistakable power and originality, although several influences were readily apparent. Penrose points out that 'Miró's treatment of reality came to a large degree from his instinctive feeling for the rhythms which underlie the traditional patterns of peasant art, and also from another equally strong native tradition which is to be found in Romanesque Catalan painting'. As a young man Miró had admired many of the Romanesque frescoes in Catalonia's churches as well as in the museum in Ciutadella Park. Other early influences included Van Gogh, Cézanne and Rousseau. 'When I loved the Douanier Rousseau,' said Miró,

'I already loved popular art. The older I grew, the greater importance this art had for me. A hayfork well carved by a peasant is very important to me.'

From 1920 to 1932 Miró spent most of his time in Paris, though he used to return during the summer months to the farmhouse at Mont-roig. In Paris he began to develop his own peculiar brand of surrealism: 'the tumultuous entrance of Miró in 1924 marks an important point in the development of surrealist art,' wrote André Breton. In 1929 Miró married Pilar Juncosa of Majorca, and from 1932 to 1937 they lived in Barcelona. Miró returned to France during the Civil War; then in 1940 he and his wife moved to Majorca, where he lived and painted (in a studio designed by Sert) until his death in 1983.

The Miró Foundation contains examples of the artist's work from his childhood to old age, although the collection is not arranged chronologically. One of the first rooms contains the magnificent *Tapis de la Fundació* (1979), a huge wool tapestry of brilliant colours: blue, yellow, green, indigo, purple. By then the curious sea-creature-like squiggles had become a leitmotiv, making his work instantly recognizable even to those with little interest in art. In the same room is a beige tapestry slung with umbrellas and a pair of gloves (*Sobre teixim de los ocho umbrellas*, 1973) and on the opposite wall there is a large white canvas, stamped with black handprints and accompanied by small blobs of blue, yellow and red paint.

From here the visitor progresses into a room of sculptures. Many are abstract figures – some painted brilliant primary colours; nearly all sprouting phallic appendages, hayforks, nails, dolls' legs, etc. – and like much of Miró's work they inspire amusement and joy rather than deep intellectual contemplation. Miró was evidently disturbed by the fact that his paintings and sculptures were often considered humorous. 'By nature I am tragic and taciturn,' he said. 'In my youth I passed though periods of profound sadness. Now I'm fairly well balanced, but everything disgusts me: life seems to be absurd ... I'm a pessimist: I think that everything is always going to turn out very badly. If there's anything humorous about my paintings, it has not been consciously sought. This humour comes perhaps from the need I feel to escape from the tragic side of my temperament.'

These early rooms – and all those which follow – leave one with a feeling of excitement and exhilaration. There are works from all phases of Miró's life: childhood doodles, drawings from his lessons with Galí, paintings of early adulthood reflecting the influence of fauvism and cubism; political posters. His later work is full of variety, but Miró's bizarre iconography – distorted insects, sea-creatures, stars, suns, hieroglyphs dancing in flat, empty spaces – informs nearly everything he did. Many a modern gallery has an enervative effect on its visitor. Here the opposite holds true: Miró's work is energizing; it is as though the passion and intensity which went into his paintings and sculptures is transmitted to all those who see them now.

Fundació Antoni Tàpies (The Antoni Tàpies Foundation)
(Carrer d'Aragó 255. Metro: L3 or L4 to Passeig de Gràcia.)

The Antoni Tàpies Foundation is housed in what many consider to be the first *modernista* building, Domènech i Montaner's Editorial Montaner i Simon (1881–6). This is a handsome structure which combines Romanesque and *mudéjar* elements with a modern approach to the use of iron and unclad masonry. The capacious windows make it a perfect setting for the display of Tàpies's work. The mesh of aluminium tubing and wire which juts from the roof and hangs like a metallic cloud above the street was created by Tàpies himself. The Foundation was opened in 1990.

Since the death of Joan Miró, Tàpies has become the grand old man of Catalan art. He was born in the Barri Gòtic in 1923, the son of a pious Catholic mother and a father of more liberal inclinations. His childhood was far from happy. He went briefly to a convent school at the age of three and was apparently harshly treated by the nuns. His teenage education was interrupted by the Civil War of 1936–9, and Tàpies has said that his art has in many ways been a product of those years and the subsequent struggles against Francoist rule. 'He shared with the former generation [of artists] an instinctive response to revolutionary ideas,' suggests Roland Penrose, 'a hatred of bourgeois complacency and a strong animosity against the tyrannical reign of a despotic government backed by the army and the church.' Like Pablo Picasso and Joan Miró, both of whom were to become friends, Tàpies suffered serious illness in his late teens. In 1940 tuberculosis led to a heart attack and Tàpies went to live for a lengthy spell in the mountains to recover. Today he lives in the foothills of the Pyrenees, and the earthy colours and textures of the countryside are reflected in much of his work.

Tàpies is venerated by the Catalans both as an artist and as a champion of Catalanism. In 1966 he was arrested, and later fined, for joining the occupation of the Capuchin Convent at Sarrià, and in 1970 he marched to Montserrat with Miró and hundreds of other intellectuals in protest against the death sentences passed on six members of a Basque separatist group. His political views often surface in his paintings: *L'Esprit Catalan* (1971) is overtly political, with its nationalist slogans written over the four bleeding bars of the Catalan flag; others, many with the symbol of the cross, hover on the edge of politics, suggestive of the battle between good and evil, light and dark.

The young Tàpies was influenced by Miró, Max Ernst and Paul Klee among others, but he has gone further than any artist this century in his exploration of texture. Walking round the Foundation, the visitor is possessed with a terrible urge to feel Tàpies's paintings and sculptures, to run fingers over the lumpy paint, the crumpled canvas, the rough wood. Tàpies makes much of his name, which means 'wall': 'It's led me to explore all the possibilities that the vision of a wall suggests – as a barrier, enclosure, the boundary of a prison. It's led me to examine what could be written on a wall, the graffiti in the streets.' This is less enigmatic than it may at first sound. All over the Barri Gòtic you will see walls where eroded bricks, cracked plaster, worm-eaten wood, chipped paint and torn posters have come together to form a haphazard collage. Created over decades, or even centuries, each collage is a small window looking back into history: there are bullet holes here, an old piece of plumbing there, and the collage reflects not just human activity but the ravages of time and the weather too. Like the walls, and using the same medium of abstract collage, Tàpies is making his own personal statement about Catalonia's past and present.

There are several other museums and galleries concerned with the arts:

Museu d'Arts Decoratives (Decorative Arts Museum)
Palau de Pedralbes, Avinguda Diagonal 686. It has a good collection of Catalan glass, especially from the 16th century; furniture, gold, silver, porcelain and enamel objects from the 16th to the 19th centuries; also Gothic and Renaissance chests. Metro: L3 to Palau Reial; bus: 7, 75.

Museu de les Arts Gràfiques (Graphic Arts Museum)
Poble Espanyol, Montjuïc. Opening times as for Poble Espanyol (see page ooo). This museum explores the art and history of printing. There is a collection of typography and lithographs from the past two centuries. There are also demonstrations of printing and copperplate engraving. Metro: L1 or L3 to Espanya; bus: 9, 27, 50, 56, 57, 61.

Museu Clará (Josep Clará Museum)
Calatrava 27. Closed Monday; 09.00–14.00, Tuesday to Sunday. A must for anyone interested in 20th-century sculpture. Josep Clará (1878–1958) studied sculpture in Toulouse at the turn of the century and thereafter lived in Paris for many years. There he met Auguste Rodin and other eminent sculptors and became a close friend of Isadora Duncan. He paid frequent visits to Barcelona, returning permanently in 1932. He left his house to the city, together with a large collection of his sculptures, drawings, paintings

and personal effects. The charming garden also contains some of his sculptures. Railway: Generalitat railway to Tres Torres.

Temporary Art Exhibitions and Galleries

At any one time in Barcelona there may be a dozen or so temporary art exhibitions outside the commercial galleries. Important venues for such exhibitions include:

- Palau de la Virreina, Ramblas 99.
- Centre d'Art Santa Mònica, Rambla Santa Mònica 7.
- Palau Robert, Passeig de Gràcia 107.
- Sala d'Expositions de la Fundació Caixa de Pensions, Carrer de Montcada 14 and Via Laietana 56.
- Saló del Tinell, Plaça del Rei.
- Fundació Joan Miró, Parc de Montjuïc.
- Museu d'Art Modern, Parc de la Ciutadella.

Barcelona's tourist office produces a monthly broadsheet in English with details of exhibitions, theatrical events and so forth; available free from tourist offices. The Àrea de Cultura (Palau de la Virreina, Ramblas 99) produces a comprehensive monthly guide, *Activitats*. Alternatively, buy a copy of Barcelona's weekly events magazine – *El Guía del Ocio* – available from newsagents and bookstores. This lists not only all the temporary exhibitions (as well as films, plays, concerts, sporting events) but gives details of the artists on show and opening times of the 50-plus commercial art galleries in Barcelona.

The main concentration of long-established galleries is to be found on or around Carrer de Consell de Cent, between Carrer de Balmes and Passeig de Gràcia. Those of international repute include:

- Sala Gaspar, Consell de Cent 323.
- Carles Taché, Consell de Cent 290.
- Joan Prats, Rambla de Catalunya 54.
- Dau al Set, Consell de Cent 333.
- Galeria Rene Metras, Consell de Cent 331.

Those wishing to acquire the latest in contemporary art – or simply to observe the latest trends – should make for the galleries which have recently sprung up in the area between Via Laietana and Ciutadella Park. Try, for example, Galeria Maeght, Montcada 25; Benet Costa, Comerç 29; and Berini, Plaça Comercial 3. The Catalan Association of Art Galleries can be contacted at Passeig de Gràcia 77 (Tel: 215 05 16).

THE SCIENCES, PAST AND PRESENT: A SELECTION OF MUSEUMS

Each of the 10 museums listed in this section is concerned, either directly or indirectly, with one of the sciences. There is nothing in Barcelona to compare with, say, the Natural History Museum or Science Museum in London, but this should not deter visitors with a keen interest in the sciences from exploring some of the relevant museums in Barcelona. A trip to the museums can always be combined with other activities: for example, the Science Museum can be taken in on a trip to Tibidabo, while both the Zoological and Geological Museums are just a few minutes' walk from the zoo in Ciutadella Park.

Museu Etnològic (Ethnological Museum)
(Passeig de Santa Madrona, Montjuïc. 15.00–20.30, Monday; 09.00–20.30, Tuesday to Saturday; 09.00–14.00, Sunday and holidays. Metro: L1 or L3 to Espanya, L3 to Poble Sec; bus: 55. The museum library is open 09.00–14.00, Tuesday to Saturday.)

This is an admirable little museum of human artefacts from various parts of the world, especially Japan, New Guinea, Indonesia and Central America. The Japanese collection includes kimonos, fishing tackle, pottery, musical instruments, rice-planting equipment, and examples of modern crafts. The selection from New Guinea will delight prurient children: there are photographs and models of large-breasted women and otherwise naked men wearing enormous penis-sheaths. The permanent displays are often augmented by temporary exhibitions.

Museu Etnogràfic Andino-Amazonià (The Andes-Amazon Ethnographic Museum)

Capuchin Monastery at Sarrià, Cardenal Vives i Tuto 2–16. Only open for two hours on the first Sunday of every month, 12.00–14.00. Closed July and August. Those with a specialist interest in ethnological matters may wish to see the collection of pre-Columbian ceramics and handicrafts, as well as more modern artefacts, housed in this monastery. Bus: 34, 66.

Museu de la Ciència (The Science Museum)

(Teodor Roviralta 55. Closed Monday; 10.00–20.00, Tuesday to Sunday. Railway: Generalitat railway to Avinguda del Tibidabo; bus: 17, 22, 58, 73.)

The Science Museum, set up in 1905, is one of the most popular in Barcelona, second only to the Picasso Museum in terms of the number of visitors it receives each year. The museum is financed by La Caixa de Pensions (the Savings Bank). There are permanent exhibitions dealing with space (there is a planetarium here), optics, perception, mechanics, computers and meteorology. Temporary exhibitions are publicized in *El Guía del Ocio*.

Gabinet de Fisica Experimental Mentora Alsina (The Mentora Alsina Physics Experimentation Centre)

(Ctra. de Vallvidrera-Tibidabo 56.)

Further up the hill of Tibidabo is another scientific museum which only admits visitors by prior arrangement. It has a display of apparatus used in the study of classical physics. For all inquiries: Tel: 417 57 34.

Planetarium Barcelona

(Escoles Pies 103. Guided visits: 09.30, 10.30, 11.30, 15.00, 16.00 and 16.30, Monday to Friday; closed, Saturday; 12.00, 13.00 and 16.30, Sunday and holidays. Railway: Generalitat railway to Sarrià; bus: 12, 22, 64, 75.)

The museum has exhibitions on space and audio-visual simulations. Those interested in outer space and not fully satisfied by the Science Museum should visit the Planetarium.

Museu de la Holografia (The Holography Museum)

Centrally located at Carrer de Jaume I 1. 11.00–13.30 and 17.30–20.30, Tuesday to Saturday; closed Sunday, Monday, and holidays. Metro: L4 to Jaume I; bus: 16, 17, 36, 45, 57.

Two museums deal with geological matters:

Museu de Geologia (The Geological Museum)

(Ciutadella Park, adjacent to Passeig de Picasso. Closed, Monday; 09.00–14.00, Tuesday to Sunday. Metro: L1 to Arc de Triomf; bus: 39, 40, 41, 51.)

The museum is housed in a handsome neo-classical building specially designed by Antoni Rovira to take the large bequest left to the city by the scientist Fransesc Martorell. The museum was opened in 1882 and it has one of the most important mineral collections in Spain; there is also a section explaining the geology of Catalonia.

Museu Geologic del Seminari (The Seminary's Geology Museum)

(Occupies rooms in the Council Seminary at Carrer de la Diputació 231. 11.00–13.00 and 17.00–19.00, Monday to Friday; closed Saturday, Sunday and holidays. Metro: L1 to Universitat; bus: 7, 14, 16, 17, 58, 59, 64.)

This museum specializes in invertebrate palaeontology and has a magnificent collection of fossils.

The biological sciences are catered for by two museums:

The Museu de Zoologia (The Zoological Museum)

(Occupies Domènech i Montaner's intended café-restaurant, built for the 1888 International Exhibition in Ciutadella Park (*see* page 75). Closed Mondays; 09.00–14.00, Tuesday to Sunday. Metro: L1 to Arc de Triomf; bus: 39, 40, 41, 51.)

The museum contains comprehensive collections of insects, molluscs, reptiles, birds and mammals. In keeping with the times, the museum is strong on environmental education. However, for those who prefer their animals alive rather than stuffed, Barcelona's zoo is on the other side of the park (*see* page 148).

Institut i Jardí Botànic (The Botanical Institute and Gardens)

(Avinguda dels Montanyans, to the west of Palau Nacional, Montjuïc. 1 April – 30 September: 15.00–19.00, Monday to Saturday; rest of year: 15.00–17.00, Monday to Saturday; all year: 09.00–14.00, Sunday and holidays.)

This is a delightful institute with gardens and greenhouses containing plants from across the world, with a special emphasis on Mediterranean flora. There is a good collection of medicinal herbs.

A FURTHER SELECTION OF MUSEUMS

Museu Arqueològic (The Archaeological Museum)

(Passeig de Santa Madrona, Montjuïc. Closed, Monday; 09.30–13.00 and 16.00–19.00, Tuesday to Saturday; 09.00–14.00, Sunday and holidays. Metro: L1 or L3 to Espanya, L3 to Poble Sec.)

This museum has a particularly good collection of prehistoric items from the Balearic islands, and it provides a thorough survey of Catalan history from Roman times through to the Visigoth invasion of the 7th century. There are also objects here from the Greek/Roman settlement of Empúries.

Galeria de Catalans Il·lustres (The Gallery of Illustrious Catalans)

(Bisbe Cassador 3. Guided visits only; for information, Tel: 315 00 10. Metro: L3 to Jaume I; bus: 7, 15, 16, 17, 34.)

The gallery contains some 50 portraits of famous Catalans from the 10th century to the present day.

Museu de la Música (The Music Museum)
(Avinguda Diagonal, 373. Closed, Monday; 09.00–14.00, Tuesday to Sunday. Metro: L3 or L5 to Diagonal; bus: 6, 15, 22, 24, 28, 34, 39.)

The museum occupies Josep Puig i Cadafalch's Casa Quadras; in the façade Gothic and Plateresque elements are combined with the floral motifs of *modernisme*. The collection is divided into three groups: keyboard instruments on the lower floor; percussion and string instruments above. The collection of guitars is one of the largest in Europe.

Museu Verdaguer (The Verdaguer Museum)
(Vil·la Joana, Vallvidrera). Closed, Monday; 09.00–14.00, Tuesday to Sunday. Railway: Generalitat railway to Baixador de Vallvidrera.)

The museum was set up as a memorial to the great Catalan poet Jacint Verdaguer and it contains his personal effects.

Museu d'Autòmates del Tibidabo (Tibidabo Robot Museum)
(Tibidabo Amusement Park (*see* also page 143). April to September: 11.00–20.00, daily; October to March: 11.00–20.00, Saturday, Sunday and holidays only. Railway: Generalitat railway to Avinguda del Tibidabo, then Blue Tram and Funicular.)

A curious museum with a collection of robots, and models of some of the attractions in Tibidabo Amusement Park.

Museu de Cera (the Wax Museum)
(Ptge de la Banca 7. 11.00–13.30 and 16.30–19.30, Monday to Friday; Saturday, Sunday and holidays the same but open till 20.00. Metro: L3 to Drassanes; bus: 14, 18, 38, 59.)

A poor man's Madame Tussaud's.

Museu del F.C. Barcelona (the Barcelona Football Club Museum)
(Stadium, Aristides Maillol. October to March: 10.00–13.00

and 16.00–18.00, Tuesday to Friday; 10.00–13.00, Saturday, Sunday and holidays. April to September: 10.00–13.00 and 16.00–19.00, Monday to Saturday; 10.00–13.00, holidays; otherwise closed.)

Football is an obsession in Barcelona and this is one of the most popular museums, with trophies, team photographs, audio-visual shows etc. Strictly for fanatics.

Museu de Carrosses Fúnebres (the Funeral Hearse Museum)

Sancho d'Avila 2. 09.00–13.00 and 15.00–18.00, Monday to Saturday: closed Sunday and holidays. Metro: L1 to Marina; bus: 6, 40, 42.

4:
PARKS, GARDENS AND
SQUARES

Barcelona is one of the most densely populated cities in Europe. On average there are 2.2 persons per room in Barcelona, compared to 0.6 in London and 0.5 in New York. Even cities like Cairo (1.5 persons per room) and Shanghai (2.0 persons per room) suffer lower levels of overcrowding. Barcelona is also one of the noisiest cities in Europe; this has less to do with the Catalan character (they are a naturally ebullient race) than with the city's infernal traffic. During rush hour, traffic flows through the city at an average rate of 10.6 m.p.h. (16.9 k.p.h.). This is marginally better than the traffic speeds in London and New York, but much worse than in many other major cities: rush-hour traffic in Tokyo, for example, moves at 28 m.p.h. (45 k.p.h.); and in Los Angeles at 19 m.p.h. (30.6 k.p.h.). Cars, buses and lorries are major contributors to air pollution, and on hot summer days the views across the city are often obscured by a dense pall of photo-chemical smog. While the crowded living conditions affect only those who live permanently in the city, congested, noisy traffic and poor air quality are an aggravation to everyone, visitors included. To escape, you must head for the city's parks and gardens – or, if you wish to remain in the old parts of town, you can retreat to the small squares tucked away from the main streets.

The Barcelonans, it seems, have always valued their public gardens. When Richard Ford visited the city in the 1840s, he was impressed by the gardens outside the city walls – one, laid out in 1816, had 'flower beds, statues, ponds with swans, aviaries, and objects of delight to the rising Barcelonese and their nurses' – and he found the environs of Barcelona 'delight-ful'.

Barcelona's green spaces range in size from the vast areas covered by Tibidabo and Montjuïc to tiny gardens like the one in the old Hospital de la Santa Creu. Some areas are wooded and little altered by man; others, like the gardens at Horta and Palau Reial de Pedralbes, have a classical formality. Over recent years – and particularly during the run-up to the 1992 Olympic Games – the city authorities have invested a consider-able amount of money and effort into smartening up existing gardens and squares and into creating new ones. This has sometimes been more than just an exercise in town planning and landscape gardening: for example, prostitutes who formerly traded in the streets around Carrer de Sant Pau were given gardening jobs in Montjuïc, and new gardens and playgrounds were established in many of the city's poorer suburbs.

It would be possible, I suppose, to give the parks and gardens a star rating, much as gourmet guides do for restaurants. I am loath to do this for the simple reason that different people will look for different things in the parks. What to one person is an attraction might to another be an abomination. When Evelyn Waugh visited Barcelona in the 1920s he was very rude about Tibidabo, which he referred to as 'a frightful hill . . . laid out as a pleasure garden with a restaurant and café, a hall of slot machines, an unfinished oratory of fantastic design, and a Great Wheel'. Well, that is Waugh's opinion, and no doubt there are others who share it; but for those among us who delight in the vulgarity of old-fashioned fairgrounds, Tibidabo comes close to paradise.

Some of the parks are very much on the tourist circuit, largely because they possess buildings of architectural interest or notable museums and art galleries. Such is the case with Montjuïc, Ciutadella Park and Park Güell. In this chapter it is their other virtues – gardens, boating lakes, fairgrounds – which come to the forefront. I have divided the city's green – and concrete – spaces into three categories. First come the major parks: each of these boasts a variety of attractions and is worthy of a visit in its own right. The second category points the visitor towards smaller parks and gardens, some of which have existed for many years, others of which are recent arrivals. Unless the visitor has a special interest in either the gardening practices of municipal authorities or the avant-garde landscaping ideas favoured by today's town planners, he or she is unlikely to make a great effort to visit any of these. These are, however, the sort of places you might visit if you happen to be in the neighbourhood, and if you are looking for somewhere to eat your sandwiches, rest your legs or have a *siesta*. If, for example, you have been to see Domènech's Hospital de la Santa Creu, you may decide to relax for a while in the Parc del Guinardó and if you have a long wait for a train at Sants Station, you could profitably spend some time in the Parc de l'Espanya Industrial. Finally, I have included a selection of small gardens and squares in the old city and around the port.

MAJOR PARKS

Tibidabo
(Railway: Generalitat railway to Avinguda del Tibidabo; Blue Tram from there to funicular; funicular to summit: 07.45–21.45, Monday to Friday; 07.15–21.45, Saturdays and holidays. The **Amusement Park** October to March: 11.00–20.00, Saturday and Sunday, except during Christmas and Easter holidays, when it is open every day. April to 11 September: 11.00–20.00, daily; later in mid-summer.)

According to local legend, the devil took Christ up to the summit of this hill during his 40 days in the wilderness and its name comes from a line in St Matthew's Gospel: *Haec omnia tibi dabo si cades adoraberis me*, 'All this will I give to thee, if thou wilt fall down and worship me'. On a clear day 'all this' includes much more than the city of Barcelona, which sprawls across the bowl of land below: to the north, you may just be able to make out the jagged contours of the snowcapped Pyrenees; to the west the weird loofah-shaped hills around Montserrat; and to the south-east, the Balearic islands. Getting to Tibidabo is half the fun: the 32-seater Blue Trams rattle up Avinguda del Tibidabo past attractive villas set in spacious gardens whose walls are submerged in bougainvillaea and plumbago. This is the Hampstead of Barcelona. There are several cafés and restaurants near the foot of the funicular, so if you wish to work off a meal, you can walk rather than take the funicular. Several rough tracks snake up the hill through the woods and it takes about 50 minutes to walk to the top. The going is steep and not suitable for the ancient or infirm. The woodland is typically Mediterranean in character, with good stands of pine, cypress and dwarf oak. It is also possible to drive to the top of Tibidabo.

The tram line, funicular and Amusement Park were built by a company set up by a Dr Salvador Andreu at the turn of the century. The Observatory (to the left of the funicular as you go up) was founded by the Marquis of Alella in 1904, the Museu de la Ciència (see page 135) was set up the following year, and in 1909 work began on the church.

The Parc d'Atractions (Amusement Park) is enchantingly archaic. The red aeroplane which wheels over the hill dates from the 1920s, and some of the other stuff looks even older. There are dozens of things to go on – magic carpets, a big wheel, a big dipper, merry-go-rounds – and rather than buy individual tickets it is best to buy a whole-day ticket and make the most of it. There are plenty of bars and food stalls as well as the Museu d'Autòmates (Robot Museum) (see page 138).

The Church of El Sagrat Cor (the Sacred Heart) is one of Barcelona's most prominent landmarks. It was built beside a tiny hermitage (established in 1886) to the design of Enric Sagnier. The main body of the church belongs to the Walt Disney/neo-Gothic style of architecture, and whilst one expects this sort of thing in Florida, one certainly doesn't in Spain. Beneath the lofty nave (one of the church's better features) is a crypt which is worth visiting for the sheer horror of the experience. Entry is by way of a large portal which almost defies description: Romanesque and *modernista* elements, along with a dash of Gothic, have come together to singularly poor effect, although nothing prepares the visitor for the ghastliness of the frescoes inside. These, quite simply, do defy description. On top of the church is a huge statue of Christ with out-stretched arms; there is a lift up to the mirador at his feet.

Montjuïc Park

(Metro: L3 to Espanya or Poble Sec; funicular from Paral·lel to Passeig de Miramar daily in summer, otherwise only Sundays and holidays. Buses: 61 and 201 go to the Amusement Park from Plaça d'Espanya and Poble Sec respectively. Montjuïc's Amusement Park is inferior to Tibidabo's but much easier to get to. June 24 to September 11: closed, Monday; 18.00–24.00, Tuesday to Saturday; 12.00–24.00, Sundays. Rest of year: 12.00–20.00, Saturday, Sunday and holidays only. For a description of Montjuïc's history and architecture, *see* page 76. For a description of its many museums, see relevant sections in Chapter 3.)

This is by far and away the most important park in Barcelona. Its northern flanks, with the Palau Nacional towering above the halls and fountains built for the 1929 International Exhibition, are home to some of the city's outstanding museums and art galleries. Behind, and to the south-west, is a large complex of sporting facilities, most of them specially constructed for the 1992 Olympic Games. To the east there is Montjuïc Castle with fine views over the port and the city below. In addition to all these attractions there is an amusement park, a cemetery and numerous gardens.

There are lovely wooded walks all over Montjuïc, and there are some fine gardens too. The largest of these occupies a wedge of land overlooking the port between the Cinturó del

Litoral and Carretera de Miramar: Els Jardins de Mossèn Costa Llobera have a large collection of sub-tropical and tropical trees, shrubs and cacti. Moving away from the sea, Els Jardins de Mossèn Jacint Verdaguer spread across sloping ground behind the upper funicular station. This is a pleasant place to rest – although there is not much in the way of shade – should you decide to walk up to the castle. Among the most attractive gardens are those named after the poet Joan Maragall, to the rear of Palauet Albéniz. Here there is an open-air theatre and the gardens are laid out to a classical design. As the Palauet is used as a guesthouse for visiting dignitaries, the public is only allowed in the gardens from 10.00–14.00, Sundays and holidays. Further to the west are the gardens of the Instit i Jardí Botànic described in the museum section (*see* page 137).

There are extensive semi-formal gardens with pergolas, trees and shrubs on the hillside below the Fundació Miró. Els Jardins del Laribal, like most of the other gardens here, were the work of the French landscape architect, Jean-Claude-Nicolas Forestier (who was also responsible for the Plaça de les Armes in Ciutadella Park) and Nicolau Rubió i Tudurí (who laid out the formal gardens around the Palau Reial de Pedralbes). Head down the winding paths of the Laribal gardens and you will come to the Jardins Amargós, open daily from 10.00 to 18.00 (or 20.00 in summer). The same combination – Forestier and Rubió – created this delightful garden, whose classical formality is beautifully complemented by the creeper-festooned cliffs and thick woods which rise behind the Teatre Grec (Greek Theatre).

Over on the other side of Montjuïc is the Cementiri del Sudoest (The South-West Cemetery). It can be reached either on foot or by bus: number 38 from Plaça de Catalunya stops outside the cemetery gates. In terms of its funereal architecture, it does not compare with Paris's Père-Lachaise or any number of London's old graveyards, but those interested in Catalan history may wish to see where some of the region's prominent heroes and villains have ended up. Lluís Companys, the President of the Generalitat, was buried here after his execution in Montjuïc Castle in 1940. His predecessor, Fransesc Macià, was also buried here, as were thousands of men and women murdered by Franco's troops after the fall of Barcelona in 1939. The cemetery officials will also point you in the direction of the grave of Salvador Puig Antich, an anarchist garrotted in 1974 and the last person to be executed in Catalonia for politically motivated crime.

Ciutadella Park

(Metro: L1 to Arc de Triomf, L4 to Ciutadella; bus: 14, 39, 40, 41, 42, 51. For a full description of Ciutadella Park's history and architecture, *see* page 70. For a description of its museums, *see* Chapter 3. The **zoo** Summer: 09.30–19.00, daily. Winter: 10.00–17.00, daily.)

This is one of the loveliest parks in Barcelona. Its proximity to the old city – it is no more than ten minutes' walk from the Barri Gòtic – means that tourists can make several visits without expending too much time and energy. That it exists at all is largely thanks to the misfortune which befell the city in the early 18th century. During the War of the Spanish Succession (1700–15) Catalonia backed the losing side, and Barcelona fell to Spanish and French troops in September 1714. Eager to subdue the restless natives, the new Bourbon king, Philip V, decreed that a large fortress should be built, and to make way for it 10,000 people in the Ribera district were evicted. For the next 150 years the fortress was a continual source of annoyance to the Catalans. Some buildings came down in 1841 and more were destroyed once General Prim (whose insurrection led to the abdication of Queen Isabel II) had handed the land over to the city authorities in 1869, thus resulting in the birth of Barcelona's oldest park, which takes its name from the despised fortress. Several buildings from the Bourbon period have survived, including the Arsenal (home of the Catalan parliament), a chapel and the Palau del Governador. During the 1870s and 1880s Josep Fontseré landscaped the park and constructed the Umbracle and the fountain, the latter with the help of Antoni Gaudí. In 1888 the International Exhibition was held in Ciutadella Park and several buildings constructed for the exhibition – most notably Domènech i Montaner's café-restaurant (now the Museu de Zoologia) – have survived to this day.

There are delightful walks throughout the park, and many quiet spots to sit and relax: Ciutadella is a favourite with courting couples and old people. Josep Llimona's famous statue *El Desconsol* sits at the heart of a lilypond in the formal gardens of the Plaça de les Armes.

The seaward end of the park is taken up by the zoo, which, with over one million visitors a year, is among the most popular in Europe. It was opened in 1892 and it now covers over 30 acres of parkland. From a purely aesthetic point of view, it is an unusually attractive zoo. There are trees and flowering shrubs everywhere and, while the big cats look somewhat bedraggled and pace up and down their cages in frustration, most of the animals are housed in clean and reasonably spacious enclosures. There are approximately 8,000 animals belonging to 500 species. There is a captive breeding programme for some of Catalonia's rarest species, including the imperial heron, the stork and the tortoise, but the main attraction for many visitors is a pitiful albino gorilla called Snowflake.

Park Güell
(Metro: L3 to Lesseps or Vallcarca, then walk along Avinguda de L'Hospital to elevators, Escales de la Baixada de la Glòria; bus: 24, 25, 31, 32, 74. 10.00–20.00, daily. For a description of the history and architecture of Park Güell, *see* page 99.)

Gaudí's architecture, wrote Evelyn Waugh, is 'the glory and delight' of Barcelona. Waugh's description of Park Güell bristles with enthusiasm:

> I paid off the taxi and entered up a double flight of china-mosaic steps, between curving machicolated walls, decorated in a gay check pattern of coloured tiles, at the base of which

was a little fountain and a kind of totem pole of mosaic . . .
There is a great terrace on which the children play games, with
a fine crinkled edge of the typical china mosaic; there is a
battlemented wall built of rough stones and clinkers, and
embellished with plaques of the word 'Güell' in contorted,
interlacing letters; there is a kind of pergola supported on a
colonnade of clinker pillars set askew and at all angles to each
other; there is a turret, surmounted by a wrought iron stand
supporting a cross; there is a little lodge that is a gem of
Gaudism, looking like a fairy cabin from the worst kind of
Rackhamesque picture book.

All this – and one or two other things, such as the Casa-
Museu Gaudí (see page 100) – is concentrated around the
lower flank of the 40-acre park. Much of the rest is covered
with a woodland of pine, olive, dwarf oak and cypress. Gaudí's
weird viaducts have clinker columns with sisal plants for
capitals and their rough surfaces seem to mimic the trunks of
the palm trees. The lower slopes have some pleasant formal
gardens and lawns. Park Güell is very busy at weekends, even
in winter. An outing here can be combined with a meal at one
of the two restaurants in the park. The views over the city are
magnificent. UNESCO recently acknowledged the park's historical significance by declaring it a world heritage site.

Parc del Guinardó
(Metro: L4 to Alfons X or Guinardó; bus: 24, 28, 31, 32, 39,
55.)
This extensive stretch of wooded hillside to the east of Park
Güell is seldom visited by tourists. The water-gardens at the
foot of the park were created by Jean-Claude-Nicolas Forestier,
who was also responsible for Ciutadella Park's Plaça de les
Armes and many of the gardens on Montjuïc. The Parc del
Guinardó is about ten minutes' walk from Domènech i
Montaner's Hospital de la Santa Creu (see page 103). It takes
rather longer to walk to Park Güell.

Parc del Laberint

(Metro: L3 to Montbau; bus: 27, 73, 76, 85.)

This delightful park is situated in the Vall d'Hebron area on the northern outskirts of the city. It takes an hour or so to get there from the centre of Barcelona and consequently the park is never too busy. The park was laid out towards the end of the 18th century to the design of the Marques of Alfarras and the Italian engineer Domenico Bagutti. It is the best example in Barcelona of a romantic neo-classical garden. There are avenues of cypresses, little temples, ponds, canals, belvederes and other elements of a classical landscape. The crowning glory, however, is the labyrinth, or maze, after which the park is named. Two Palladian temples (encrusted with pigeon muck and, at the time of my visit, in sore need of attention) overlook a cypress-hedge maze which has also seen better days. At the centre of the maze there is a statue disfigured by vandalism and graffiti. Both the gardens and the Moorish-looking palace at the entrance were about to be renovated at the beginning of the 1990s. There is a nature trail in the gorge beside the park.

SMALL PARKS, BIG GARDENS

Parc Joan Miró

(Metro: L1 or L3 to Espanya; bus: 9, 27, 38, 50, 56, 109.)

This is probably the grimmest park in Barcelona. It occupies four blocks of the Eixample immediately behind the bullring in the Plaça d'Espanya. With its swathes of concrete, monotonous rows of pines and ugly backdrop of highrise flats, the park is about as welcoming as the abattoir which it has replaced. The westerly corner is dominated by Miró's monumental phallic sculpture, *Dona i Ocell* (*Woman with Bird*).

Parc de L'Espanya Industrial

(Metro: L3 or L5 to Sants Station; bus: 27, 43, 109, 544.)

This park occupies some 5 hectares of land to the south of Sants Station, and it is the most intriguing – though not the most successful – of Barcelona's modern parks. Designed by Luis Peña Ganchegui and Fransesc Rius i Camp, it was built in 1982–85 on the site of an old factory. The park is dominated by 10 towers which look as though they have been salvaged from a 1930s Futurist film set. White steps descend from the towers to a lake, beside which is a small copse of cypress trees. A few weeping willows look distinctly out of place in this bleak, impersonal landscape. The park is liberally sprinkled with sculptures: there is a particularly ludicrous one of Neptune on a podium in the lake, and a giant dragon-like creature for children to clamber over beside it. The city authorities are very proud of this park, though it is hard to see why. It has not been improved by the abundance of litter and graffiti. It is significant, I think, that if you come here on a weekday you will find that most visitors congregate below the avenue of plane trees on the opposite side of the park from the towers. Here the old men of the neighbourhood chatter, play *petanca* or snooze on the park benches.

Parc del Clot
(Metro: L1 to Clot; bus: 34, 35, 43, 544.)
Another modern park in the city's northern suburb. The walls of the old railway roundhouse have been incorporated into the design of the park.

Parc de l'Estació del Nord
(Metro: L1 to Arc de Triomf; bus: 19, 39, 41, 42, 55, 141.)
This is another green phoenix which has risen from the ashes of an old station. The station ceased operations many years ago but the buildings have largely survived. The platforms have been turned into a sports hall and there is a broad expanse of grass outside.

Parc del Palau Reial de Pedralbes
(Metro: L3 to Palau Reial; bus: 7, 75. The **gardens** November to February: 10.00–18.00; March to April: 10.00–20.00; May to August: 10.00–21.00; September to October: 10.00–19.00.)

These lovely classical gardens were laid out by the landscape architect Nicolau Rubió i Tudurí in 1925. Gaudí's pavilions for the Güell estate are on the nearby Avinguda de Pedralbes.

Jardins d'Eduard Marquina
(Railway: Generalitat railway to La Bonanora; bus: 6, 7, 14, 34, 66.)
These delightful gardens, named after the poet, were also laid out by Rubió i Tudurí. There is a small lake, a formal garden, an open-air theatre and a playground. At the entrance there is a monument to the great Catalan cellist Pau Casals.

Other parks in the suburbs include:
- **Parc de les Aigües** (Metro: L4 to Alfons X). Not far from Domènech's hospital but closed to the public as it incorporates some water works.
- **Jardins de la Vil·la Amelia** (Metro: L3 to Maria Cristina). Formal gardens north of the Diagonal.
- **Jardins del Turó de Monterois** (Railway: Generalitat railway to Padua) and Jardins del Turó del Putget (Metro: L3 to Vallcarca). Pleasant gardens in smart suburbs.
- **Plaça de la Sagrada Familia and Plaça de Gaudí.** Good places to rest after a visit to the famous cathedral. The street which runs from the cathedral up to the Hospital de la Santa Creu – Avinguda de Gaudí – is also an agreeable place to relax.

GARDENS AND SQUARES IN AND AROUND THE OLD CITY: A SELECTION

Some of the squares listed here have already been described in Chapter 3 'A City Guide'.
Plaça de Catalunya: A large square at the top of the Ramblas and the foot of Passeig de Gràcia. Popular venue for political demonstrations. The Café Zurich *cerveseria* is a good place from which to watch the action.

Plaçeta de Ramon Amadeu: This charming, secluded little square is next to the church of Santa Anna. Flower stall at the entrance.

Plaça Nova: Once the site for public executions; today a popular haunt for visitors. Hundreds of Catalans gather in front of the cathedral to dance the *sardana* on Sunday evenings (*see* also page 163).

Plaça de Sant Felip Neri: Possibly the prettiest of all Barcelona's squares, dominated by the baroque façade of the church of Sant Felip Neri (*see* also page 30).

Plaça del Rei: A Gothic square bordered by the chapel of Santa Agata and the Saló del Tinell. Concerts are sometimes held here.

Plaça de Sant Jaume: A magnificent square sandwiched between the Renaissance façade of the Palau de la Generalitat and the neo-classical façade of the Ajuntament. A great gathering place for political events; also for festivals. The *sardana* is danced here on Sunday evenings. Unfortunately there are no seats or benches (*see* also page 34).

Plaça del Pi, Plaça de Sant Josep Oriol and Plaçeta del Pi: These three delightful little squares run into one another beside the fine Gothic church of Santa Maria del Pi. The flea/antique markets, held on Saturdays, are always worth investigating. The Café del Pi is popular with students.

Plaça Reial: A neo-classical gem lined with serious beer halls and popular with tramps, drunks, nutcases, thieves and dope-dealers. The wrought-iron lamps were designed by Gaudí. There are plenty of places to sit, though the company may not be to your liking. There is a coin and stamp market here on Sunday mornings (*see* also page 42).

Plaça de la Mercè: Dominated by the baroque church of La Mercè. Rather seedy (*see* also page 38).

Plaça del Duc de Medinaceli: This square, tacked onto the noisy Passeig de Colom, must once have been lovely, but even the palm trees look worn out now.

All the squares mentioned so far are to be found east of the

Ramblas between Plaça de Catalunya and the sea. If you are looking for a quiet spot in which to relax to the west of the Ramblas, there is little in the way of choice. There is nowhere in the overcrowded slum quarters below Carrer de Sant Pau, although you could sit in the garden of the church of Sant Pau del Camp. Plaça de Josep Maria Folch i Torres is a very popular square near the Avinguda del Paral·lel: men play *petanca*; children play ball; adolescents flirt. There is a shady square in front of the church of Santa Agusti, not far from La Bouería market, but the benches are often occupied by tramps. By far and away the pleasantest place to relax is in the Jardins de Rubió i Lluch: these are the gardens in the old Hospital de la Santa Creu. Nobody will mind if you rest for a while in the courtyard of the Casa de Convalescència. While you are there you can admire the 17th-century ceramic scenes by Llorenç Passoles. The Jardins del Doctor Fleming are a few yards away on Carrer del Carme (*see* also page 61).

The old quarters between Via Laietana and Ciutadella Park are also poorly served by squares and gardens. Among the more convivial places to loiter are Passeig del Born and Plaça de Sant Pere. Much better, however, to walk a little way further and spend time in either Ciutadella Park or in Passeig de Lluís Companys.

There are plenty of places to rest your legs along the seafront. The Moll de la Fusta, the recently tarted-up wharf beside the Passeig de Colom, strikes me as disappointing. Rows of palms are embedded in sterile concrete but there are plenty of benches and several cafés. *Golondrinas* pleasure trips round the port leave from the wharf beside the Columbus monument; highly recommended. (Summer: 10.00–20.00, every 30 minutes; Winter: 10.30–13.00 and 15.00–17.00.)

5:
ENTERTAINMENT IN
BARCELONA

Barcelona is a city of enormous vitality. It is blessed with one of the finest opera houses in Europe, half a dozen notable venues for orchestral and choral music, over fifty cinemas and a dozen decent theatres. It even has some old-fashioned music and dance halls. Unfortunately, the peak tourist season – July and August – coincides with a period of cultural dormancy, but by September everything is back in full swing.

To get the most out of Barcelona requires considerable stamina, as the evening entertainment tends to begin late and continue long after most northern Europeans would rather be in bed. The opera disgorges its audiences the wrong side of midnight, and most Barcelonans then spend a couple of hours in a restaurant. In Catalan society it is not unusual to be invited for a meal at one o'clock in the morning, and at four o'clock there are still large numbers of people wandering the streets. If you do manage to stay the course during the night, you can always have the pleasure of observing – through a silky screen of Ducados smoke – the early risers, the street-sweepers and transport workers, downing their first brandies of the day while you contemplate the last of yours.

It is worth planning – and booking – your evening entertainment well in advance, especially if you hope to get a seat at the opera. The weekly entertainment guide, *El Guía del Ocio*, lists everything from opera and jazz to the theatre and performance art; from the week's sporting events to what's on in the galleries and on television. The guide is in Spanish, but easy to decipher even for those who don't speak the language. The various tourist offices around the city (*see* page 239) will also provide information about entertainment, and the Patronat de Tourisme's monthly guide to activities is widely distributed in hotels, museums and galleries.

Operatic, Orchestral and Choral Music

By the time the English traveller Richard Ford arrived in Catalonia in the 1840s, Barcelona's reputation as a centre of operatic excellence was well-established. Ford, however, was unimpressed: 'The new theatre is good,' he wrote, 'although the lighting is bad and the odour worse, for the atmosphere is impregnated with the filthy fumes of a garlic-fed audience; the edifice was built on a suppressed convent; now the farce and fandango have supplanted the monastic melodrama. There is sometimes a second-rate Italian opera.' If there was much truth in this – and Ford's acidulous prose is sometimes more entertaining than it is instructive – then things have since changed for the better: the audience today is relatively sweet smelling and the operas are invariably of the highest quality. The theatre referred to here is, of course, the magnificent Gran Teatre del Liceu on the Ramblas.

For the past century Barcelonans have been besotted with Wagner. Though *Tannhäuser*'s 'Triumphal March' was first performed in Barcelona in 1862, it was to be another twenty or so years before the Wagnerian cult really took root. A Wagnerian Society was formed in 1882, but it folded soon after despite Wagner's growing popularity among the Catalan bourgeoisie. However, in 1901 another Wagnerian Association was set up, this time in that great *modernista* meeting place, Els Quatre Gats café (*see* page 119). The association not only organized concerts and lectures, but had all of Wagner's libretti translated into Catalan. By 1910, every major opera by Wagner had been performed at the Liceu with the exception of *Parsifal* and, in 1913, Barcelona became the first city outside Germany to stage *Parsifal*. The degree to which Barcelonans took to Wagner was reflected in curious ways: one café was called Oro del Rin, and another La Walquiria; light bulbs were named after *Wotan* and Wagner-lovers could smoke *Lohengrin* cigarettes. Since its creation in the 1840s the Liceu has been Barcelona's main opera house, although the older Teatre Principal, further down the Ramblas, was for some time a keen rival. Indeed the police were occasionally called upon to break up the fights between the supporters of the two factions

Josep Anselm Clavé (1824–74) had a profound influence on choral life in the city. Clavé set up several choirs – *Cors de Clavé* – which brought together Catalan singers who hitherto had performed largely in bars and on the streets. A choral contest held in 1891 led to Lluís Millet and Amadeu Vives forming the Orfeó Català and, in 1895, Enric Morera established a workers' choir. Both flourished, and their legacy is a large number of active choral groups today.

The Orfeó Català commissioned Domènech i Montaner to build a new concert hall. The Palau de la Música Catalana, which is one of the great *modernista* buildings (*see* page 102), was inaugurated in 1908 by Richard Strauss conducting the Berlin Philharmonic Orchestra. In terms of its sophistication and popularity, orchestral music was a latecomer to Barcelona and its rapid development following the opening of the Palau de la Música was largely due to the flair and energy of the great Catalan cellist Pau Casals (1876–1973). In 1920, he founded his own orchestra, and from then until the Civil War the orchestra put on some 20 performances a year. 'It was a modern orchestra,' wrote Roger Aliér in *Homage to Barcelona*, 'with an efficient organisation, which confirmed Barcelona's international standing in the concert field. The Orquestra Pau Casals not only put on a remarkable and extremely active season each year, but also brought to Barcelona some of the foremost composers and conductors of those years. Stravinsky, for example, conducted his own works at the Liceu in 1924 and 1925 with Pau Casals' orchestra.'

Casals is one of a score of great musical talents born and raised in Catalonia. The province has had more than its fair share of composers, the two best-known being Isaac Albéniz

(1860–1909) and Enric Granados (1867–1916). Albéniz's *Suite Ibèria* for piano is probably his most popular work. Pre-eminent among the singers of Catalonia are Josep Carreras (150,000 people turned up for an open-air concert in Barcelona celebrating his recovery from leukaemia), Montserrat Caballé, Dalmau Gonzàlez and Victòria de los Ángeles.

The Liceu and the Palau de la Música remain the twin citadels of classical music in Barcelona. Worth visiting for their architectural splendour alone, they are seen at their best during performances. In fact being seen at one's best also applies to the audiences: there is so much chattering and looking about at concerts that one suspects many Catalans are more concerned with being noticed in the right places and in the right company than with the music itself.

GRAN TEATRE DEL LICEU:

(La Rambla 61–65; Metro; L3 to Liceu.)

For a description of its history and architecture, *see* page 53. There are 90-plus performances during the Liceu season, which runs from September through to early June. Opera predominates (Wagner being especially popular) but there are also programmes of ballet and orchestral music. The booking office is round the corner at Carrer de Sant Pau 1 (Tel: 318 92 77). For information about advance booking, contact the booking office during July, either by writing or telex: 99750 LICEU E. Normal opening hours, Monday to Friday: 08.00–15.00; Saturday: 09.00–13.00. For tickets on the day of performance, go to Rambla dels Caputxins 65, 11.00–13.30 and 16.00 to the beginning of the performance. The Liceu seats 3,000 people, and prices range from 500 to 8,500 pesetas.

PALAU DE LA MÚSICA CATALINA:

(Amadeu Vives 1; Metro: L4 to Plaça Urquinaona.)

For a description of its history and architecture, *see* page 102. Magnificent though this building was, it has benefited from improvements over the last decade: the musicians now have proper dressing rooms (which they hadn't before); the seats have been replaced; a new annex built; air-conditioning installed; and the acoustics upgraded from being good to exceptional. The Palau is the home of the Orquestra Ciutat de Barcelona, which gives some 50 concerts a year, most starting at 21.00. Information and tickets from the box office (Tel: 317 10 96). The Palau frequently receives visiting orchestras, and it is also used for concerts organized by the Orfeó Català, Fundació Caixa de Pensions and others.

There are several other important venues for classical music, including: Casal del Metge (Via Laietana 31), Saló de Cent (Barcelona City Hall), Teatre Mercat de les Flors (Lleida 47), and even the Plaça del Rei (for example, for the choral concert during the festival of La Mercè on September 24). For all information about classical music, contact Amics de la Música de Barcelona (Tel: 302 68 70), open Monday to Friday: 10.00–13.00 and 15.00–20.00.

Jazz, Flamenco, Folk and Rock

Ever since Jack Hylton brought his big band to play at the Palau Nacional during the 1929 International Exhibition, jazz has been popular in Barcelona. During the 1930s many other bands from England and the United States made their way to Barcelona, and local jazz bands grew in number and popularity. The Hot Club Barcelona, set up in 1935, produced publications about jazz and brought such famous figures as Django Reinhardt and Stephane Grappelli to the city. The Hot Club was also instrumental in setting up the annual Barcelona Jazz Festival.

There are a dozen or so local bands worth watching out for. The best-known Catalan jazz musician today is Tete Montoliu. La Locomotora Negra and A-Free-K play excellent trad jazz, while Globo Feroz veer more towards the blues. Madagascar, Ictus and Azucar Imaginario also deserve a mention, as do the big bands attached to the Aula de Música Moderna i Jazz and the Taller de Músics (the Musicians' Workshop). There are two jazz festivals in Catalonia, one in the town of Terrassa in the spring, the other in Barcelona in the autumn. In the past the festivals have attracted outstanding musicians like Louis Armstrong, Dizzy Gillespie and Count Basie; the tradition of excellence continues today. For details of the festivals, contact the tourist offices. *El Guía del Ocio* provides a weekly up-date of the jazz scene. The best places to hear jazz outside the festival period include:

- La Cova del Drac, Carrer de Tuset 30.
- L'Auditori, Carrer de Balmes 245.
- Abraxas, Carrer de Gelabert 26.
- L'Eixample Jazz Club, Carrer de Diputació 341.
- Harlem, Carrer de Comtessa de Sobradiel 8.

Flamenco, the passionate gypsy music of Andalucia, was imported to Catalonia by the men and women who came north last century in search of work. To hear flamenco at its best you must travel south still to the taverns of Seville and Córdoba, but it has become increasingly popular in Barcelona. There are excellent shows twice nightly (at 22.00 and midnight) at **Los Tarantos**, Plaça Reial 17. Try, also, **El Patio Andaluz**, at Carrer d'Aribau 242, for dinner and flamenco.

Barcelona, like most European cities of its size, regularly hosts big rock concerts with international stars. More interesting in many ways are the home-bred Catalan singers and groups, some of whom are popular beyond the province. Lluís Llach is a much-revered Catalan version of Leonard Cohen: he persisted in performing songs in Catalan, often of a very political nature, during Franco's era, and he is a favourite with the French as well as the Catalans. Several bars and discos have live rock music; among the best (and they are all expensive) are **Zeleste** (Carrer d'Almogàvers 122), **Studio 54** (Avinguda del Paral·lel 65), **Otto Zutz** (Carrer de Lincoln 15) and **K.G.B** (Carrer d'Alegre de Dalt 55).

Music Halls and Dance Halls

Perhaps it is unfair to lump saucy music halls together with old-fashioned dance halls, but they have one factor in common: in both cases legs are raised – albeit in differing manners – for public entertainment. Barcelona's equivalent of Montmartre's Moulin Rouge is **El Molino** (Carrer de Vila i Vila 99). El Molino, as you would expect, puts on variety shows in which the females shed their sequined swimwear and feather boas with great regularity. This is a popular venue with visiting sailors and a ribald evening is guaranteed. (There are afternoon shows Tuesday to Sunday: 18.00; late shows Tuesday to Sunday: 23.00, except Saturday: 22.15 and 01.00.) The **Belle Epoque** (Carrer de Muntaner 246) is an upmarket version of the same thing (shows every day except Sundays, 23.30). **Barcelona de Noche** (Carrer de les Tàpies 5) is in an appropriately sleazy setting just north of the Avinguda del Paral·lel. It specializes in transvestite numbers. (There are two shows nightly, 23.45 and 01.30.) However, far more entertaining than any of these is the famous **Bodega Bohemia** (Carrer de Lancaster 2). Here men and women who were fully grown by the time Franco came to power sing their old favourites, often very badly.

There are several old-fashioned dance halls of the sort that died out in Britain soon after the Second World War. If you feel inclined to dress up and do the fox trot or the waltz, in gorgeous *fin-de-siècle* surroundings, head for the ineffable **La Paloma** (Carrer de Tigre 27). Check before going as La Paloma sometimes stages boxing fights. Other dance halls with their own orchestras include: **Bolero** (Avinguda Diagonal 405), **Cibeles** (Carrer de Córcega 363) and **Sutton** (Carrer de Tuset 13). The audiences tend to be middle-aged and conservatively dressed.

Theatre

During the rule of Franco (1939–73) theatrical performances in Catalan were banned. They are now back with a vengeance, and consequently theatrical life in Barcelona is a closed book to most foreigners, including those who speak Spanish. However, ardent theatre-goers may wish to catch the flavour of the performance, so a few brief pointers are in order. The Josep Maria Flotats company is said to be one of the best in Europe. The company tends to perform classical works translated into Catalan and its main venue is the **Poliorama** (Rambla 115; Tel: 317 75 99). The Centre Dramatic de la Generalitat puts on Catalan productions at the **Romea** (Carrer de l'Hospital 51; Tel: 317 71 89). For non-Catalan speakers, far and away the most exciting theatre is provided by Els Fura del Baus, or the 'Vermin of the Sewers'. Their performances succeed in stimulating, outraging and embarrassing. Highly recommended. One of the most attractive theatres is in the old flower market near Montjuïc, the **Mercat de los Flors** (Carrer de Lleida 59; Tel: 426 18 75). The painting in the dome is by Miquel Barceló. **Teatre Lliure** (Carrer de Montseny 47; Tel: 218 92 51) has plays by its own theatre company, and is also a venue for concerts. For details about what's on and where, refer to the listings in *El Guía del Ocio*. Two new theatres – one designed by Ricard Bofill, another by Rafael Moneo – will be opening during Olympic year in the Plaça de les Glòries.

Cinemas

There are two major film festivals in Catalonia each year. The Barcelona International Film Festival occupies the last two weeks in June and the first two in July (Tel: 215 24 24, FX: 215 29 66). The Sitges International Festival of Horror Film takes place in the seaside resort in early October. There are over fifty cinemas in Barcelona and most have an afternoon show around 16.00, an early evening show at about 19.00, and a late one at 22.30 or 23.00. There are often long queues for the late shows of recently released films. Most foreign films are dubbed in Spanish, but some cinemas show films in their original language with Spanish subtitles. At any one time there will be a dozen or so un-dubbed English language films, and several German, French and Italian. *El Guía del Ocio* lists these under the heading *Peliculas en V.O.*

Festivals

The Spanish have an unrivalled passion for *fiestas*, or *festes* as the Catalans call them. Some of those held in Barcelona are observed throughout Spain; others are peculiar to Catalonia. In addition to these every village and urban district (*barri*),

19. Tibidabo amusement park with the church of El Sagrat Cor behind.

20. Art nouveau shop front, Carrer de Girona.

22. Above: Ripoll: Romanesque cloister, monastery of Santa Maria.

23. Below: Tarragona: cathedral cloisters, a splendid blend of Romanesque and Gothic.

21. Left: Barcelona's Gothic cathedral, dedicated to the Holy Cross and Santa Eulàlia.

24. Sitges: Church of Sant Bartomeu and Santa Tecla.

25. Sitges: Maricel de Mar and (left) Maricel de Terra.

26. Sitges: *modernista* detail.

27. Sitges: capital by Pere Jou, Maricel de Terra.

28. Ripoll: Romanesque capital in monastery cloister.

29. Girona: the cathedral's baroque façade conceals a fine example of Catalan Gothic architecture.

30. Tortosa: baroque side entry – Porta de l'Olivera – to cathedral.

31. Tarrogona: Roman amphitheatre.

32. Vall de Boí: ploughing by mule beside the village of Durro.

33. Vall de Boí: the church of Sant Climent at Taüll, one of the world's greatest Romanesque monuments.

34. Vall de Boí: Romanesque portal, Coll.

35. Ebro Delta: traditional peasant dwelling.

36. Vall de Boí: farm buildings in the village of Durro.

will set aside time to celebrate its own patron saint. The nature of celebration varies according to the festival's purpose and setting, but just as there are several common ingredients to most Catalan food (garlic, olive oil, nuts, tomatoes) so there are certain activities which link many of the festivals. Frequently, the *sardana* will be danced to the sound of the *coblas* (brass bands). This national dance is somewhat like a Scottish reel in slow motion: a group of people hold hands in a circle and jig to left and right in time with the music. It is enchanting to witness and the footwork is not nearly so easy as it may at first appear. Spaniards from further south are fond of ridiculing the *sardana*, but to the Catalans it is no laughing matter, a fact borne out by the solemnity of their expressions when performing it. (On Sundays hundreds of people come together to dance the *sardana* outside Barcelona cathedral and in Plaça de Sant Jaume. The festivals are often accompanied too by the parading of *gegants* and *cap grossos* (giants and big heads), and in some areas (especially in and around the town of Valls) *xiquets* come together to build human towers. The festivals described below are among the more important in the Catalan calendar.

REIS MAGS This is held on 6 January, or Epiphany, following the Feast of the Three Kings. On the evening of the 5th, children leave out a shoe so that the Three Kings from the Orient can fill it with sweets and presents. There is a quid pro quo: they must leave a bucket of water beside the shoe so that the Kings' camels can slake their thirst. On the 6th, the Kings arrive by boat and are greeted by the Mayor at the port. Then follows a noisy procession through the streets.

CARNIVAL In Barcelona, Carnival was banned from 1930 to 1980. It is once again celebrated with great verve, especially in Sitges, but also in Barcelona and other towns and villages. Carnival in Catalonia is similar in character to the *Mardi Gras* festivities in southern France: people dress up in masks, make mischief, drink too much and celebrate, on the festival's conclusion, the burning of an effigy of Carnestoltes, King of the Vices.

SETMANA SANTA Holy week, from Palm Sunday to Easter Day, remains a sombre religious occasion and has not been hijacked by *bon viveurs*.

SANT JORDI Catalonia celebrates its patron saint, Sant Jordi (St George), on 23 April. At one time there used to be jousting in what is now the Passeig del Born. Nowadays the festival has a literary flavour. In 1923 the 23 April, which was the day of Cervantes's death, was declared the 'Day of the Book'. Young men give their girlfriends red roses, and the latter reciprocate by giving books. From a writer's point of view, this is an admirable practice.

CORPUS CHRISTI This festival, which is held in honour of the Eucharist, is celebrated on a Thursday in May (consult an ecclesiastical calendar to find out which one). The procession held in Sitges (*see* page 179) features *gegants* and *cap grossos*, and is particularly famous. The streets are filled with fabulous displays of flowers.

MIDSUMMER'S EVE AND THE FESTIVAL OF SANT JOAN The summer solstice on 23 June is celebrated by spectacular bonfires and firework displays. Being a noisy race, the Catalans are fond of bangers, so don't expect much sleep. The biggest of the bonfires attracts tens of thousands of people to Montjuïc. On Sant Joan's Day the Catalans eat *coca*, cake made from pine nuts and crystallized fruit.

DIADA DE CATALUNYA The Catalan National Holiday on 11 September is curious in that it commemorates defeat, not victory. On 11 September 1714 Barcelona capitulated to the troops of Philip V at the end of the lengthy War of the Spanish Succession. This led to the abolition of local government institutions, the banishing of the university, and the building of the fortress in Ciutadella Park among other things. During the Franco era, public celebration of the Diada was banned. Today the festival celebrates, in belligerent style, the strength of feeling for Catalan self-determination. There are political gatherings and demonstrations, and the Senyeres (the Catalan flag) flutters above every roof and balcony. The Diada is a good excuse for Catalans to sing their national anthem 'Els

Segadors' ('The Reapers'). The anthem is derived from a ballad which described the revolt on 7 June 1640 – Corpus Christi day – when the Catalan peasantry, encouraged by Pau Claris, President of the Generalitat, rose against the Spanish Crown. The Republic survived till 1652, when the rebellion was put down.

SETMANA GRAN A week of festivities – including concerts, parades, dances and so forth – is organized around the Feast of Maré de Déu de la Mercè (Our Lady of Mercy) on 24 September. There is a tremendous meeting of *gegants* from all over Catalonia in Plaça de Sant Jaume, and a spectacular procession of devils, dragons and other beasts through the old city. The much-venerated image of La Mercè – a 14th-century wood sculpture – can be seen in the baroque church dedicated to Our Lady in Carrer de la Mercè (*see* page 38).

Sports

On 17 October 1986 the city of Barcelona received the nomination to hold the 1992 Olympic Games. By then over 70,000 had already signed up as volunteers. This indicated a remarkable confidence on the part of the Catalans that their city would be chosen to host the games; it was a manifestation too of the great enthusiasm for sport in Catalonia.

Barcelona had its first Olympic winner in the year AD 129 when Lucius Minicius Natalis Quadronis Verus won the chariot race at the 227th Olympiad. The province's sporting history since then has been chequered: though Catalonia provided 40 per cent of the Spanish athletes who took part in the last three Olympic games, few of them won medals. Until recently sport has fared badly in the Catalan education system. 'Those who are now over 30,' wrote the journalist Eduard Boet, 'still remember what sport was like at school during their childhood and adolescence. The Physical Education classes were given once a week by a teacher who also gave lessons in political theory, which in those days was called "Formation of the National Spirit". Very little love of sport was learnt in those classes, where the teacher often directed gymnastics dressed in a jacket and tie.' Fortunately, those days are long gone, and local authorities and sports federations in Catalonia have put tremendous effort into encouraging sports activities both at school and at club level. Further impetus to the development of sport has come from the Olympics, and many of the new facilities will be available for public use after the games.

Poor sports education, however, never did anything to diminish the Catalan love of spectator sports. The most popular – it is nearly a religion here – is football. There are two First Division clubs in Barcelona. The more prestigious, **Barcelona Football Club**, or Barça for short, plays at the superb 120,000-seater Nou Camp Stadium (details of matches, Tel: 330 94 11; metro: L5 to Collblanc). The club was founded in 1899 and its turbulent history has to some extent mirrored the province's political vicissitudes. During Franco's era, the board of directors could only meet in the presence of a member of the dictator's armed forces, and the government in Madrid used all sorts of ploys to weaken Barça, the main rival of Real Madrid. During the dictatorship Catalans were able to channel their nationalist sympathies, otherwise sternly suppressed, through support for their football team: victory over Madrid assumed a level of importance difficult for outsiders to appreciate. The Club's yearning for continual success means a ruthless regime at the top, with even successful managers like Terry Venables getting their marching orders when the team has faltered. There are more than 100,000 members of Barça, four-fifths of whom have permanent seats. There is no such thing as football hooliganism in Barcelona. The other club in the city is **Real Club Deportivo Español** (Tel: 203 48 00; Railway: Generalitat to La Bonanova).

Much to their credit, the Catalans do not care for bullfights, which in Barcelona are attended mainly by tourists and immigrants from Andalucia. Bullfights are held on Sundays at 17.30 at the **Monumental Bull Ring** (Gran Via de les Corts Catalanes 749). There is a box office at Carrer de Muntaner 24 (Tel: 253 38 21). The season is from March to September.

Apart from football there are several other spectator sports which may be of interest to visitors. Details about basketball, rugby, water polo, tennis and other sporting events can be found in Barcelona's two daily tabloid papers devoted solely to sport: *El Mundo Deportivo* and *Sport*.

There are over 1,200 sports facilities in and around Barcelona, and many of these are open to visitors from abroad. It would be pointless to attempt a comprehensive listing, but the following should give you an inkling of what is available.

GOLF This sport is becoming increasingly popular in Catalonia. To play, you will need proof of membership of a club in your home country and it is wise to bring your handicap card. Green fees in Spain are very stiff indeed; the expense of playing rises further if you hire clubs and trolleys. A round of golf costs about the same as the best seat at the opera. The closest course to Barcelona is the **Real Club de Golf del Prat de Llobregat** (Tel: 379 02 78). A scenically more attractive course is **Club de Golf Terramar** at Sitges, some 25 miles (40 km) south of Barcelona (Tel: 894 05 80). To the north of Barcelona is the **Club de Golf Vallromanos** at Montores del Vallés (Tel: 568 03 62).

SWIMMING There are swimming pools dotted throughout the city. Of the open-air pools one of the most pleasant is the **Bernat Picornell Pool** on Montjuïc (Avinguda del Estadi 34; Tel: 325 92 81). This is open only in summer, 10.00–15.30. Nearer the centre of town there are several good covered pools, for example, **Montjuïc Swimming Club**, Plaça de Folch i Torres (Tel: 241 01 22; 11.30–13.30, Monday to Friday); and **Ronda Swimming Pool**, Ronda de Sant Pau 46 (Tel: 329 98 06; 07.00–21.00, Monday to Friday). Further out of town there are two swimming pools, one outdoor, at the **Can Carraleu Sports Centre**, Carrer Esports (Tel: 203 78 74; bus: number 94 from Tres Torres). There are also tennis and volleyball courts and an indoor football pitch. Opening times for the public are restricted (08.00–10.00 and 14.00–15.30 for indoor facilities, Monday to Friday; 10.00–13.00, Sunday). Outdoor facilities are open in summer from 10.00–17.00, although tennis courts are open 08.00–23.00.

* TENNIS AND SQUASH As above for tennis at the Can Carraleu Sports Centre. Tennis and squash courts can also be hired at the **Vall Parc Club**, Carretera a Sant Cugat 79 (Tel: 212 67 89). Open daily, 08.00–24.00. **Can Melich Club** at Avinguda 11 de Septembre, San Just Desvern, has 20 squash courts and 10 tennis courts as well as a sauna and gymnasium. Open daily, 08.00–24.00. If you want to combine a game of squash with a complete physical overhaul, then the **Squash Club Barcelona**, Avinguda Roma 2 (Tel: 325 81 00) is recommended. Gymnasium, sauna, solarium and massage available (07.00–22.00, Monday to Friday; 08.00–14.00, Saturday; 09.00–12.00, Sunday).

BOWLING There are three bowling alleys in Barcelona. **Pedralbes Bowling Alley**, Avinguda Doctor Marañón 11 (Tel: 333 03 52); open daily, 10.00–01.30. The **AMFF Bowling Centre**, Sabino de Arana 6 (Tel: 330 50 48); open daily, 11.00–01.30. **Boliche**, Avinguda Diagonal 508 (Tel: 237 90 98); open daily, 18.00–02.00.

For information about water sports and skiing, contact the Tourist Offices (*see* page 239).

6:

FOOD AND DRINK

Catalan cuisine has many virtues, one of the more obvious being its variety. To some extent this is a reflection of culinary ingenuity: the Catalans are brave mixers, setting chicken beside prunes, spinach with pine nuts, rabbit with snails, and even lobster with chocolate sauce. However, nature must take much of the credit, for the variety of raw materials available in Catalonia is largely a function of the region's geographic diversity. From the Ebro Delta come rice, artichokes and soft fruit; from the high Pyrenees, wild mushrooms, walnuts and game. The rolling countryside inland supports that familiar Mediterranean trinity of olives, vines and wheat, while the irrigated *huerta* provides all manner of vegetables from summer aubergines to winter cabbage. Inevitably, factory farming supplies much of the province's chicken and pork, but there is plenty of good meat to be had from beasts reared outdoors: the salt marshes of the Ebro Delta are grazed by beef and lamb, while the wooded Pyrenees supply not only good pork and mutton but wild boar and partridge, too. That a relatively small area – Catalonia is only one and a half times the size of Wales – can provide such a wealth of food is fortune enough, yet this is only half the story: Catalonia has 312 miles (500 km) of coastline, and a great variety of fish and shellfish ends up in the local markets.

Catalan cuisine, which is said to be Spain's oldest, has received many influences from outside. The Greeks and Romans both left their mark, as did the Arabs, whose influence lingers still in the widespread use of lemon, cinnamon and honey. There is some debate about whether it was the Arabs or the Italians who first introduced pasta to Catalan cooking. Between 1282 and 1444, Sicily, Sardinia and Naples (that is to say, southern Italy) were brought under the rule of the Catalan–Aragonese crown. Thus the arrival of many pasta dishes, though the celebrated *canalons* – a Catalan version of *cannelloni* – probably didn't arrive from Italy until the 19th century. *Canalons* is to the Catalan Boxing Day what turkey is to our Christmas. Other very obvious influences have come from the French provinces across the border, and especially from Roussillon and Provence.

Markets provide the visitor with the best introduction to Catalan food. The finest in Barcelona is **La Boqueria**, just off the Ramblas. Arabella Boxer, writing about this market in her *Mediterranean Cookbook*, was particularly impressed by the ladies who ran the fish stalls: 'No fish wives these, but superior-looking matrons such as one might find running a Women's Institute sale in aid of the Red Cross; complete with hair-dos, dark glasses, pearl earrings and twin sets protected by white plastic aprons, they were immensely efficient.' I suppose that in the average English fish market one might find half a dozen species of sea fish, not many more. Here, there are scores: cod (both fresh and salted), sole, eel, anchovy, sea bass, angler fish, hake, tunny, red mullet, bream, gilthead, turbot, mackerel and manta ray to name just a few. There is a similar profusion of shellfish on sale at the market, from bulbous squids and spiny lobsters to minute crabs and tiny butterfly shells. The meat stalls are impressive too; some deal in red meats, some in smoked hams and a multitude of sausages, others in poultry and game. Beside conventional game like pheasant, partridge and hare, the Catalans are partial to wild boar, woodcock and song thrushes. These stalls may dismay vegetarians (and conservationists), who are advised to ponder the extravagantly colourful displays of fresh fruit and vegetables. There are also several stalls near the entrance which specialize in dried fruit, nuts and herbs.

There are half a dozen ingredients essential to Catalan cuisine: they are the pillars, so to speak, on which the entire edifice is built, and all are grown locally. These are olive oil, tomatoes, garlic, onions, nuts and dried fruit. Colman Andrews in his *Catalan Cuisine: Europe's Last Great Culinary Secret* identified four key Catalan sauces, which between them utilize the ingredients mentioned above: *allioli*, a garlic and oil paste often served with grilled meats and fish; *sofregit*, a sauce made with oil, onions and tomatoes; *picada*, a thickening or flavouring agent made from pounded nuts, garlic, fried bread, parsley and oil; and *samfaina*, which is an elaborate version of *sofregit*. The same four sauces are cited too by Marimar Torres, though she adds to this list *romesco*, a sauce made of almonds, tomatoes, peppers and garlic – a speciality of Tarragona, where it is used to accompany fish dishes.

The Catalans sometimes claim that their cooking is comparable to French cuisine at its best. This strikes me as wishful thinking, though the disparity between the two is not so great as to preclude a good debate on the subject. However, there is one thing that is beyond dispute, and of profound relevance to visitors on modest budgets. It is much easier to eat well in France than it is in Catalonia; indeed, south of the border I have had more meals than I care to remember which have led me to reflect on the gulf in quality between the raw materials available in the markets and the finished product on the plate. There are several things a visitor can do to avoid disappointment or, at least, to lengthen the odds against a poor meal. Adopt the eating habits of the locals: that way you are less likely to receive reheated food left over from a previous meal. It is best to avoid hotel breakfasts, and instead take a light snack in a café or bar. If you have had your fill of *croissants* or *brioches*, then try *pa amb tomàquet*, bread rubbed with tomato and sprinkled with olive oil, salt and pepper. If you stray into Barceloneta in the morning you will see fishermen and dock workers eating hearty fish breakfasts, and indeed manual workers throughout the region take their cooked breakfasts seriously, often with a glass of brandy.

For Catalans, lunch is the main meal of the day; it should be yours too. Between 13.00 and 16.00 most shops and offices close, and everyone heads either for home or a restaurant. Most restaurants have a 3- or 4-course *menú del día* at lunch, whereas few do in the evening. For the visitor, this is the most economical way to eat. A first course – perhaps a salad or soup – is generally followed by a substantial meat or fish dish, then a dessert. The evening meal in Catalonia is a lighter affair and often taken between 22.00 and midnight: the Catalans favour *verduras* (a vegetable dish), perhaps with a *tortilla* (a Spanish omelette), or some fish. As their figures often attest, the Catalans are very partial to snacks between meals. Barcelona's pastry shops are deservedly famous and should be patronized. A plate or two of *tapas* will also stave off the pangs of hunger brought on by strenuous sightseeing, though *tapas* are an Andalucian import, and the Catalans do not take such meagre fare seriously.

There are said to be more than 10,000 restaurants and bars in Barcelona, a tiny fraction of which are listed in the recommendations in the section on 'Where to Eat and Drink' (*see* page 233). No doubt there are hundreds of restaurants, unmentioned here, which are equally worthy of the visitor's attention. Wherever possible, however, you should avoid those establishments which rely solely on the tourist trade: with their multilingual menus and glossy photographs of *plats combinats* (combination dishes), places such as these are little more than fuel stops. If it is simply calories you are after, you may as well go to fast food restaurants like McDonald's or Burger King. Most restaurants will have menus in both Spanish and Catalan and those who speak neither language should arm themselves with a dictionary. It would be a pity to miss choice Catalan dishes because they went unrecognized on the menu. The brief survey below may be of some assistance.

Soups, Salads and Other Starters
The soup closest to the heart of many Catalans is *escudella i carn d'olla*. This is a meat and vegetable broth – akin in many

ways to an English hotpot – which is virtually a meal in itself. It is much favoured in the Pyrenees, and in other parts of Catalonia during the winter months. The Catalans are exceedingly fond of fish soups, especially along the coast, and there are endless variations on the theme. *Suquet* – or *sopa de pescadors* – combines potatoes with scorpion fish, halibut, bass and monkfish; in some recipes rice replaces the potato, and mussels, prawns and clams join the fish. The autumn is a good time to try *sopa de bolets*, which should preferably be made with the strong-flavoured wild mushrooms rather than the bland cultivated variety. Two other good soups – neither native to Catalonia – which often appear on menus are *sopa de ajo* (garlic soup) and *gazpacho*. The latter is an Andalucian soup, made from tomatoes, green peppers, cucumber and onion, served chilled with a garnish of chopped eggs and vegetables. Perfect on a hot summer's day.

The politest thing one can say about many Catalan salads is that they are robust. The one which takes the region's name – *amanida catalana* – is the sort of thing that gives salads a bad name: lettuce, tomatoes, peppers, onions and carrots, each practising culinary apartheid and heaped in a pile on its own, keep company with anchovies, boiled eggs and whatever *charcuteria* the chef feels he can spare. Of much greater interest are several salads based on fish. If you are in Sitges or Vilanova i la Geltrú you should try the delicious *xató* (you can get it in Barcelona, too): cod, tuna and anchovies tossed in a *romesco* sauce (*see* page 171). Fish is also the main ingredient in the popular *esqueixada* (shredded salt cod salad).

Of the vegetable dishes served as a first course, one of the most popular is *espinacs a la catalana* (Catalan spinach): the greenery is lightly boiled, then chopped up and fried in oil with raisins and pine nuts. *Espinacs a la catalana* is easy to reproduce back at home; unfortunately the same cannot be said for *calçotada*, a dish of grilled green onions served with a piquant sauce made with almonds, tomatoes, garlic, chilli powder and oil.

The Catalans, like the French, have a fondness for snails,

which are served in a variety of ways: they are especially good cooked over tin – *al la llauna* – and accompanied by *picada* and *sofregit* sauces. This dish generally goes under the name of *cargols picants*.

Rice and Pasta Dishes

Paella is the dish that Spain has given to the rest of the world; it is actually a Valencian invention, but the Catalans show as much fondness for it as their southerly neighbours, who still maintain that they are the only ones who really know how to cook a *paella valenciana*. There are many variations of *paella*. Onions, tomatoes, garlic, peppers, peas and short-grained rice are simmered with a combination of the following: chicken, pork, rabbit, snails, frogs' legs, eels, mussels, clams, prawns, monkfish, bass, halibut. Aesthetically this is one of the most attractive Spanish dishes.

There are two other superb rice dishes worthy of mention: one from the coast to the north of Barcelona, the other from further south. The best place to eat *arròs negre* is in the region which invented it, the Costa Brava. Stuffed squid or cuttlefish is served with rice cooked in the creatures' ink: hence the name of the dish, 'black rice'. The other rice dish comes from Valencia, but is a great favourite in and around the Ebro Delta (*see* page 197). *Arròs a banda* is a rice and fish dish (the fish generally being scorpion fish) served with *allioli*.

Of Catalonia's pasta dishes, *canalons* is one of the most popular. A direct descendant of Italian *cannelloni*, the pasta is stuffed with a variety of meats (for example, chicken and veal, or sometimes something more exotic like duck) and baked with a coating of Parmesan cheese. Catalonia's other pasta dishes are based on *fideus* (noodles).

Fish Dishes

Colman Andrews suggests that 'if *suquet* is Catalonia's most famous fish soup, *sarsuela* is its most notorious'. *Sarsuela*, he goes on to say, even has a bad reputation among many Catalan chefs, 'both because it seems too much of a good thing and because, in unscrupulous hands, it can provide an easy way to use up bad fish'. The ingredients of *sarsuela* are, roughly speaking, the ingredients of the sea. *Sarsuela* gets its name from the light opera – the Spanish equivalent of Gilbert and Sullivan – which caught on in Spain in the 18th century, 'the implication being that this is a sort of variety-show dish, presumably not to be taken too seriously,' says Andrews.

For those who prefer a simple approach to the serving of seafood there is no end of choice in Catalonia. Shellfish – cockles, lobster, prawns, crayfish, clams – are often eaten grilled (*a la braisa* or *graellada*) and accompanied by a bowl of *allioli*. Mussels are generally served much as they are in France with a *marinière* sauce. Most species of fish are available either grilled or baked in an oven (*al forn*), though frequently they are subjected to more elaborate treatment. In the Tarragona area fish dishes are often served with *romesco* sauce.

If there is such a thing as a fish staple in Catalonia it is the *baccalà* (Atlantic salt cod). As long ago as the 15th century salt cod was imported by the Spanish from Newfoundland. For those not reared on salt cod, which bears little resemblance in taste to fresh cod, it is definitely an acquired taste. The cod is used in a variety of ways, having first been desalted by soaking in fresh water. In *baccalà a la catalana amb panses i pinyons*, the cod is stewed in a combined *picada* and *sofregit* sauce together with raisins and pine nuts. Another dish – *bacallà a l'escuma d'allioli* – matches the cod against an *allioli* mousse.

Meat Dishes

Some of the robust meat stews typical of inland and upland Catalonia are reminiscent of the Languedoc classic, *cassoulet*. *Favas* (beans) are essential to most of these, and in the case of *faves a la catalana* they are the main ingredient, with *botifarra negra* (blood pudding), *botifarra* (white Catalan sausage) and belly pork playing second fiddle. Other stews of a similar type have the benefit of pig's trotters and mutton too. Catalan bangers-and-beans is far superior to our own variety; whole *botifarra* are fried till brown and laid on a bed of white beans. Another popular stew – a *fricandó* – is made from veal and mushrooms.

Catalan cooking is seen at its most adventurous when it comes to dealing with game and poultry; the Anglo-Saxon treatment of pheasant, rabbit and duck seems prosaic and unimaginative by comparison. The richness of game is often beautifully complemented by the presence of fruit, cooked or uncooked. Dishes to watch out for include *ànec amb peres* (duck with pears), *ànec amb figues* (duck with figs), *conill ambs herbes al vi negre* (rabbit in red wine), and *pollastre rostit amb samfaina* (chicken with *samfaina*).

The Catalans are expert at grilling meat, and chicken, lamb and pork are especially good when cooked outdoors over a charcoal barbecue. A green salad and bowl of *allioli* make an ideal accompaniment. The Catalan aversion to bloody meat may come as a relief to many British and American visitors. However, some Catalan chefs have a tendency to cremate meat which deserves to be left more sanguine.

Desserts and Cheeses

When it comes to putting the final touches to a good meal in a Catalan restaurant, one is often sorely disappointed. All too often the bulk of desserts involve a variation on a theme – the theme being ice cream. One local standard available almost everywhere is *crema catalana*, a viscous custard sealed with a coating of burnt caramel. If you are fortunate you may hit upon a restaurant whose chef believes in doing justice to Catalan desserts. Look out for *menjar blanc* (almond milk pudding), *flam* (fruit flan) and *pastís de pinyons* (pine-nut tart). If you have a yearning for pastries (and in the manufacture of these the Catalans excel) I suggest you buy them direct from patisseries and eat them on a park bench.

If anything the cheese situation in restaurants is even more depressing. Many often serve none at all, some just a slice of imported Camembert – yet the Catalans produce a number of excellent and distinctive cheeses. Some of the best come from the Pyrenees. The smoked cow's cheese from the Vall d'Aran is particularly admired, and if you like a strongish sheep's cheese, try Serrat. There are several good goat's cheeses too. *Mató* (the soft cheese) is often served with honey and lemon (*mel i mató*).

Wine

The Catalans take their drinking seriously. On their way to work in the morning businessmen often stop off at a café for a coffee and a brandy. Beer is consumed in mid-morning with a sickly pastry, and as a refresher throughout the day; and in the evenings the young and chic resort to cocktails, of which the Catalans have a bewildering array. Spirits are popular too, and the standard measure far exceeds its equivalent in Britain. However, the blood of Catalonia is wine, which is drunk in hearty quantities at meal times, and in the case of the sparkling *cava*, between meals as well.

Catalonia is the second largest wine-producing region in Spain. North Europeans and Americans are probably better acquainted with the produce of La Rioja, but there are some excellent Catalan wines which deserve the visitor's attention. The best wines carry the mark D.O., which means *Denominació d'Origen* (the equivalent to the French *appellation contrôlée*); this is a guarantee of both authenticity and quality. Among the best-known wines of Catalonia are those of Penedès, a large area to the south-west of Barcelona. Light white wines, slightly fruity in taste, are produced from the Xarel·lo and Parellada grapes; they make an excellent accompaniment to fish dishes. Penedès rosés and reds are more than drinkable, the latter being less heavy than the full-bodied reds of Priorat, a hill area inland from Tarragona. As well as its potent red table wines, Priorat also produces sweet wines which go well with the region's sickly desserts. Wines of *Denominació d'Origen* Tarragona fall into three categories. The Cap de Tarragona, which adjoins Penedès, supplies light white wines and some well-perfumed rosés. The Comarca de

Falset wines are similar to the heavy reds of its neighbour
Priorat. The third sub-division of D.O. Tarragona takes in the
wines of the Ribera d'Ebre (the River Ebro). Immediately to
the south-west is Terra Alta, whose reds are aggressively
provincial (more suited, perhaps, to a farmworkers' lunch
than a candlelit dinner), and whose whites make a good match
for a strong-tasting dish of *sarsuela*.

In pleasant contrast to the heavy wines of Terra Alta and
Priorat are those of Alella, a small area just to the north of
Barcelona. The dry Alella Marfil is one of the best whites in
Catalonia. If you are visiting the Costa Brava to the north of
here, try the wines of Empordà. The rosés are tart and fruity,
the reds lively and warm.

Catalonia produces over 100 million bottles a year of *cava*,
a sparkling white wine made by the *méthode champenoise*.
The best quality *cavas* have *brut* or *brut nature* on their labels.
Cava is widely drunk on feast days and at Sunday lunch.
Visitors are urged to sample the region's many *cavas* in
Barcelona's *xampanyeries* (champagne bars), some of which
are recommended in the section 'Where to Eat and Drink' (*see*
page 233).

7:
BEYOND BARCELONA

SITGES

Sitges is one of the most delightful towns on the Catalan coast. It is small, compact and beautifully situated in the lee of the rugged Garraf Mountains. Its proximity to Barcelona – it is less than 25 miles (40 kilometres) to the south – has made it very popular with day-trippers and weekenders, and even in the winter months this quiet town of some 13,000 people livens up considerably come Friday evening. During the peak summer months, when the population rises to over 70,000, the beaches seethe with bronze bodies and the narrow streets are clogged with human flesh, but Sitges is seldom vulgar and never crass. I have spent time in Sitges both in high summer and mid-winter, and each season has its appeal.

Sitges has little in common with the tacky, jerry-built resorts which have sprung up along much of the length of Mediterranean coast over the past few decades. Though tourists have been coming here for a century or so, it retains much of its old charm. It possesses one of the loveliest seafronts imaginable: a great curving arc, lined by palms and culminating in the spectacular rose-pink façade of the parish church. The church is built on a small promontory and surrounded by some of the town's most interesting buildings and museums. It is a pleasant place to stroll around on a summer evening, when scores of swifts and house martins wheel noisily over the roofs in search of insects. At ground level there is the dubious attraction of a large population of feral cats, which live and breed among the jumble of rocks on the breakwater.

The **Parish Church**, which is dedicated to Sant Bartomeu and Santa Tecla, was consecrated in 1672. The best thing about it is the tentatively baroque façade, with a towering, octagonal bell-tower on the seaward side, and a smaller clock tower on the other. The latter is a modified version of the old *comunidor*, where prayers used to be offered when there were storms at sea.

Behind the church is a small square bordered by the town hall, an indoor market and an imposing monument to Dr Bartomeu Robert. More notable, from an architectural point of view, is the complex of buildings to the north of the church. **Maricel de Mar** is a bizarre pastiche cobbled together for Charles Deering, an American, between 1910 and 1913. Miquel Utrillo, who directed the renovation, succeeded in creating an extraordinary palace, which, despite its eclectic pretensions, is thoroughly pleasing to the eye. Maricel de Mar is linked to **Maricel de Terra** by a small bridge across Carrer Fonollar. There are Romanesque arches, Gothic windows, medieval crenellations and some fine sculptural details, including an avenging angel and some exquisitely carved capitals by the sculptor Pere Jou, who spent much of his life in Sitges and died there in 1964. The capitals portray a variety of scenes such as farmers carrying sheaves of corn, a bearded gentleman tweaking a cook's ear, a funeral procession, a group of fat-bottomed men and women dancing the *sardana*, and joiners and masons at work. More of Jou's work can be seen on the façade of the restaurant/cinema in Carrer F. Guma.

Maricel de Mar houses a small museum which contains the art collection of Docteur Jesús Pérez Rosales. You may feel inclined to rush through the first rooms on the lower floor: gathered here are examples of Gothic and baroque church art, together with some good 18th-century Catalan ceramics and some ghastly 16th-century Renaissance-style angels. The best room overlooks the sea and contains four fine marble sculptures, including Joan Rebull's *Descans*. This, one feels, is how marble should be displayed, with plenty of space, and behind the deep blue of the Mediterranean. The other notable feature on the lower floor is Josep Sert's colossal mural depicting, in allegorical form, the events of the First World War. The gloomy colours would benefit from better lighting, but the whole thing is fittingly cataclysmic. The upper floor of the Maricel de Mar contains a collection of furniture, paintings, bric-à-brac, ceramics and so forth. I particularly liked the sombre oil portrait of Christ carrying the cross, *Via Dolorosa*, by a 17th-century Spanish artist, and the crystal chandelier in the form of a Spanish galleon.

Next door to the Maricel de Mar is the **Museu Cau Ferrat**. This building was converted from the ruins of two old fishermen's cottages for Santiago Rusiñol, who arrived in Sitges in 1891, promptly fell in love with the town and settled here. It was Rusiñol who put Sitges on the cultural map of Catalonia and his generous spirit lives on in the museum. Rusiñol was one of the outstanding Catalan painters of his time. With Utrillo and Ramon Casas he founded Els Quatre Gats café in Barcelona and at Sitges he arranged a number of influential *Festes modernistes*, or *modernista* festivals. In 1894 Rusiñol returned from a trip to Paris with two paintings by El Greco, whose work at that time was largely ignored. He led a procession of the paintings from the station to his home, and over the following years he did much to revive interest in El Greco, a statue of whom was erected beneath the palms on the Passeig de la Ribera. A little way beyond, incidentally, there is a singularly unfeminine statue of a mermaid by Pere Jou, and, further still, a touching little bas-relief of G. K. Chesterton, who was '*enamorado de Sitges*'.

Rusiñol bought Cau Ferrat as a home not only for himself, but for his impressive collection of Spanish ironwork. The most significant pieces come from the 5th to the 10th centuries, though there are later objects as well. The ironwork is mostly confined to the upper floor, on whose walls hang the two El Grecos (one a portrait of St Peter; the other of Mary Magdalene). As one would expect, the museum also has a good collection of Rusiñol's paintings. 'At his best,' suggests Alastair Boyd, 'Rusiñol has an elegance reminiscent of Sir William Nicholson, but his work was to drift into symbolism, allegorical murals and finally a sugary series on the great gardens of Spain.' All the same, some of his serious portrait work (for example, the female drug addict in La Morfinomana) are compellingly good. The lower floor of this small museum has some fine decorated ceramic tiling from the 17th century, and more paintings. Picasso's small Corrida de Toras in pastel and gouache dazzles; there is also a portrait of Rusiñol by his friend Casas. (For more about Rusiñol, see the section on Barcelona's Museu d'Art Modern, page 119.)

It would be a shame to visit Sitges and miss either Museu de Maricel or Museu Cau Ferrat. However, I cannot claim the same for the **Museu Romàntic** (the Romantic Museum), which is housed in Casa Llopis, a handsome neo-classical building of the 1790s at the southern end of Carrer Sant Gaudenci. This house, which belonged to the Llopis family, is got up in the style favoured by the 19th-century bourgeoisie. There are some good pieces of furniture and a valuable collection of musical instruments, but the overall impression is of barely restrained bad taste, epitomized by the marble statues of little girls sporting soppy, pre-Raphaelite expressions. These are to be found on the second-floor balcony, at the end of which is a three-holer lavatory. The top floor of the museum contains an extensive collection of antique dolls donated by the artist Lola Anglada.

Sitges has some interesting modernista buildings, most of which are to be found within a few minutes' walk of one another. On the corner of Pl. Cap de la Vila and Carrer Major there is a wedge-shaped building with a marvellous turret-cum-clock-tower. It is decorated with blue, white and beige ceramic tiles arranged in such a way as to appear like waves breaking over sand. Other modernista buildings are to be found in Carrer St Bartomeu, Carrer Gaudenci, Carrer St Isidre and Carrer Illa de Cuba. This area is partly residential, partly commercial. There are many galleries here selling paintings by local artists. The quality varies, with oils, often crudely applied by palette knife, generally being favoured above watercolours.

For such a small town, Sitges is remarkably cosmopolitan. Tourism, of course, is one of the main reasons for this, but it has also become a cultural centre in its own right. The first great event of the year is Carnival, which is celebrated with processions and festivities at the time of Mardi Gras. Sitges has become the gay capital of Spain and many flock to the town for Carnival (there are even gay clothes shops in Sitges selling such things as leather cod-pieces). The main religious festivals are Corpus Christi and the Fiesta Mayor de Sant Bartomeu, the former being in spring, the latter during the last week in August. Since the 1960s Sitges has played host each year to an International Horror Film Festival and to an International Theatre Festival.

A brief guide to Sitges

GETTING THERE: Sitges is less than an hour by train from Barcelona. There is a regular service leaving from Passeig de Gracia and Sants stations (180 pesetas). From the station it is about 10 minutes' walk to the seafront, the Passeig Maritim.

WHERE TO STAY: Sitges has over 70 hotels. For details contact the Tourist Office (Tel: 93–894 47 00). For those wishing to self-cater, there is the pricy four-star **Mediterráneo Apart-hotel** (Tel: 93–894 51 34). An excellent middle range hotel is the two-star **Subur**, which overlooks the seafront from Carrer Espanya (Tel: 93–894 00 66). There are plenty of modest and relatively cheap hotels and pensions on the side streets running up the hill from the seafront. If you visit Sitges during the high season, it is essential to book in advance. From October to April, you can simply turn up and take your pick, though many hotels close for the winter months.

WHAT TO EAT AND WHERE: There are as many restaurants as there are hotels. Seafood is excellent, though often pricy: try the Swiss-run **Bar Chez Nous**, Passeig Villafranca 2, or the **Costa Dorada**, Port Alegre 26. The latter serves superb *paella*.

Cheap meals can be had at **El Superpollo**, Carrer Sant Josep 8. For less than the price of a beer in some of the trendy bars nearby, you can get a quarter chicken with bread, olives and a glass of champagne. This is fast food at its best. There are two old-fashioned cafés which are strongly recommended: **Bar Xatat** on Carrer St Francesc (the walls are covered with paintings and drawings by local artists) and **Café Roy** (marble tables, dignified service) on Carrer de Parrelades. Many young people spend their time in the brash bars on Carrer 1er de Maig, otherwise known as the Street of Sin (which is probably wishful thinking). The music is loud and the drinks are expensive; you will be deafened and robbed simultaneously. Some bars are frequented almost entirely by gays; some by straights; and some by both. For delicious and outrageously priced fruit drinks and fancy cocktails, head for **Villa Lola**, Passeig de la Ribera.

TARRAGONA

Tarragona is a thoroughly agreeable city, much smaller than Barcelona, much less polluted, and more conspicuously wedded to the sea. Walk down Barcelona's famous Ramblas and you end on the fringes of dockland: a large, placid pond of not-so-clean water surrounded by cranes and jetties. Walk along Tarragona's Rambla Nova and the blue sea hits you square on. Tarragona is perched on a rugged bluff and its breeziness seems to have rubbed off on the character of its citizens. As a rule the Catalans are rather a sombre race, lacking the indolence and exuberance of their Castilian-speaking neighbours, but in Tarragona there's more than a hint of the effervescent south. In many ways, Tarragona is a pleasanter city to visit than Barcelona, especially during the foetid heat of the summer months. It would be possible to take a day trip from Barcelona and see something of the city, but to do Tarragona justice you should give it two or three days. It is blessed with some of the finest Roman monuments in Spain, and the old town around the cathedral is every bit as attractive as its equivalent in Barcelona.

Tarragona lies 62 miles (100 kilometres) to the south-west of Barcelona at the centre of the Costa Daurada. The region behind the city is known as the Camp de Tarragona; in places it is quite mountainous, but much of the land undulates gently beneath a veneer of nut-bearing trees. You will see hazelnut, carob and almond, as well as the more familiar vine and olive. The poet Pliny was enchanted by the region's wines and its equable climate. The Romans, it seems, had chosen this site for their administrative centre with good care. Once the Carthaginians had been driven south, the Romans made it the capital of Hispania Citerior. Under Julius Caesar it became known as Colonia Julia Urbs Triumphalis Tarraconensis, or Tarraco for short. The city was built on a steep incline and three distinct terraces emerged during the Roman occupation: the upper part with temples and forum (roughly approximating to the old city around the cathedral); the middle part with its circus (around the present Plaça de la Font); and a lower part, where there was a local forum, an amphitheatre and living quarters.

Before embarking on a tour of the city – it makes sense to begin with the Roman remains – it is worth getting a feel of its layout. This is easily done. Head for the Rambla Nova and make your way towards the sea. If I have any quibble with this handsome street it is that it seems to slope the wrong way: it goes up to the seafront, not down. Looking back over the Plaça Imperial Tarraco you will see the mountains rising behind the city; and once you reach the Balco del Mediterráneo, you have the sea itself. This is a popular gathering place for both young and old. Some sit beneath the statue of the corsair Roger de Llúria; others beneath the trees on the Passeig de les Palmeres, which leads from the Balco down towards the amphitheatre. The cliffs below the Balco drop sheer to a patch of scruffy pine forest, beyond which lies the railway line, the coastal road and the beach. The great thing about Tarragona is that you can see, smell and hear the sea.

Away to the right you will glimpse the cranes and ware-houses of the port. Tarragona was an important trading centre during Roman times, as indeed it still is. The last century saw an unparalleled period of expansion. In the early 1700s less than 5,000 people lived here (compared with 30,000 during the Roman heyday), but the industrial revolution was followed by a rapid rise in the city's numbers. By 1900, there were over 23,000 inhabitants; today there are well over 100,000. To the south and west of the city there are some large industrial complexes, many of them related to the petro-chemical industry.

From the Rambla Nova I suggest you make your way through the upper city – the **Nucli Antic** or **Ciutat Alta** – to the **Passeig Arqueològic**. Here you will see the best remaining section of the old Roman wall. The Passeig is actually a pathway between the old wall and the outer ramparts built in the 18th century. The wall is over half a mile long and in places more than 30 feet high. Its base, laid down in the 3rd century, consists of monumental blocks of granite, layered upon which are narrower courses of mellow sandstone. There are six 'Cyclopean' gateways and a number of towers built into the wall, the most noteworthy being the Torre de Minerva and the 15th-century Torre de l'Arquebisbe. The grounds between the walls are beautifully kept. Slender cypress trees are etched like green pencils against the ochre wall, and there are several statues, including one of Augustus, one of Romulus and Remus, and another, less predictably, of a semi-naked Wagner. A row of old cannons along the ramparts points across the suburbs towards the hills behind.

I have never seen a wall more alive than this one: as you wander along its length you half expect to hear the stones breathe. In some places windows have been cut into the wall; framed by the soft browns and pinks of the stone you will see a washing line, some geraniums and perhaps a brown-skinned, deep-bosomed woman relaxing with a cigarette. It is all very picturesque when seen from the outside, but there is a fair amount of squalor once you penetrate within the walls. A dank gloom hovers over many of the streets, as well as the smell of urine, and some of the occupants of the old city appear very down-at-heel.

Having seen the wall, I suggest you head back across the city to the **Museu Nacional Arqueològic**, which is in a newish building beside an old Roman house wrongly termed the Pretorium (from whose roof there are fine views back across the city and down to the port). The Pretorium houses the Museu d'Història de la Ciutat, but unless you are very historically minded, I would head straight for the superb archaeological museum. Most of the exhibits are from the Roman city, but there are some objects from earlier times, and some from the Visigoth period. Everything is beautifully laid out, but this being Catalonia there is no guide and all the labels are in Catalan. One hopes that by the time the city hosts the 1993 World Archaeological Conference, a little more help might be given to non-Catalan speakers.

Room I contains a section of the old wall which used to run from here down to the site of the present railway station and up to where it begins in earnest today, a few hundred yards north along the Passeig de Sant Antoni. In the same room there are some small, though impressive, funerary monuments. **Room II**: columns, friezes, capitals and statuary from temples, theatres, fora, amphitheatre and other Roman buildings. There is a wonderful purity and economy of purpose about the calligraphy. **Room III**: some notable mosaics: one of Medusa, snakes licking round a face of Byronic appeal; another depicting partridge, antelope and peacock; and another of tigers pulling a chariot. **Room IV** is devoted to beautifully crafted household implements: bottles, needles, lamps, pottery, metal rings, brooches and so forth. On the walls leading up to the third floor there is a large 'marine' mosaic. All the creatures depicted here are instantly recognizable, from the dolphins to the octopuses, from the pipe fish to the eels. It might easily be an illustration for a book on cooking *paella* or *romesco*, the latter being a famous Tarragona sauce which accompanies fish dishes. **Rooms V** and **VI** contain examples of Roman sculpture: Bacchus, Apollo and Venus predominate.

The other Roman monuments in the centre of town can be seen in the course of an hour or two. The most impressive is the vast **amphitheatre**, which occupies the area between the Via Augusta, below the museum, and the Platja del Miracle (Miracle Beach). The amphitheatre is elliptical in shape, and at its heart lie the remains of a 12th-century Romanesque church, which was built on the site of an earlier basilica commemorating Sant Fruitós and his deacons, who were martyred here in the year AD 259. Above the amphitheatre there are some pleasant gardens; higher still is the monstrously ugly Hotel Imperial Tarraco, whose glass and concrete façade mimics the curve of the arena.

There were two **Roman fora** in Tarragona. The main one was in the upper city, but little remains save a stretch of wall in the Plaça del Forum. The **Local Forum** is to be found a few minutes' walk below the Rambla Nova on Carrer Cardenal Cervantes. There is rather more to see here, including some slender Corinthian columns, which stand as white as snow against the grey background of the surrounding tenements. The last significant Roman port of call within walking distance of the town centre is some way to the west of here. The **Palaeo-Christian necropolis** is on the left hand side of Avinguda S. Ramon i Cajal, just before you reach the River Francoli. It was discovered when the foundations for a tobacco factory were being excavated. The cemetery – and the associated museum – contain tombs from the time of the Roman conquest up to the 7th century AD. Among those buried here were Fruitós and the martyred deacons, Auguri and Eulogi.

Christianity's fortunes, like those of Bishop Fruitós, were mixed. In 716 Tarragona fell into Arab hands. The city was laid waste and abandoned, its bishop fled to Italy, and it was not until the 12th century that Tarragona was brought to life again and back into the Christian world. Its importance as a centre of Christian belief can be gauged from the fact that its Archbishop is the Primate of the Spains, as well as Metropolitan of the Catalan dioceses.

Tarragona **Cathedral** dominates the old city. It was begun in 1171 and consecrated in 1331; it is the best example to be found in Catalonia of the transition between the Romanesque and Gothic styles of architecture, having been begun in the former and finished in the latter. It is an immensely impressive, though somewhat gloomy building. The west front, which is approached up the stairs from Carrer Major, sets the tone for the rest of the cathedral, the central Gothic section being flanked by smaller façades in the Romanesque style. Unfortunately, the Gothic section is unfinished, but there is an impressive rose window above a large portico which boasts some fine sculpture. Master Bartomeu, the great 13th-century sculptor, was responsible for the statue of the Virgin which adorns the pier that divides the door and for some of the apostles on either side of the entrance.

Entry to the cathedral is through the cloister, which is one of the loveliest in Catalonia. Here the Romanesque and Gothic combine splendidly. The cloister is square, with six pointed (Gothic) arches on each side. Each arch is subdivided into three smaller, rounded arches, these being supported by double columns whose carved capitals boast a great diversity of themes. Depicted here are monsters, mythical beasts, biblical scenes, and even a procession of rats. There is a small museum in the Chapel of Corpus Christi, at the north-east corner of the cloister.

The basic plan of the cathedral is that of the Latin cross, with nave, aisles and transept. There is no ambulatory, but there are over a dozen side chapels off the aisles. The semi-circular apse is Romanesque, as is the lower part of the transept and the magnificent door which leads from the cloisters into the cathedral. The piers throughout the cathedral are heavy and square, their influence being carried up to the Gothic vaulting. There is a fine octagonal lantern above the transept. The choice work of art in the cathedral is undoubtedly the main retable, sculpted in marble and alabaster by Pere Joan in 1426 to 1434. The predella has some powerful scenes portraying events in the life of Saint Tecla, whose statue stands to the right of the Virgin in the retable's middle section.

On either side of the retable there is a door leading to the apse behind; above the one on the left is the figure of the martyred Bishop, Saint Fruitós.

There are a number of other good buildings in the vicinity of the cathedral, including the Palau Arquebisbal, the Casa dels Canonges and the Casa Rectoral, immediately below which is a Gothic arcade on the Carrer Merceria. On Casa del Dega at number 27 are inscriptions in both Roman and Hebrew. There are several evocative little squares in the old city, the most intriguing being the Plaça del Pallol, where styles from various epochs are jumbled together: especially striking is the heavy Romanesque door supporting a delicate Gothic window.

OUTSIDE TARRAGONA

To visit the Roman monuments outside Tarragona you will need a car. The most spectacular is the **Roman Aqueduct**, otherwise known as the Pont del Diable (Devil's Bridge). There are photographs in the archaeological museum, taken a century ago, of the aqueduct spanning a cultivated valley, with scarcely a tree in sight. Since then the land has been abandoned and the valley is now thickly wooded. Though the aqueduct is only a couple of miles from the city it is far from easy to find. Follow the CN 240, signposted for Lleida. Approximately 200 yards after passing beneath the southbound carriageway of the A-7 motorway, pull into a small lay-by on the right. From here walk through the shabby gateway and follow the track through the woods. There are disgraceful quantities of litter and junk the whole way along. After five minutes or so, the aqueduct will come into view. It is possible to walk along the top.

The aqueduct was built during the 1st century BC to bring water from the River Francoli to Tarragona. It is some 183 yards (167 metres) long and consists of two tiers of arches, 11 on the lower level, 25 on the upper level. It is built out of the same warm, honey-coloured stone used for the old walls of the city and much else besides. It is a great shame that it is so near the motorway: the constant drone of traffic is infuriating.

Unfortunately, the other three Roman monuments outside Tarragona also suffer from their proximity to roads. A few miles north of the city, on the CN 340 (the old Via Augusta), a lay-by on the crest of a hill signals the point where the **Torre dels Escipions** stands. This funerary monument was erected in the 1st century BC; the two eroded figures are apparently not, as the name of the monument suggests, the brothers Scipio, who founded Roman Tarraco. Several miles further along the road there is an old Roman quarry, worth seeing again, but hard to find. At a sign for La Mora, turn right; cross the bridge over to the west of the motorway; follow the track on the left as far as you can, which is to say about half a mile. From here it is a five minutes' walk through the pine woods to the quarry of **Mèdol**, a deep scoop with a thin 'obelisk' poking through the trees. L'Agulla de Mèdol, as the obelisk is known, was used as a gauge to show how much stone had been excavated from the quarry. Finally, another ten minutes' drive northward will bring you to the **Arc Roma de Berà**, which sits in the middle of the CN 340 surrounded by tarmac and traffic. This is a superb and relatively simple arch, exemplifying the power and nobility of Roman architecture. It was erected in memory of Licinius Sura during the 2nd century BC.

Having investigated the aqueduct, the quarry and the arch, you will be in urgent need of refreshment, and I advise you to take the track down to the **Castle of Tamarit**, which was restored by Charles Deering (*see* Maricel del Mar, Sitges) early this century. Within the castle, which is situated on a small cliff, there is a Romanesque church and a rectory. This is one of the least spoilt stretches of the Costa Daurada: the swimming is excellent and there is an unpretentious café attached to the campsite.

A brief guide to Tarragona

GETTING THERE: A good train service links Tarragona with Barcelona to the north, Valencia to the south. If you are driving down to Tarragona from Barcelona, take either the A-7 motorway, or the coast road, the CN 340. Obviously, the journey along the latter will take longer, but that way you can see the Arc Roma de Berà and the Torre dels Escipions. There is also a motorway linking Tarragona with Reus, which has an airport served during the holiday season by charter flights.

WHERE TO STAY: The local tourist board (Passeig de Sant Antoni 100; Tel: 977–23 33 13) lists over twenty hotels in Tarragona. I am inclined to advise against the **Imperial Tarraco** (Rambla Vella, Tel: 23 30 40) purely on aesthetic grounds. It is the only four-star hotel in town, and evidently the plushest. The three-star **Hotel Lauria** (Rambla Nova 20; Tel: 977–23 67 12) is reputed to be very good. Of similar standard is the clean and pleasant **Hotel Urbis** (Reding 20; Tel: 977–21 01 16). The following fall into the cheapest bracket: the **Abella** (Apodaca 7 pral. Tel: 977–23 42 24); **El Callejon** (Via Augusta 213; Tel 977–23 63 80); **La Noria** (Pl. de la Font 53; Tel: 977–23 87 17.) If you wish to camp, then I recommend **Tamarit** (977–65 01 28).

WHAT TO EAT AND WHERE: Tarragona is famous for *romesco*, a sauce which accompanies many fish dishes. The ingredients include hazel nuts, olive oil, red pepper and red wine, all of which should come from the Camp de Tarragona. An idea of the agricultural – and piscatorial – wealth of the region can be gleaned from a quick walk around the **Mercat Central**, the *modernista* market in the Plaça Corsini. This, incidentally, is where you should shop if you are cooking for yourself. Other popular dishes include *el rosseja* (fried rice boiled in broth) and eaten with that great favourite, *allioli*; and *espineta amb caragolinas*, which is based on tuna and snails. The latter is associated with the major festivals.

There are plenty of eating places to choose from in Tarragona. **Sol Ric** (Via Augusta 227; Tel 977–23 20 32) is one of the best restaurants for seafood; it is also expensive. I have eaten reasonably well at **La Rambla** (Rambla Nova 10; Tel: 977–23 87 29): a delicious plate of *espinaca catalana* (spinach with pine nuts and raisins) was followed by a succulent, though disappointingly small, pork cutlet. I ate one of the worst meals of my life at **Café Cantonada** (Carrer Fortuny 23; Tel: 977–21 35 24). One side of this establishment is a bar – and great fun too, with many young people, racy music, chess games and a pool table. But do not even contemplate eating in the adjoining restaurant.

TORTOSA AND THE EBRO DELTA

Having consulted two guidebooks, I expected the worst when I reached Tortosa, the most southerly town of consequence in Catalonia. 'Unusually for Catalonia,' said one, 'Tortosa is a rather dirty town with beggars and gypsies . . .' The other was equally damning: 'No one seems to like it much . . . If fate brings you to Tortosa, there are two sights worth your time . . .' Well, I liked Tortosa very much indeed; the dirt and dilapidation in the older parts of the town in no way detracted from its considerable charms. The town is dominated by the remains of an Arab fortress, below which is a magnificent cathedral whose monumental baroque façade conceals a fine example of airy Catalan Gothic. There are many other buildings of interest here, ranging from a Renaissance college to a *modernista* abattoir. Even for those who feel no compulsion to look at architecture, Tortosa is a pleasant place to spend a couple of days. The Ebro River gives Tortosa a certain freshness, the traffic is tolerable and there are some delightful walks along the riverside.

Half an hour away from Tortosa is the Ebro Delta. With its rice paddies, reed-lined lagoons and explosions of feathery palms, the Delta has a distinctly oriental look about it. There are no large tourist developments here, and with luck there never will be. The regional tourist authorities are keen on promoting 'eco-tourism' and indeed the Delta's main attraction is its wildlife. This is one of the finest remaining wetlands in the Western Mediterranean; during the summer months, visitors can see flamingoes, cattle egrets, purple heron and dozens

of other species. It would be quite possible to visit Tortosa
and ignore the Ebro Delta, or vice versa: but it would be a pity
to miss either.

Tortosa was an important city during Roman times, and by
the 6th century it had its own bishopric. The city fell to the
Moslem invaders between 715 and 717 and it remained in their
hands until 1148, when it was liberated by Ramon Berenguer
IV. In 1018 Tortosa became an independent *taifa*, or kingdom,
and enjoyed a period of splendour. Unfortunately, little
remains from the Moorish times save the imposing remains of
the **Suda Castle**, which dates from the 10th-century rule of
Abd-al-Rahman III. The fortifications are ranged across the
small hills immediately behind the cathedral. Once the
Moslems had been driven south the castle became the property
of the Knights Templars. Later it was used as a palace for royal
visitors. Over the years it has been much modified and today
it houses the Parador Nacional, which commands long views
across the winding river and expansive valley. Even if you are
counting your pennies, I urge you to stay at the Parador. You
will appreciate it all the more if you've spent a long, hot day
scouring the Ebro Delta for flamingoes. In the failing light of
evening, the jagged mountains to the south take on the soft
blues and grey of dusk while swifts wheel raucously above the
pantiled roofs of the town below.

From here you get the best view – an oblique aerial view –
of **Tortosa Cathedral**. It is even more hemmed in by neighbouring buildings than the cathedral at Tarragona, where there is
at least a vista of the main façade. Given some space, Tortosa's
baroque façade would appear truly impressive; at present it
reminds me of some forgotten treasure, tucked out of sight
and gradually being left to decay. Work on the cathedral
began in 1347 and the altar was consecrated just under a
century later. On feast days entry is by the main door;
otherwise you must enter by the Porta de l'Olivera – also
baroque – and the cloister. The cloister is small and trapezoid.
All but two of the columns separating the pointed Gothic

arches possess unadorned capitals; the exceptions are those on either side of the gateway which leads to the garden of scruffy pines and cypress trees. These figure capitals are in the Romanesque style and have been much despoiled by the elements and neglect. The cloister is something of a disappointment, especially if your last port of call was Tarragona cathedral, and it does nothing to prepare the visitor for the splendid mature Gothic interior.

There is none of the heavy gloom of Tarragona here. Gone are the heavy piers and thick walls of the Romanesque, and in their place come delicacy and diffuse light. Of particular beauty is the double ambulatory (supported by flying buttresses outside), best seen behind the main altar. Outstanding among the cathedral's works of art (it contains relatively few, as it happens) is the main retable of Santa Maria, which dates from 1351. It is in the Italian style, with gilt-painted sculptures on the front, and paintings on the back. One of the great things about this cathedral is that it is relatively uncluttered, although the baroque side chapel dedicated to Maré de Déu de la Cinta goes someway towards dispelling this notion. The chapel contains a belt which is said to have belonged to the Virgin, and consequently it is much venerated. When I first visited the cathedral there were only three people present: two old ladies prayed in the chapel, while an elderly priest smoked in the chapter house.

The baroque façade was begun in the early 17th century and finished midway through the 18th. This powerful, relatively unfussy piece of architecture may lack the florid exuberance generally associated with Spanish baroque (one thinks, for example, of such gaudy masterpieces as the *Transparente* in Toledo Cathedral), but it is among the best examples of the style to be found in Catalonia. Rising from base to cornice is a series of composite half-columns and pilasters. Above the three doorways are small alcoves which once contained statuary, all now missing. The façade is in a desperately sad state of repair, a thick crack running from top to bottom on the right-hand side. There is pigeon muck everywhere, weeds sprout from the stonework, and a large colony of swifts and martins nests in the upper reaches of the façade.

Among the other Gothic buildings in Tortosa is the 13th/14th century **Palau Episcopal** (Bishop's Palace), which has a magnificent courtyard and a delightful chapel. Also worth visiting is the **Llotja de Mar**, the 14th-century stock exchange which now stands in the wooded park in the heart of the town.

Renaissance architecture is even more poorly represented in Catalonia than the baroque, but Tortosa does possess two fine examples. Both were built as royal colleges for young Moorish converts. The older of the two is the **Col·legi de Sant Jaume i Sant Maties**, founded by Carlos V in 1544. At the centre of the building is a square patio, around which are ranged three tiers of arcades. At the time of my visit the building was closed, but some of the interior could be seen through a window on the upper floor, this being reached from the steep alley leading up to the Suda, the Carrer del Castell. The intricately decorated entrance with the imperial coat of arms can be glimpsed through an overgrown garden. Nearby is the **Col·legi de Sant Jordi i Sant Domènec**, whose Renaissance façade dates from 1578. It is a work of considerable delicacy, with alternating Ionic and Doric orders, but sadly the statues in the small niches above and beside the doorway have lost their heads. The façade conceals a Gothic church which now houses the curious Museu-Arxiu Municipal. The Museum was set up in 1910 and indeed, on entering, one feels as though one has stepped back several generations. Half a dozen employees sit at heavy desks studying musty manuscripts. The displays seem distinctly haphazard. There are various Roman remains, medieval manuscripts and even some modern paintings.

Tortosa has been ravaged by several wars, the latest being the Civil War of 1936–9. On 15 April 1938 the Republican army retreated to Tortosa, blew up the bridges and established itself on the left bank. Franco's army took up positions on the right bank. The battle of the Ebro, fought in January 1939, was won by the latter. Needless to say, the town suffered considerable damage. A monument to the battle, and to the 35,000 who died – appropriately fascistic in design – was erected in the middle of the river, just upstream from the new bridge on a pier which belonged to its predecessor. If you happen to walk along the left bank at this point you may witness one of nature's more spine-chilling sights. Thousands of white-mouthed fish gather here to feed at a waste outfall, and at times the river surface is a heaving mass of grey scales. (You may see similar scenes in the river at Girona.)

Fortunately, the two best buildings of the *modernista* era survived the Civil War. Pau Montguió's **L'Escorxador Municipal** (municipal abattoir) is a large edifice built between 1906 and 1908, a little way upstream of the bridge (and the fish) on Av. de Felip Pedrell. The design of the building is entirely in keeping with its function. A wealth of spiky ironwork summons up images of callous brutality, while the patterned ceramic tiles interspersed among the brickwork suggest the butcher's knife and the cleansing hose. Altogether more welcoming is the earlier (1880s) **Mercat Public** by Joan Abril, who was also responsible for the Església del Roser.

The **Ebro Delta** consists of some 125 square miles (325 sq kilometres) of low-lying, fertile land where the silt-laden River Ebro meets the Mediterranean. It is an area of great agricultural importance: approximately a third of the cultivated land is devoted to riziculture; most of the rest produces fruit and vegetables, and there is a striking abundance of artichokes. The Delta has only recently been settled by humans. Salt was collected from the lagoons in medieval times and saltmarsh plants were burnt for the manufacture of soap; there was also hunting and fishing in those days, but agricultural settlement began much later. The canal along the right bank of the Ebro was dug midway through the last century, and this enabled the irrigation of the southern part of the Delta. A canal on the left-hand (northern) side was completed in 1912. Gradually more land came under the plough and the population rose, though for a while the scourge of malaria acted as a limiting factor. The population of the Delta stood at 5,000 in the 1850s; today it is over 40,000. Most families are involved in farming, fishing and related industries.

During the summer months, as the rice sprouts from the paddies, much of the Delta is a lush, watery green. In the winter, once the harvest is in and the paddies are drained, the landscape turns a drab brown. The planting and harvesting of rice is mostly done by machine nowadays, but a few farmers can still be seen wading through the paddies in bare feet and carrying out their tasks by hand. Not all of the Delta is waterlogged, and herds of fearsome-looking horned cattle can be seen grazing the rough pasture in the company of rangy sheep.

The **Parc Natural del Delta de l'Ebre** (the Ebro Delta Natural Park) covers just under 20,000 acres (8,000 hectares) of land and water. It exists not as one unit, but several, with half the park lying to the north of the river, half to the south. Detailed maps and guides can be obtained from either the park information offices at Deltebre and beside the lagoon of L'Encanyissada (near El Poblenou del Delta) or from local tourist offices (*see* page 201 for addresses). The Generalitat's publication *Parc Natural del Delta de L'Ebre* is printed in several different languages (including English) and provides an excellent survey of the Delta's wildlife. Each section of the park consists of a strip of land surrounding either a lagoon or an inlet of the sea. Some parts are only open to those with official permits, but other areas can freely be visited, though visitors should keep to footpaths and observe whatever restrictions are indicated. Watchtowers and bird-hides are provided in some areas.

The wildlife is by no means confined to the park. Follow any of the narrow roads which run from Amposta coastwards and you will see cattle egrets, heron and black-winged stilts strutting about the paddies and canals in search of eels and frogs. Apparently their presence is resented by some farmers, who feel the birds are taking food from their own mouths, frogs and eels being popular human fodder in these parts. You may also see marsh harriers, purple herons and hoopoes as you make your way through the farmland. However, to see the best of the bird life you must visit the lagoons within the park boundaries. Flamingoes come to the Delta to feed, but they do not breed here. I saw a score or more off the old salt pans on Punta de la Banya, the weird lobe of desolate land in the south, reached by way of the thin sand-bar known as the Barra del Trabucador. They might equally well have been feeding in the Port del Fangar in the north or on one of the other lagoons around the Delta's perimeter. Among the other birds which can be seen in summer are short-eared owl, little bittern, collared pratincole, great-crested grebe, squacco heron, kestrel, various terns and several species of gull, including a large breeding population of Audoin's gull. During the winter months the Delta supports over 50,000 ducks and 13,000 coot. Some 300 species have been recorded here, making it one of the richest areas for birds in Europe.

Human pressures have inevitably led to the decline and disappearance of some species of wildlife. There are no longer any red deer – they were hunted to extinction long ago – and wild boar are exceptionally rare today, though otters are still found on the Delta. Turtles too have virtually died out, and sturgeon and lamprey have become rarities. Along the river banks you will see large numbers of nets. There are set to catch eels, some 30 to 50 tons of which are taken from the Delta each year.

The main town at the heart of the Delta is **Deltebre**, which sits in the left bank of the Ebro. It is a modern town, dating from midway through this century, and it is here that the rice factories are to be found. Further south there is the intriguing settlement of **Poblenou del Delta**, which was founded 50-odd years ago to house 97 immigrant families. The neat rows of whitewashed houses have a very Mexican look about them. The museum-cum-information centre beside the neighbouring lagoon looks like a Canadian hunting lodge. And that is precisely what it is, or was: it was imported by a wealthy gentleman from Tarragona around the same time that El Poblenou was built.

On the edge of the Delta are the more substantial towns of **Amposta** and **Sant Carles de la Ràpita**. Both, in their very different ways, are rather attractive. Amposta clings to the right bank of the river, and is connected to the other side by a handsome suspension bridge. There is an unusual church opposite the town hall. The lower half, begun in 1773, is neo-classical in character; the upper half, which was completed 92 years later, is in the *modernista* style. Sant Carles de la Ràpita is named after its founder, Carlos III, who intended it to become a major port. The town has a neo-classical layout and is among the most vibrant along this stretch of coast. There are some rather grand neo-classical buildings in the oval Pl. de Carlos III, and there is also a thriving fishing industry. The best time to visit the harbour is late afternoon when the fish catches are being auctioned off under signs which warn against cartel-fixing.

A brief guide to Tortosa and the Ebro Delta

GETTING THERE: There is a direct rail link between Barcelona and Tortosa. If you intend to visit the Delta you will need a car (or bicycle). To get to Tortosa from either north or south take the A-7 motorway or the CN 340. Leave the motorway at exit 40, or the CN 340 at Paitrossos, and head west for about 8 miles (13 kilometres) along the CN 235 to Tortosa. The CN 340 passes by both Amposta and Sant Carles de la Ràpita. There is a dense network of narrow roads throughout the Delta; signposting is poor and in places non-existent, so it is easy to get lost. There are no bridges across the River Ebro downstream of Amposta, but crossings can be made at Deltebre on the admirable *transbordadors* (motorized rafts) which take cars from one side to the other for a modest fee. There are tourist ferries which ply the route between Deltebre and the river mouth during the summer months.

WHERE TO STAY: Tortosa is surprisingly ill served by hotels. The best is the four-star **Parador Nacional Castell de la Suda**

(Tel: 977–44 44 50). Coming down the scale there is the two-star **Berenguer IV** (Carrer Cevantes 23; Tel: 977–44 08 16). Sant Carles de la Ràpita is comparatively well served by hotels, most possessing a single star. Deltebre has three two-star hotels, and Amposta two one-star hotels. For detailed information about the accommodation in these towns contact the tourist offices: Sant Carles de la Ràpita (Tel: 977–74 01 00); Amposta (Tel: 977–70 00 57); Deltebre (Tel: 977–48 95 11). Tortosa's tourist office is at Pl. d'Espanya 1–3 (Tel: 977–44 00 00). The natural park information office is at Pl. del 20 de Maig, Deltebre (Tel: 977–48 95 11), open mornings and afternoons every day except Sunday, when it is closed during the afternoon.

WHAT TO EAT AND WHERE: The fruits of the sea play a major role in the cuisine of the Delta. Indeed, many Catalans believe that the best seafood dishes of the region are to be had in the restaurants in and around the Delta. One of the most popular dishes is *arròs a banda*, more commonly associated with Valencia than Catalonia. This is a rice and fish dish (the fish generally being scorpion fish) served with *allioli*. Spiny lobster is a local delicacy, as are freshwater eels and elvers. For authentic and unpretentious local cooking, try **Restaurant Nuri** at Riumar. If you wish to splash out in Tortosa, eat at the **Parador**, where the menu is varied and excellent. For those averse to seafood, lamb reared on the Delta pastures is highly recommended. For a cheaper meal in the lower town I suggest **Restaurant Rosa**, which specializes in Italian food, at Marques de Bellet 13 (Tel: 977–44 20 01).

VALL DE BOÍ

In the Vall de Boí, man and nature have conspired to perfect effect. This is one of the loveliest of all the Pyrenean valleys. It may be smaller and somewhat less dramatic than the celebrated Vall d'Aran, which lies to the north, but its landscape is altogether more subtle and appealing. The valley is best known for its remarkable collection of Romanesque churches. The naves are generally squat and small, but their towers, some reaching sixty feet or more, give them tremendous grandeur. In 1989 the first ski development came to the valley, and consequently new buildings are springing up in some of the villages. Despite this, the valley retains its atmosphere of down-to-earth rurality. The cobbled alleys in Durro, Erill-la-Vall and Taüll are spattered with cowdung and straw, and many farmers still live above their byres and plough with mule and single-furrow plough. The spring is especially lovely: sleek yellow cattle graze up to their bellies in cow parsley and stitchwort; sandpipers and wagtails feed along the bubbling streams; and beside the mellow-stoned churches pollarded walnut break into bronze leaf.

As both this section and the next deal with two valleys in the Pyrenees – the other being the Vall de Camprodon, midway between the Vall de Boí and the Mediterranean – it helps to know a little about the mountain range. The Pyrenees stretch over 270 miles (430 kilometres) from the Atlantic to the Mediterranean, separating the Iberian peninsula from France and the rest of Europe. In terms of their size, they are second only in Europe to the Alps: there are several peaks over 10,000 feet (3,000 metres), the highest being Aneto at over 11,000 feet (3,404 metres). Over half the length of the Pyrenees falls within the province of Catalonia, and it provides its freshest and most spectacular scenery. Needless to say, there are great differences between the north-facing (French) Pyrenees and the south-facing (Spanish) Pyrenees. The former, under the influence of an Atlantic climate, are generally wetter and cooler than the latter, whose climate is predominantly continental. However, the eastern parts of the Catalan Pyrenees, being closer to the Mediterranean, tend to be damper and more verdant than the westerly regions. The Vall d'Aran is an exception to the rule, being the only Catalan valley with an Atlantic climate.

Of the 3,500 species of plants found in Catalonia, three-quarters are present in the Pyrenees. That the mountains possess such a diversity of species is very much a reflection of the range of habitats found here. Within a matter of half a day or less one can journey from dry Mediterranean scrub through temperate mixed woodland, then into pine forest and finally on to an alpine grassland. Indeed, the three-hour drive north from Lleida to the Vall de Boí provides a good insight into the great variety of landscapes to be found in Catalonia. To the north of Lleida the olives, so dominant further south, begin to die out, and in their place are orchards of citrus fruit. The first foothills of the Pyrenees are modest and dry, supporting little in the way of trees apart from scrub oak and gnarled pine. In the valley bottoms there are vast fields of barley, blood-red with poppies in May and early June. Once past Benabarre (here the CN 230 has deviated across the provincial border and into Aragon) the scenery becomes increasingly rugged and imposing; by the time you reach the small market town of Pont de Suert, just before the turn-off to the Vall de Boí, poplars and willows fringe the lush meadows, and the architecture, like the scenery, takes on a distinctly alpine character.

The Vall de Boí is a glacial valley some 19 miles (30 kilometres) long. A narrow road runs most of its length along the right bank of the Noguera de Tor. The golden era for the valley was the 12th century, when most of the churches were built. It is said that at that time the only way into the Vall de Boí was by the narrow pass protected by the fortress at Cardet; the archway is alleged to have been just wide enough to let one horseman through at a time. A little way to the north of Cardet is the settlement of Barruera. This is the capital of the valley, and a good base from which to explore the villages and mountains. The name Barruera, incidentally, is a corruption of Val-osera, or 'valley of the bears'; bears and wolves were once plentiful in this region, and indeed a small population of the former still clings precariously to their mountain habitat on the French side of the Pyrenees.

Villages and Churches
I was first drawn to the Vall de Boí not by guidebook recommendations, but by the wonderful collection of

Romanesque church paintings in Barcelona's Museu d'Art de Catalunya. Perhaps the finest example in the museum is the magnificent Pantocrator taken from the apse of Sant Climent de Taüll, but many other murals were also rescued from the valley's churches. The man who spear-headed the operation to rescue Romanesque church art was the politician and architect Josep Puig i Cadafalch (*see* page 105).

Altogether, Catalonia has some 1,800 Romanesque churches and 200 castles. At the mention of Romanesque many will think immediately of great cathedrals and abbeys such as those at Cluny, Durham, Ely, Toulouse, Santiago de Compostella or Worms; however, the churches of the Vall de Boí are slight and rudimentary when compared to these noble works. The Romanesque style of architecture emerged as a coherent entity after the death of Charlemagne, as the Carolingian Empire began to crumble towards the end of the first millennium. It follows in the classical tradition, taking from Rome such features as the groin-vault and the semi-circular arch. The walls of Romanesque buildings are generally thick, and doors and windows thus possess a very broad undersurface. In mature Romanesque buildings the arches were moulded, and the simple Roman column thus developed into the compound Romanesque pier – though not in any of the valley's churches. In a Romanesque church light is seen as something distinct from – and contrasting to – the massive structure of the walls; whereas in Gothic churches light seems to permeate the buildings, suggesting a porosity entirely absent from Romanesque churches, though the latter are not necessarily darker within than those built in the Gothic style. In the Romanesque church the surfaces are seen as scaffold for murals and ornament; in Gothic architecture ornament is subordinate to structure, but the structure itself is sculptural.

Puig i Cadafalch recognized two distinct phases in Catalonia's Romanesque period. The early phase arrived from Lombardy by way of southern France. The ground plan of the churches tends to be basilican or on the lines of the Latin cross. Sometimes there is a single nave, with one or three semi-circular apses; sometimes there are aisles as well. The walls inside are generally smooth, while the outside is often decorated with Lombard bands, a series of blind arcades, slightly recessed, surmounted by a row of semi-circular arcuations. This first phase of Romanesque architecture endured throughout the 11th century and was confined to Old Catalonia (which is to say, the north) and the areas around Segarra. The second phase, which spread throughout all Catalonia, began before the end of the 11th century and saw Romanesque architecture reach full maturity. It was characterized by greater structural complexity, and by an increasing use of sculpture, especially on portals, windows, capitals and so forth. As Nikolaus Pevsner pointed out, 'In the eleventh century and still about 1100 Spain led Europe not only in the art of the figure capital but also in major figure sculpture.'

The churches of the Vall de Boí had many functions apart from the obvious one of worship. They were used for public meetings and for trials; they were also used as places of refuge and as food stores. With their soaring bell-towers, many command long views down the valley, so they undoubtedly fulfilled the role of look-out posts too. It also seems likely that the churches were an expression of civic pride, different communities vying with one another to produce great monuments to themselves (and God). I should point out that the visitor may find some or all of the churches closed on his or her visit. If you are hell-bent on getting inside a locked church, then ask around for a villager with a key. As it happens, many of the churches are rather disappointing when seen from the inside, and the reproductions of their murals, where they exist, are no more than poor imitations of the originals.

Of the two churches at **Taüll**, Sant Climent is undoubtedly the finer, although it is a close-run thing. The church is situated at the foot of the village (and invariably photographed in such a way as to conceal the road which runs round it). Its outstanding feature is the six-storey tower, whose configuration of mullioned windows is particularly remarkable. The bottom storey has a single, arched slit; the second is double-arched; the third, triple-arched; and the fourth, fifth and sixth, double-arched again, with the windows of the sixth being larger than those below. The windows are set in recessed arcades with Lombard bands, and the Lombard bands are repeated around the three apses. The tower is detached from the main body of the church, which consists of a nave and two smaller aisles beneath a pitched slate roof. The round piers which separate aisles from nave are without capitals; the murals are reproductions of the originals. Sant Climent was consecrated on 10 December 1123, a day before Santa Maria, which stands a few minutes' walk away at the heart of the village.

Santa Maria is built along similar lines to Sant Climent, with a nave, two aisles and three semi-circular apses. The bell-tower rises from the south aisle and is slightly less ambitious than that of Sant Climent. The main apse contains a reproduction of a mural of the Virgin Mary, the original having been taken to the Museu d'Art de Catalunya in 1922. Surrounding the church are buildings typical of these alpine areas, with heavy stone walls, wooden balconies and shingle roofs with wide, overhanging eaves. On the outskirts of the village new apartment blocks are being built to cater for winter skiers. The impression of modernity is partially offset by the presence of old ladies in black and cattle in the street: this is still a peasant town.

The village of **Boí** lies midway down the hill between Taüll and the main road. It has rather more in the way of hotels and cafés, and this is where visitors can hire four-wheel drive vehicles to take them up to the national park of Sant Maurici i Aigüestortes. The church, which is dwarfed by the neighbouring buildings, has a nave and two aisles, each culminating in a semi-circular apse. Again, the paintings are copies of the originals, all removed to the Museu d'Art de Catalunya. The bell-tower is of the Lombardy type; the upper storey, containing the bells, has recently been modified.

Across the valley, and facing Boí and Taüll, is the village of **Erill-la-Vall**. This has a particularly beautiful, and rather unusual church dedicated to Santa Eulàlia. It possesses a single barrel-vaulted nave with semi-circular apse; there are two apses on either side, arranged as though wings of a transept. The church is extremely gloomy inside. An arcaded porch runs along one side of the nave to the rear of the bell-tower; this may once have served as a village forum. The magnificent six-storey bell-tower is similar to the one at Sant Climent de Taüll.

These four churches, together with the Església de la Nativitat at **Durro**, are the architectural gems of the Vall de Boí. The church at Durro also has an arcaded porch; the nave is long and narrow. The four-storey tower lacks the elegance of those at Erill-la-Vall and Taüll; it is also in need of restoration. Durro is one of the least spoilt villages in the valley. There are some magnificent farmsteads, linked by narrow, cobbled alleys. Small meadows encroach into the village and here you will see sheep lambing in the open and men ploughing with mules. There is a very pleasant walk of a mile or so up a dirt track to the tiny chapel of Sant Quirc. There are good views down the valley from here. It looks a very long way from the chapel down to Barruera, but you can walk it in little more than an hour.

There are other churches well worth visiting at Barrucra (in terms of its situation, this is one of the most attractive), Cardet and Coll (which has a fine portal).

Spas, Snow and the High Mountains

The paved road up the valley comes to a halt at **Caldes de Boí**, one of Catalonia's leading thermal spas. If you come here out of season, the two big hotels will be closed and there will be no sign of life other than trout splashing in the stream. Traditionally the spa season runs from 24 June to 30 September. However, there were plans afoot during 1990 to open the spa hotels in winter too, and thus cash in on the influx of skiers into the valley.

These spas, the highest in the province at 4,920 feet (1,500 metres), were probably first enjoyed by the Romans. During the middle ages a sanctuary (Maré de Déu de Caldes) and a House of Charity were built at Caldes de Boí. Midway through the 19th century the church ceded the land to the state; subsequently it came into private ownership and commercial exploitation of the spas began in 1895. There are 37 springs at Caldes de Boí, their temperature ranging from 4 to 56 degrees C. The waters are said to be beneficial to those suffering from rheumatism, digestive disorders, skin problems, and respiratory and kidney disorders. There are swimming pools, attractive gardens, a discothèque and many other modern facilities. The spas have their own medical personnel.

Alastair Boyd, in *The Essence of Catalonia*, suggested that the spas at Caldes de Boí helped to preserve the valley from 'the brasher developments of ski culture'. Alas, though understandably, that is no longer the case. In 1989 skiing began for the first time at Boí-Taüll, on the slopes immediately above the two villages. The first season got off to an excellent start, not least because there was insufficient snow at traditional ski resorts like Baqueira, an hour's drive north in the Vall d'Aran. In general most of the young people in the valley welcome the new developments, which should help to stem that widespread scourge of the uplands, depopulation. Many farmers' wives run bed-and-breakfast establishments, and indeed husbands often lend a hand dishing out the evening meals.

At the head of the Vall de Boí is the **Parc Nacional de Sant Maurici i Aigüestortes**. This is a fine area for walking if you come during the summer months, the climate always being cool, and sometimes downright chilly. Getting to the park is something of a problem. Ideally, you need a four-wheel drive vehicle with good chassis clearance to travel up the rutted and pot-holed track to the park. The park is sign-posted from the main road; turn right midway between Erill-la-Vall and Caldes de Boí. If you do not have a four-wheel drive car, you must either walk (it will take you several hours, but there is a camp site near the park entrance), or hire a vehicle at Boí (ask in the cafés if the park office is closed). In 1990 vehicle hire cost 5,000 pesetas, and the greater the number of passengers, the cheaper the trip. These vehicles only go a short distance into the park, and after an hour or so walking around some small lakes, you are obliged to return down the valley. Serious naturalists and walkers will be disappointed.

The scenery in the park is magnificent, with steep granite slopes falling almost sheer down to icy lakes. During the short time I spent walking through the juniper and pine scrub, I only saw redstarts, buzzards, and several common species of bird. Were you to spend longer and explore the park on foot you might be fortunate enough to see pine marten, chamois, wild boar, capercaillie, golden eagle, and perhaps even wild cat. A visit to the park is certainly not obligatory, and I suspect most people will be just as happy walking through the meadows and woods lower down the valley.

A brief guide to the Vall de Boí

GETTING THERE: The nearest railway station to the Vall de Boí is at Pobla de Segur, so to get there you really must have a car. From Barcelona, take either the A-2 motorway or the CN 11 to Lleida, then follow the CN 230 north to Pont de Suert (189 miles (305 km) taking the motorway; 177 miles (285 km) using the N 11). A short distance north of Pont de Suert take the road to the right to Barruera.

WHERE TO STAY: New hotels and bed-and-breakfasts are being built at present, so this list is by no means exclusive. Information about hotels, pensions and so forth can be obtained from the Patronat de la Vall de Boí, Barruera (Tel: 973–69 60 00). For information about skiing conditions and winter accommodation, contact Boí Taüll S. A., C/. La Granada 25, 6è, 1a, 08006 Barcelona; Tel: (93) 238 04 73. There are two hotels at Caldes de Boí: the four-star **El Manantial** (Tel: 973–69 01 91) and the older and more traditional one-star **Hotel Caldes** (Tel: 973–69 04 49). At Boí there are several hotels, including the two-star **Beneria** (Tel: 973–69 60 30) and the one-star **Pey** (Tel: 973–69 60 36). Reasonably priced and excellent value is the **Hostal Ferrer D'Avall** (two-star) at

Barruera (Tel: 973–69 60 29). The hotels at Erill-la-Vall are **L'Aüt** (Tel: 973–69 60 48), the **Plaza** (Tel: 973–69 60 05) and the **Noray** (Tel: 973–69 60 50), all of which are one-star. There is a pleasant camp site beside the river at Barruera (Tel: 973–69 60 29).

WHAT TO EAT AND WHERE: I am very partial to the no-nononsense cuisine in these mountain areas: it is homely and wholesome. *Escudella i carn d'olla*, which is a sort of cross between a soup and a hot-pot, is one of the oldest Catalan dishes. It consists of a stewed hodge-podge of meat, turnips, chickpeas, sausages, cabbage and so forth. In other words, it's the sort of meal a man needs after calving a cow or ploughing a field. Another popular dish is a *girella*, made with rice and lamb, and indeed lamb is eaten frequently round these parts. Trout served with almonds or pine nuts is popular, and in season the wild mushrooms should be savoured. I visited the valley off-season, so many restaurants were closed. This may have been a blessing in disguise: we ate every night at the **Hostal Ferrer d'Avall** in Barruera, where we were staying. Here visitors experience farmhouse cooking at its best.

FROM RIPOLL TO CAMPRODON

The district of Ripollès – one of the thirty-eight which make up the province of Catalonia – lies midway between the small principality of Andorra and the Mediterranean coast. The landscape is distinctly mountainous to the north, along the border with France, and pleasantly hilly to the south. The mountains are drained by two rivers, the Ter and the Freser, at whose confluence is the region's largest town, Ripoll. There are approximately sixty Romanesque religious buildings within the region, including the three great monasteries of Ripoll, Sant Joan de les Abadesses and Camprodon. These alone make a trip to this region worthwhile, but there is much else to enjoy, both in town and countryside, in this part of the Pyrenees.

Ripoll, as it happens, is rather gloomy and unprepossessing, not unlike one of the small wool towns of the Lancashire Pennines. It has had a long and prosperous industrial history, and from the 16th to 18th centuries it was one of Europe's leading producers of armaments and other metal goods. I can think of only one good reason to spend time in Ripoll – and that is the **Monastir de Santa Maria**, which is easy to find in the centre of town (it is best to park down by the river and walk from there). The original monastery was founded in 879 or 880 by Count Guifré el Pilos (Wilfred the Hairy), whose remains are in a casket where nave meets transept. The church was remodelled by Abbot Oliba, a friend of Pope Benedict VIII, in 1032. Such was the influence of the monastery that Ripoll became known as the *bressol de Catalunya* (cradle of Catalonia). The monastery has had a turbulent history: it was damaged by earthquake in 1438; burnt and pillaged in 1837. Much of what the visitor sees today is a 19th-century reconstruction of the original, with some modifications. For example, there used to be two Lombardic bell-towers; now, there is just one. The 19th-century stonework jars the senses (as well as the spirit), but all is redeemed by the cloister and the extraordinary porch.

The church has a nave with double aisles on either side, and a wide transept with seven apses. Romanesque architecture is much more than a sum of its parts – the semi-circular arch, the groin vault and so forth. It distinguished itself from what came before by exploring new ways of dealing with space. During the latter half of the 10th century, the growing trend towards worshipping saints, and the relatively novel habit of each priest celebrating Mass every day, led to a demand for more than one altar in each church. The solution was twofold, and in both cases the innovations came first in France. Several apses, each with its own altar, were arranged either radially around the east end of the church, or staggered side by side. The latter solution was adopted at Ripoll.

The two-storey cloister is entirely Romanesque, though parts of it were built well after the Gothic style had taken root in Catalonia. The gallery adjoining the church was built between 1170 and 1200, and the remaining sections of the lower storey around the end of the 14th century. The upper galleries were eventually completed in the early 16th century. The arches of the galleries are supported by double columns, many of which have fine sculptured capitals portraying saints, beasts, plants and so forth. This is one aspect of Romanesque art in Catalonia which I find particularly uplifting. The orna- ment in Norman (which is to say, Romanesque) churches in England tends to be abstract or absent, whereas in the Catholic countries around the Mediterranean, from the 10th century onwards, there emerged a strong tradition of decorating capitals with biblical scenes, animals, foliage and so forth.

Sculpture, of course, can be used to tell a story, and for the vast majority of Christians during medieval times knowledge of the scriptures came not from the written word, which to the illiterate was unintelligible, but from sermons and the scenes depicted in murals or carved in wood and stone. One of the supreme examples of Romanesque sculpture is the large porch at Ripoll, protected now from wind and rain by a modern extension. Unfortunately the stonework is in poor condition, but it is still possible to 'decipher' the 87 panels depicting scenes from the Bible. The porch dates from the 12th century and is in the shape of a triumphal arch. St Peter and St Paul support the archivolts, which themselves are decorated with sculpted figures beneath the central image of Christ.

The second great monastery on the River Ter is at **Sant Joan de les Abadesses**, some 6 miles (10 kilometres) upstream from Ripoll. It sits at the heart of a delightful town which has long been popular with holiday-makers. There are two bridges across the river at Sant Joan de les Abadesses, a modern one carrying the main road, and a medieval bridge whose central pointed arch spans the river from large stepped piers. The monastery was founded by Count Guifré in 885 for his daughter Emma, who headed a community of Benedictine nuns. The 12th-century Romanesque church lost its ambula- tory during an earthquake in the 15th century. Its plan is that of a Latin cross, with five apses, three deriving from the old ambulatory and the others from the transept. In the main apse there is a fine group of seven wooden figures depicting the descent from the cross and dating from 1251. According to the brief guide presented to visitors on entry, there is a piece of holy bread on Christ's forehead which has been 'preserved untouched for 700 years'; it seems to have disappeared. The acoustics of the church are unusually good: sermons need only be whispered, not declaimed. There is a feeling of great sanctity in this church, something noticeably absent at Ripoll.

Between the church and the cloister there is a small baroque chapel whose pietà by Josep Viladomat is a sumptuous affair. The Gothic cloister is modest yet graceful. On your way out it is worth spending a little time in the museum, which contains retables, choir stalls, church furniture, religious garments and ecclesiastical memorabilia from the monastery. The choir stalls boast some enchanting carvings: a monkey playing drums; a pig playing a pipe . . .

Neither Ripoll nor Sant Joan de les Abadesses is blessed with good hotels, and I would strongly advise visitors to stay in the town of **Camprodon**, whose monastic church is one of many attractions. Camprodon is a short journey upstream from Sant Joan de les Abadesses, and it too has a superb bridge, the **Pont Nou**, the original structure here dating from the 13th century. There is a fortified tower protecting one end of the bridge. Two rivers meet at Camprodon, the Ter and the Titort, and the houses overhanging the water are very picturesque with their shabby balconies, clothes lines and pots of geraniums.

Camprodon's popularity as a holiday resort has its origin in the days, around a century ago, when Dr Bartomeu Robert, Mayor of Barcelona, used to come here. (If you go to Sitges you will see his statue in the square behind the parish church.) The town has a good collection of *modernista* buildings, many of which are found along Passeig de la Font Nova and Passeig de Maristany. On the whole they are intriguing rather than memorable, and one or two are in sore need of repair.

The **Monestir de Sant Pere de Camprodon** – or, rather, the church which served it – stands at the top of town. Consecrated in 1169, it is a Romanesque building in the form of the Latin cross with five square apses. Externally, its most striking feature is the bell-tower, a two-storey, square Lombardic tower (with mullion windows, arcuations and so forth) which is anchored to an octagonal dome over the crossing. I was unable to gain entry, so I must leave a description of the interior to Alastair Boyd: 'It is a great building with a domical vault on squinches and two curious little passages leading from the nave into the transepts, which have semi-circular barrel vaults, while those over the nave are slightly pointed as the church caught up with the times during its construction.'

I did, however, get inside the **Església Parroquial de Santa Maria**, which stands a little way down the hill from the church of Sant Pere. This is a 14th-century Gothic building with an admirably wide vaulted nave and small side chapels between the buttresses.

Camprodon is a good base from which to explore the surrounding villages. Beget and Molló, both with marvellous Romanesque churches, lie some way to the east in rolling, green countryside; while some way to the north-west, and deeper into the Pyrenees, there is the small resort of Setcases.

A brief guide to Ripoll and Camprodon

GETTING THERE: Ripoll is 62 miles (100 kilometres) from Barcelona and easily reached along the scenic CN 152. This road continues up the valley to Sant Joan de les Abadesses and Camprodon. Ripoll is also linked to Barcelona by rail. There is a regular bus service between Ripoll and the other two towns.

WHERE TO STAY: The best place to stay is Camprodon, which has six hotels. I particularly recommend the stately **Hotel Güell**, which inexplicably boasts just one star. It is well situated in the Pl. d'Espanya (Tel: 972–74 00 11). Beware the local parking restrictions. Other hotels of a reasonable standard are the **Rigat**, Pl. del Dr Robert 2 (Tel: 972–74 00 13) and the **Edelweiss**, Ctra. Sant Joan 28 (Tel: 972–74 09 13). If you must stay in Ripoll, then I suggest the **Hotel Solana del Ter**, which is actually some way outside town on Cra. Barcelona-Ripoll (Tel: 972–70 10 62). There is a camp ground here and a swimming pool, all set in open woodland. At Sant Joan de les Abadesses your best bet is the one-star **Ter**, Vista Alegre 1 (Tel: 972–72 10 05).

WHAT TO EAT AND WHERE: As one might expect, the cuisine in this region is robust, with many of the specialities reflecting the good hunting to be had in the Pyrenees. Rabbit, partridge, wild boar are all available in season, as are river trout and a great variety of wild mushrooms. The best restaurant for Catalan cooking is Ripoll's **Solana del Ter** (*see* above for address). Further up the valley, in the small village of Llanars, **Restaurant Celler** is renowned for its fine range of Catalan dishes. Do not be put off by the ludicrous Swiss-chalet-style hotel which houses the restaurant. There are several simple restaurants serving honest food in Camprodon. For example, **Restaurant San Roc**, Pl. del Carme 4 (Tel: 972–74 01 19).

GIRONA AND THE NORTH-EAST

The Catalan poet Eugeni d'Ors had this to say about Girona: 'You, City, are a dry walnut of stony wrinkled shell, but white inside, tender, milky, exceedingly sweet.' The description fits perfectly: from the outside – and certainly when seen from a distance from the A-7 motorway – Girona looks dour and unprepossessing; but the drab apartment blocks and belching factories of the suburbs conceal a city of singular beauty. Girona is about an hour's drive north of Barcelona on the main route to France. One could see most of the city's important monuments on a day trip from Barcelona, but it really deserves more of the visitor's time than that. Those staying on the Costa Brava – 40 minutes' away by car – may feel inclined to pay the city several visits.

Girona is the capital of the region and an important link between the Frankish north and the Hispanic south. The Via Augusta, the great Roman road, passed through Girona (whose people, during Roman times, were known as Gerundenses), and since then the city has always straddled the principal route into France. In terms of its surroundings, Girona is well situated: it lies in the fertile valley of the River Ter within easy reach of both the mountains and the sea. However, its proximity to France has led to it being one of Europe's most besieged cities. The first serious siege took place in 1295, when Philippe III of France invaded Catalonia. The city was under siege again during the Civil War of the 1460s, and during the War of the Reapers in 1640 and 1642. The last quarter of the 17th century was especially traumatic, the city being besieged during the wars with France in 1675, 1683–4 and 1694. Then came the sieges during the latter years of the War of the Spanish Succession (1701–13). Lastly, and most famously, Girona was besieged by Napoleonic forces in 1808. There is a monument to the defenders of Girona in the Plaça de la Independencia. Two thousand Gironese under the command of Mariano Alvarez held out for seven months against 35,000 French. Girona thus became known as the 'City of Sieges', famous both for the heroism of its citizens and their intolerance of outsiders.

Faced by such frequent acts of aggression, Girona defended itself with stout walls. Most were dismantled at the end of the last century, but one superb section remains intact. A walk along the wall gives the visitor a bird's-eye view of *el barri vell* (the old city), which huddles on the eastern bank of the River Onyer. Unlike most of Girona's religious buildings and museums, the wall stays open at lunchtime and this is a good place to relax with a sandwich and a drink. Before climbing the steps up to the wall (from Plaça del General Marva), I suggest you arm yourself with a map of the city, which can be obtained from the Tourist Information Office on Rambla de la Llibertat. Seen from the walls the skyline is dominated by the vast bulk of the **cathedral**, dedicated to Santa Maria, and the broken spire of the church of Sant Feliu.

The cathedral is one of the most impressive buildings in Catalonia. It is approached by way of a dramatic flight of steps constructed between 1690 and 1694. The baroque façade was begun ten years earlier; further work was carried out during the 1730s, although the statuary which fills the alcoves dates from the 1960s. The monumentality of the square frontage emphasizes the sculptural grace of the three-storeyed baroque 'reredos', surmounting which is a rose window bordered by floral bas-reliefs. The octagonal bell-tower was completed in 1764.

This elegant baroque façade conceals one of Catalonia's Gothic masterpieces. When work began on the cathedral in 1312, the architects envisaged a central nave flanked by two aisles. The form it would have taken can be gauged by observing the cathedral to the east of the transept: the piers separating the ambulatory from the chancel would have continued towards the back of the church, thus separating nave from aisles. However, once the east end was complete, the original plan was abandoned with the architects arguing in favour of a single nave. Such were the uncertainties within the church about the wisdom of building such a wide nave, that it took the affirmation of two councils of architects to convince the authorities that it could be done. The architect Antoni Canet and the builder Guillem Bofill finally began work on the nave in 1416. At 75 feet (22.9 metres) this is the widest Gothic nave in Europe.

Natural light flows into the church through the clear glass of the rose windows – one at either end – and the large stained-glass windows above the triforium; the latter looks especially lovely when back-lit at night. The silver and enamel altarpiece and baldaquin (canopy) are among the outstanding examples of medieval craftsmanship in Catalonia; their author was Pere Bernès.

The **cloister** belonged to an earlier Romanesque church, and it is one of the loveliest in Catalonia. The galleries, with half-barrel-vault ceilings, have round arches supported by twin columns; these and the capitals are exquisitely decorated with biblical themes as well as birds, animals, monsters and abstract designs. There are dozens of tombs dating from Romanesque times and there is a charming well at the centre of the enclosure. Rising from one corner of the cloister is a five-storey Romanesque bell-tower complete with Lombard arcuations and mullioned windows; it now serves as a buttress for the cathedral.

The small **cathedral museum** occupies the old Chapter Rooms. It contains some of the finest religious art of the medieval period. There are illuminated manuscripts, Gothic and Renaissance sculptures and paintings, Arab and Romanesque chests and various other church treasures. The museum's outstanding possession is the *tapís de la Creació* (the Creation Tapestry), a Romanesque work of the 12th century. With Christ staring serenely from the centre of the wheel of time, surrounded by images of rural life, the seasons and the stars, this beautifully embroidered tapestry gives one a remarkable insight into the preoccupations of the medieval world.

The nearby church of **Sant Feliu** is thought to stand where the African missionary was either martyred or interred at the beginning of the 4th century. The ground plan of the church is Romanesque, but by the time the builders reached the triforium this style was abandoned in favour of the Gothic: thus the contrast between the heavy rounded arches separating the central nave from the aisles and the graceful triforium.

The Gothic spire was partially destroyed by lightning in 1581. There are eight pagan and early Christian sarcophagi (dating from the 2nd to 6th centuries) set into the Presbytery wall. A Gothic cloister was replaced in the late 1700s by the baroque chapel of Sant Narcís; the baroque façade was built around the same time.

Carrer Ferràn el Catòlic leads from Sant Feliu to the **Banys Àrabs** (Arab Baths). These alone make a trip to Girona worthwhile. They were built in the 12th and 13th centuries, not by Arabs, but in the style favoured in North Africa at that time. The *frigidarium* (the cold-bath room) has a tiny octagonal pool beneath a lantern supported by eight columns with Romanesque capitals, mostly decorated with plant motifs. Light enters the *frigidarium* through the overhead lantern and the horseshoe doorway. The *tepidarium* (warm-bath room) and *caldarium* (steam-bath room) are somewhat smaller, rectangular rather than square, with half-barrel and barrel-vault ceilings.

From here you could almost hurl a bar of soap to two lovely Romanesque buildings. The larger of the two, **Sant Pere de Galligants**, dates from 1130. There is a high nave, flanked by two aisles and supported by columns with decorated capitals. The three-storey octagonal bell-tower is particularly fine. The cloister, constructed between 1154 and 1190, exemplifies the virtues of mature Romanesque; note in particular the marvellous sculptures on the capitals, some telling of Christ's life as recounted in the New Testament, others depicting animals and mythical beasts. The church houses Girona's **Archaeological Museum**. There is a good collection of Greek and Roman artifacts, but most interesting of all are the Jewish tombstones with Hebraic inscriptions. Beside Sant Pere is the tiny church of **Sant Nicolau**, with three semi-circular apses (with Lombard arcuations outside) and a single nave.

How much else you see in Girona depends on both your time and inclination. There are a dozen or so other buildings of considerable architectural interest, and there are two more museums besides those already mentioned. The **Museu d'Art** in the Episcopal Palace opposite the south door of the cathedral is one of the best museums in the region, with sculptures and paintings from the Romanesque periods as well as a collection of Catalan art (including works by the Olot School of landscape painting; *see* also page 118).

The old city is a delightful place to walk around. There are plenty of places to relax – the verdant Jardins de la Fransesa beside the old wall, for example, or the nearby Passeig Arqueològic – and there are dozens of narrow alleys and courtyards to explore. The old Jewish quarter is well worth investigating. A Jewish community lived in the *call* from the end of the 9th century to 1492, the year of their expulsion from Spain. Carrer de la Força, which runs along the old course of the Via Augusta, was the principal thoroughfare in the *call* and the birthplace of Spain's first group of cabbalists (rabbis who sought secret meanings in the Bible). The Jews were frequently persecuted by their Gentile neighbours, and on one occasion in the late 14th century a mob broke into the *call* and beheaded 40 Jews. The **Isaac el Cec Museum** on Carrer Sant Llorenç keeps alive the memory of Girona's Jewish community.

AROUND GIRONA

Most visitors to this north-easterly corner of Catalonia stay by the sea on the Costa Brava. However, those who are weary of the tourist-induced desecration of the Mediterranean shoreline may prefer to avoid the crowds and stay inland. Girona makes an ideal base from which to explore the surrounding area.

The worst parts of the coast – by which I mean the most despoiled – are to the south of Sant Feliu: in places like Lloret, Blanes and Tossa you can get Watney's Red Barrel, fish and chips, and British T.V. soaps beamed out by satellite. Further north, and due east of Girona, the rugged coastline around Begur still has a few quiet coves: **Sa Riera** and **Sa Tuna** are good places for a swim and a snack, and there are easy walks around the headlands. On summer nights you will hear nightingales singing in the pine trees.

Further north still, beside the small fishing port of L'Escala, are the ruins of **Empúries**, a town founded by the Greeks in the 6th century BC and taken over by the Romans in the 3rd century BC. Empúries was eventually abandoned at the end of the 3rd century AD. The ruins and the associated museum are well worth a visit, though there are always large crowds in summer.

The most dramatic section of the coast is to the north of the Golf de Roses where the rocky Cap de Creus juts into the sea.

The fishing port of **Cadaques** has long been a favourite haunt of artists, Salvador Dalí being one of the many who lived here or nearby. There are less than 2,000 people in Cadaques in winter; more than 20,000 in summer.

Twenty minutes' drive inland from Roses is **Figueres**, an attractive little town with a distinctly French feel about it, and the home of the **Teatre-Museu Dalí**. This is one of the most popular museums in Catalonia, busy even in winter with coachloads of French and Germans. Dalí supported what most Catalans considered to be the wrong side during the Civil War (the fascists), and consequently he is not revered in the way Miró and Tàpies are. After an hour in this museum you realize that Dalí was as daft as he looked.

To the north and west of Girona the countryside is volcanic and voluptuous: devotees of 19th-century Catalan painting will enjoy the works of Vayreda, Alsina, Nonell and others at the **Museum of Modern Art** in **Olot**. Those with an appetite for Romanesque architecture should visit the magnificent **cathedral** at **Vic**, an hour's drive to the south-west of Girona.

A brief guide to Girona and the north-east

GETTING THERE: Girona is 59 miles (95 kilometres) from Barcelona, and linked both to the Catalan capital and to the French border at Le Perthus by the A-7 motorway. A word of warning: this road is jammed on Friday afternoons and evenings when the Barcelonans head north for the weekend, and again on Sunday evenings when they return. If you must travel north on Friday it may be wisest to follow the coast road, the N 11, to Malgrat, then head inland and join the A-7 at Junction 9. There is a good train service connecting Girona with Barcelona to the south and Perpignan to the north.

WHERE TO STAY: A good hotel in the centre of town is the three-star **Ultònia** at Gran Via de Jaume I 22 (Tel: 972–20 79 00). Of similar standard are the **Costabella**, Av. de França 61 (Tel: 972–20 25 24) and the **Sol Girona**, Ctra. de Barcelona (Tel: 972–24 32 32). Down at the cheap end are the **Peninsula**, Nou 3 (Tel: 972–20 38 00) and the **Margarit**, Ultònia 1 (Tel: 972–20 10 66).

For more information, contact the Tourist Office (Tel: 972–20 26 79).

WHAT TO EAT AND WHERE: Girona's position midway between the Pyrenees and the sea is reflected in its cuisine: you can sample both mountain fodder like *escudella i carn d'olla*, and the seafood (try the spiny lobster) caught off the Costa Brava. For a real treat you should head to Figueres: **Hotel Ampurdán** has what is possibly the best restaurant in Catalonia (Tel: 972–50 05 62). There is nothing in this class in Girona, but there are several restaurants serving honest Catalan and Spanish food. The old-fashioned **Cal Ros** in the gloomy basement of Cort Real 9 is a good family restaurant. The vast helpings may have something to do with the city's siege mentality. The lamb and beef dishes are good, but the *riñones al jerez* (kidneys in a sherry sauce) have a bouquet of pigsty which is rather too strong for my liking.

A PRACTICAL GUIDE

GETTING THERE AND GETTING AROUND

Barcelona has a superb public transport system. I have heard people rail against the scruffiness of the Metro, but those with complaints have obviously spent little or no time on the London Underground or New York subway. Services are efficient and regular, and those areas which cannot be reached by Metro are served by bus. As soon as you arrive in Barcelona it is worth getting a map titled *Guía Transporte publico de Barcelona y su area Metropolitana*. Most Tourist Offices will have copies; otherwise, it can be had from news stalls. It shows all the bus routes for the city, and has a Metro map as well. Of course, the best way to get to know a city is by walking the streets. Lack of public transport pretty much means that you must cover the sites within the old city (within the Rondas) by foot, but there is no reason why you shouldn't propel yourself further afield. Montjuïc, the Eixample below the Diagonal, Barceloneta, Ciutadella Park – all these are within range for the moderately fit person. Tibidabo, Park Güell, Horta, the Sagrada Familia and Nova Icaria are rather too far out to walk from the city centre, but are easily reached by public transport.

For information about all forms of public transport, Tel: 336 00 00

Flying in and out
Barcelona's international airport, El Prat de Llobregat, is 7.5 miles (12 kilometres) from the city centre. There are rail connections every 30 minutes to Barcelona Sants and Passeig

de Gràcia. The first train in the morning leaves Sants for the airport at 6.00; the last at 22.30. There are always plenty of taxis, and when arriving at the airport you can pick up a broadsheet, 'Barcelona Taxi', which gives details of the fares. Expect to pay around 1,500–1,800 pesetas for the journey to Plaça de Catalunya.

Iberia has more flights in and out of El Prat than any other airline. Information, Tel: 301 39 93; domestic reservations, Tel: 301 68 00; international reservations, Tel: 302 76 56. Iberia's main offices are at Passeig de Gràcia 30 and Diputació 258. Many other airlines have offices in Barcelona, including:

		Tel:
Air France	Passeig de Gràcia 63	215 28 66
British Airways	Passeig de Gràcia 85	215 21 12
Pan Am	Rbla. Catalunya 26	301 03 58
TWA	Passeig de Gràcia 55	215 81 88

Rail services

Barcelona has international rail connections with major cities in Western Europe. For example, there are daily services to Geneva via Montpellier, Avignon and Grenoble; to Paris via Limoges; and to Rome via Nice and Genoa. Trains of varying speeds run the length of the coast up to Port-Bou on the French border, and there are frequent connections with major Spanish cities such as Valencia and Madrid. The rail service in Spain is not noted for its speed or efficiency – but it is much cheaper than, say, British Rail or the French SNCF.

The two main terminals are Barcelona Sants (in the southern part of the city) and Estació de França (between Ciutadella Park and Barceloneta). Smaller rail stations are at Plaça de Catalunya and Passeig de Gràcia. In addition to the RENFE (national) network, there is also the FGC (Ferrocarrils de la Generalitat de Catalunya) local rail network which connects the city centre with places like Tibidabo, Güell Colony,

Montserrat and Manresa. RENFE information, Tel: 322 41
42; FGC information, Tel: 205 15 15.

Long-distance coach services
Coach transport is a complicated business in Barcelona, involv-
ing many different companies. Tourist offices will steer you in
the right direction. One of the main bus stations is Norte
Vilanova (Metro: L1 to Arc de Triomf). There are services
from here to the deep south (Granada, Algeciras, Seville, etc.),
Madrid, Burgos and Salamanca. From Ronda de Universitat,
coaches depart for Vall d'Aran and the neighbouring Pyrenean
valleys, Huesca, Zaragoza and Andorra. Most international
services leave from Plaça de la Universitat.

Getting round the city – public transport
There are six Metro lines, two of which are run by the
Generalitat. Trains run 05.00–23.00, Monday to Friday;
05.00–01.00, Saturday; 06.00–01.00, Sundays and holidays. The
system is easy to use. Each line has a number and colour code
(for example, L1 – red; L3 – green) and the names of the
stations are announced prior to arrival. There are only two
things wrong with the Metro system. For one thing, it closes
down too early at night; for another, the connections from one
line to another may look simple on the map, but often they
entail long walks down drab corridors. One ticket buys one
journey, and thus you pay the same to go fifteen stops as for
one stop (as in Paris). A single ticket costs 60 pesetas (65
pesetas at weekends), but it is more economical to buy a book
of 10 tickets, a *targeta*. A T-1 *targeta* (390 pesetas) is valid on
buses, Metro, the Blue Tram, the Generalitat's urban rail
service and the Montjuïc funicular. A T-2 *targeta* (325 pesetas)
does all of these except buses. *Targetas* are available at all
stations.

The bus service looks – and is – daunting. But with a little
perseverance you will manage to decode the bus map. Buses
run during roughly the same hours as the Metro, but there is
also a network of night buses, most of which pass through the

city centre. Taxis are yellow and black and, when free, a green light is illuminated on the roof. Foreigners are likely to be overcharged, so stand your ground and ensure that the meter is running when you begin your journey. For long distances, negotiate a price before starting out.

In addition to trains and buses, Barcelona boasts other exotic, if limited, forms of public transport, most of which link up with the Metro. There is a short funicular railway linking the Paral·lel station (L3) with Parc Montjuïc. This only runs at weekends, from 11.00 to 22.00. A cable car (*teliféric*) links the funicular to the castle on the top of the hill: daily from June to September (12.00–15.00 and 16.00–19.30); otherwise only at weekends and on holidays (11.00–14.45 and 16.00–19.30). There is also a cable car (*Transbordador Aeri*) linking the docks of Barceloneta with Montjuïc. This looks terrifying; it only runs at weekends. At the other side of the city there are two more funiculars, one up to Vallvidrera Superior, the other up the flanks of Tibidabo. The latter is linked to the Metro at Av. del Tibidabo by an ancient Blue Tram (the *Tramvia Blau*). Finally, there is the admirable system of escalators which takes pedestrians up the steep hill to Parc Güell (Escales de la Baixada de la Glòria); these operate 05.00–23.30, weekdays; 05.00–01.30, weekends.

Car Hire

Not long ago, car hire in Spain was reasonably cheap. It no longer is. I have found that the cheapest way to proceed is to hire a car through a travel agency in Britain, some of whom do fly-drive deals. Many of the big companies (Hertz, Budget, Avis and so forth) have offices at El Prat airport and in the city.

WHERE TO STAY IN BARCELONA

There are over 300 places to stay in Barcelona, ranging from luxurious five-star hotels to insalubrious flea-pits. At the end of this section there is a list of the hotels, hostels, tourist apartments, cheap guest-houses and pensions metioned in the text. It is always best to book hotel rooms in advance.

The system by which accommodation is classified in Spain is unnecessarily confusing, and visitors may find themselves wondering why their choice is a hostel rather than a hotel, or vice versa. The following is a rough guide to the classification system, which is always posted on a blue sign outside the entrance of the building: H = hotel; HR = residential hotel; HA = apart-hotel; RA = residential apartment; HS (the 's' being written in the upper arms of the 'H') = hostel; HSR = residential hostel; P = pension; CH = guest house.

Hotels and hostels are given a star rating; for the hotels the range goes from one star to five; for hostels, from one to three. Five-star hotels are luxurious, having everything one would expect in a top-class international hotel. At the lower end of the scale, one-star hotels offer relatively simple accom- modation: some rooms may have a wash-basin, but up to seven rooms will share the same bathroom. A three-star hostel is equivalent to a two-star hotel. For those who have a car, the presence or absence of a garage may be important (petty theft is so widespread that many locals who leave their cars on the street remove their stereos at night). Five- and four-star hotels in the city always have a private garage, three-star hotels and hostels may or may not.

No prices are given in this guide, but it goes without saying that the greater the number of stars, the more expensive the hotel is likely to be. Expect to pay the following for a night in a double room:

Star rating	Cost (pesetas)	Cost (£)
H *****	20–35,000	115–200
H ****	10–14,000	55–80
H ***	8–9,000	45–50
H **	4–8,000	22–45
H *	3–4,000	17–22
HS ***	4–6,000	22–35

At the bottom of the range, in guest houses and pensions, double rooms can be had for 1,000 pesetas or less (£6). As a general rule a single room will cost four-fifths of a double. The prices of all accommodation are governed by the local Tourist Boards, and by law they must be displayed both at the hotel entrance and in the rooms. The Barcelona Hotels Association publishes an annual guide to the city's hotels (Via Laietana 47; Tel: 301 62 40). For information and advice about bed-and-breakfast arrangements, contact Café-Colcha Agency (Trafalgar 52; Tel: 301 26 97).

When choosing a hotel, it is important to take two factors into account: noise and crime. I have had my stay at some hotels ruined by noise. This is not much of a problem in the more expensive hotels, as they are generally air-conditioned and the double-glazing will keep the sound of traffic and late-night revelry out. But be warned: on the main roads in Barcelona, traffic (and people) keep going throughout the night. The Ramblas is never quiet, and neither are the Passeig de Gràcia nor the Diagonal. For this reason I am inclined to advise against staying at the cheaper hotels on these streets, *unless* you can get a room at the back. Of course, if you intend to spend your nights in bars and clubs, this is irrelevant. The other precaution you should take is against crime. Those in search of the cheapest places to stay must head for the pensions and hostels in the narrow alleys and squares off the lower end of the Ramblas. During the daytime these areas may seem very picturesque, but at night the atmosphere can be distinctly nasty. There is a serious hard-drug problem in Barcelona, and both dealers and addicts frequent these areas in large numbers. The nearer you are to Plaça de Catalunya, the safer you will be.

If you intend to spend more than a few days in Barcelona, I strongly recommend the city's 'apart-hotels'. These are self-catering apartments, with bedroom, kitchen and bathroom. Some have sitting rooms, televisions and so forth. They are particularly popular with business people, or families spending some time in the city. They are very reasonably priced, and indeed I have found them a better deal than most hotels. Naturally, being able to cook for oneself saves eating out every day.

Recommendations – The Ramblas and Barri Gòtic
Two of the best modern hotels on the Ramblas are just a few yards away from one another. Both the **Ramada Renaissance** (****) and the **Royal** (****) have recently been refurbished. Neither possesses quite the elegance of the **Oriente** (***), which is further down the Ramblas, midway between the Opera House (Liceu) and the Plaça del Teatre. The hotel ballroom incorporates part of an old monastery, and indeed a sense of history hovers about the public rooms like an intoxicating perfume. The hotel is highly recommended, though the bedrooms are distinctly ordinary. In a similar price bracket is the **Montecarlo** (***), which from the outside looks deceptively grand: the entrance hall, with its gilded mirrors and marble statuary, promises a degree of elegance not to be found in the bedrooms, which are nevertheless clean and comfortable. The **Continental** (HS***) also looks stylish from the street, but the bedrooms are somewhat gloomy and dusty. George Orwell and his wife stayed here during the Civil War: some of the carpets look as though they date from that era. Also on the Ramblas is the popular **Internacional** (*), whose modern interior is concealed by a handsome baroque façade. The hotel is immediately opposite the Opera House. There are four good, moderately priced hotels just off the Ramblas; one advantage of staying in these establishments is that they are more peaceful than similar hotels on the Ramblas, though the streets are narrow and some of the rooms never see sunlight. The **España** (**) on Carrer de Sant Pau is very handy for the Opera and for London Bar (*see* page 235) and you should certainly have a meal in the *modernista* splendour of Domènech i Montaner's dining room. The other three clean, competently run hotels in this price bracket are the **Cortés** (**), the **Cataluña** (**) and the **Nouvel** (*), all on Carrer de Santa Anna.

Superbly situated opposite the cathedral, at the heart of the Barri Gòtic, is the famous **Hotel Colón** (****). Its neighbour is the less expensive but somewhat dowdy **Regencia Colón** (***). If you are looking for cheap accommodation in this area, it is mostly to be found further towards the port, between Carrer de Ferran and Passeig de Colom. **Hostal Cervantes** (HS*) is said to be good value, as is **Pension Fina**. The latter, being on Carrer Portaferrisa, is in a safer area. Many travellers like to stay in Plaça Reial, whose neo-classical buildings are a good deal more appealing than some of its night-time denizens. This area is notorious for drug-dealing and theft, despite an almost permanent police presence. **Hostal Roma** (HS**) has rooms overlooking the square and a good restaurant; **Hostal Mayoral** (HS**) is also popular. Nearer the cathedral – and in a pleasanter environment – are **Hostal Rey Don Jaime I** (HS**) and **Hostal El Casal** (HS***).

Recommendations – Eixample

Within a few minutes' walk of Plaça de Catalunya are three of the best hotels in Barcelona. The **Avenida Palace** (*****) and the **Ritz** (*****) are on Gran Via de les Corts Catalanes; the **Diplomatic** is on Carrer de Consell de Cent. If I could afford to stay in any of these hotels, I would plump for the Ritz, whose décor is utterly sumptuous. It is worth stepping through the doors just to look at the lobby, through which Salvador Dalí once rode on a white horse; the restaurant is one of the best in Barcelona, and one of the most expensive. In between the Ritz and the Avenida Palace is the **Gran Via** (***), which is an architectural gem and the sort of place one might wish to spend one's honeymoon: there are some fine art nouveau fittings, including the main staircase, and the bedrooms have a *fin-de-siècle* charm. Two hotels occupying *modernista* houses deserve special mention: the **Duques de Bergara** (****), just off Plaça de Catalunya, and **Condes de Barcelona** (****), on Passeig de Gràcia.

There is not much in the way of cheap or even moderately priced accommodation in the Eixample. The **Urbis** (HS***), on Passeig de Gràcia, is one of the best hostels in the city, but it suffers from the problem of noise. It is popular with student groups. On Rambla de Catalunya, the **Líder** (HS**), the **Windsor** (HS**) and the **Neutral** (HS**) offer respectable rooms at a reasonable price. The **Universitat** (HS**), on Ronda de la Universitat, is a great favourite and often full. There are a number of hotels along the Diagonal, which is possibly the noisiest street in Spain: people who live along the street have triple- and sometimes quadruple-glazing, and even then the noise and dust filters through. The **Princesa Sofía** (*****) is massive – it has over 500 rooms – and ugly; it is also too far from the old city to walk back at night, although trend-setters might point out that the most fashionable clubs and discos are near the Diagonal. In fact, the Princesa Sofía has its own disco, Regine's. All the same, if you can afford to stay at the Princesa Sofía, I suggest that you stay at the Ritz, the Avenida Palace or the Gran Via instead. They have real class.

Apart-hotels

Apart-hotels, or *apartamentos turisticos*, range from the splendid to the seedy. They are subject to a rating system which uses keys instead of stars (4 keys = luxury; 3 keys = first class; 2 keys = second class; 1 key = third class). Some apart-hotels have minimum-stay times of a week, and in some cases, a month. The rates generally decrease the longer the stay. One of the best apart-hotels (although it does not call itself that) is the **Victoria** (****), which is some way out from the centre on Avinguda de Pedralbes. This is a pleasant area; across the road from the Victoria are the gardens of the Palau Reial. One of the better apart-hotels in the Eixample is **La Equitativa** (3 keys), which occupies the upper floors of the tall office block opposite Casa Lleó-Morera, Domènech i Montaner's gaudy wedding cake of a building on Passeig de Gràcia. The staff are very helpful, and the only drawback is the incessant noise of traffic. Rather further away from the centre is the modern **Senator** (3 keys), which is more expensive than La Equitativa but less spacious. If you are determined to stay on the Ramblas there is the **Mur Mar** (2 keys). The street life here is never dull.

Youth Hostels and Camp sites
Barcelona has two youth hostels which are run under the umbrella of the International Youth Hostels Federation. One is near the main entrance to Ciutadella Park at Passeig de Pujades 29 (Tel: 300 31 04). The other is a fair way out on Passeig de Nostra Senyora del Coll 41–51 (Tel: 213 86 33). To stay here you must have a YHA membership card. For details about camp sites, contact the Barcelona Camping Organization: Carrer Diputació 279 (Tel: 317 44 16).

Recommended Hotels
N.B.   If calling from the U.K., you should add '010 34 3' before the hotel number for a direct line through.

H *****

Avenida Palace	Gran Via 605	301 96 00
Diplomatic	Carrer de Consell 122	317 31 00
Ritz	Gran Via 668	318 52 00

H ****

Colón	Av. Catedral 7	301 14 04
Condes de Barcelona	P. de Gràcia 75	215 06 16
Duques de Bergara	Bergara 11	301 51 51
Ramada Renaissance	Rambla 111	318 62 00
Royal	Rambla 117	301 94 00
Victoria	Av. Pedralbes 16 bis	204 27 54

H ***

Gran Via	Gran Via 642	318 19 00
Montecarlo	Rambla 124	317 58 00
Oriente	Rambla 45	302 25 58

H **
Cataluña	Santa Anna 24	301 91 50
Cortés	Santa Anna 25	317 91 12
España	Sant Pau 9	318 17 58

H *
| Internacional | Rambla 78–80 | 302 25 66 |
| Nouvel | Santa Anna 20 | 301 82 74 |

HS ***
| Casal, El | Tapineria 10 | 319 78 00 |
| Urbis | P. de Gràcia 23 | 317 27 66 |

HS **
Lider	Rbla. de Catalunya 84	215 50 65
Mayoral	Pl. Real 2	317 95 34
Neutral	Rbla. de Catalunya 42	318 73 70
Rey Don Jaime I	Jaume, I 11	315 41 61
Roma	Pl. Reial 11	302 03 66
Universitat	Rda. de la Universitat 10	317 13 41
Windsor	Rbla. de Catalunya 84	214 11 98

HS *
| Cervantes | Cervantes 6 | 302 51 68 |

APART-HOTELS
La Equitativa	P. de Gràcia 44	215 93 00
Mur Mar	Rambla 34	318 27 20
Senator	Via Augusta 167	201 14 05

WHERE TO EAT AND DRINK

I advise the serious gourmet to consult two specialist books before setting out on an eating expedition in Barcelona. These are the *Michelin Guide* and the *Gourmetour Guía gastronomica y turistica*, both of which provide a comprehensive survey of the city's best restaurants. The list below is to some extent idiosyncratic, reflecting my own personal preferences as well as those of friends and acquaintances. It is far from exhaustive. Barcelona has a great number of bars and restaurants catering for all tastes and pockets. No mention is made here of those serving Italian, Indian, Chinese or South American food. There are two reasons for this. First, I assume that visitors want to savour Catalan and Spanish food; and second, the Italian, Indian and Chinese food in Barcelona is generally of poor quality, and in no way comparable to the equivalent fare in cities like London or Paris.

A few years ago it was possible to eat very cheaply in tapas bars. Unfortunately, times have changed. Three dishes of tapas – for example, a slice of tortilla, some mushrooms and some cockles – may now set you back as much as a 'straight' meal in a restaurant. Many restaurants have a low-priced *menú del día*, but this is often available only at midday. Most restaurants are closed for at least one day a week, generally a Sunday or a Monday.

Bars and Tapas Bars

Barcelona is blessed with an astonishing wealth of bars, and it would take half a lifetime to visit them all. They range from the small and seedy to the plush and palatial. My preferences veer towards the more modest. A good place to start and end the evening is the tiny, ceramic-tiled bar of **Mesón del Café** in Carrer Llibreterie. Here you get the best coffee in town, and there is a satisfyingly wide range of spirits and liqueurs. Of the bars on the upper reaches of the Ramblas one of the more intriguing is the **Viena**, which serves good draught beers and Austrian snacks. The fresco on the ceiling – angels hovering in a light-blue sky – looks like a bad Tiepolo. In the evenings a morose pianist plays old favourites of the play-it-again-Sam genre. Across the street is **Café Moka**, a glitzy, air-conditioned bar and restaurant. In *Homage to Catalonia*, Orwell describes taking pot-shots from the roof of the Poliorama at the communists who were holed up inside the café. The Moka's history strikes me as being more interesting than its cooking, but this is not a bad place for a quick drink. Up in Plaça de Catalunya the most popular café is the **Zurich**, a great beer-hall of a place frequented by young people and students. Those who like this sort of ambience should also try the *cerveseries* (beer houses) of Plaça Reial.

For the best tapas and some of the most atmospheric bars in Catalonia you must head down towards the waterfront. **Bodega de la Plata** on Carrer Ample is a classic of its type: sawdust floors, tiled walls, no frills. Here you should order a *porrón* of roughish wine (you simply ask for red, white or rosé) and a dish of small, silver fish fried in oil. Nearby is another bar (no name for this one) whose ceiling is slung with hams and sausages.

Barcelona is renowned for its champagne bars. There is a particularly good one on Carrer Reina Cristina, sandwiched between shops selling radios, watches, cameras and so forth. The bar has no seats and is always packed; by the end of the day the customers – tarts, stockbrokers from the Llotja, sailors, students, respectable old ladies – have to wade through an ocean of cigarette stubs, discarded napkins and leftovers. A couple of glasses of champagne and a Camembert or ham sandwich costs less than 200 pesetas. This is an ideal stopping-off place if you are walking to Barceloneta. There is another good champagne bar, **Magic**, at Passeig de Picasso 40; and if you head down Carrer Montcada from here you will find plenty of tapas bars around the church of Santa Maria del Mar.

There are two bars in the lower regions of the Ramblas whose decor has much to do with their popularity. The **Café de la Opera**, which sports a turn-of-the-century look, is immediately opposite the Liceu. The drinks here are rather pricey, but if you get a table near the entrance you can watch life passing along the Ramblas. A more genuine article – though closed during the day – is **London Bar**, Carrer Nou de la Rambla. Red and white marble lines the walls like Punch-and-Judy awnings; there's a trapeze above the bar and a piano in one corner. The waiters and waitresses are delightful.

Several delicatessens serve drinks and tapas. **La Castellana** at Ramblas 41 is a good place to sample wine and *charcutéria* simultaneously. Further afield, but of the same type, is the expensive *jamoneria* on the corner of Carrer Consell de Cent and Carrer d'Enric Granados.

Rather far out for most visitors, but well worth dropping in to if you are near by, is the extraordinary **Bar-Llibreria Cristal-City** at Carrer Balmes 294. Here you can find excellent tapas and browse through the bar's book collection – there's everything from Hess to Le Carré, Marquez to Flaubert, and some of it is in English.

All these bars have been around for some time and none can be accused of being trendy. You certainly won't meet the international smart set, nor will you be fleeced of your money (except perhaps in the streets outside). A very different world of *bars modernos* attracts the young and rich, with bars going in and out of fashion from one month to the next. Drinks tend to be expensive in these places. Most of the 'hip' bars are found in the Eixample, to the north of the Diagonal. Here are a few which were in fashion at the start of the decade. Most stay open well into the night. **K. G. B.**, Carrer Alegre de Dalt 55; **Nick Havanna**, Carrer Rosellon 208; **Tres Tres**, Carrer Amigo 33; **SiSiSi**, Diagonal 402; **Network**, Diagonal 616; **Ars Studio**, Carrer Atenas 25; **Universal**, Carrer Mariano Cubi 184.

Eating Reasonably

Colman Andrews, in his seminal work, *Catalan Cuisine*, gives a short list of his favourite restaurants serving Catalan food. One of his more revealing entries is **Bar Pinocho**, at stall 66–67 in La Boqueria market: 'Ten stools at a funky counter in the middle of the market, with food good enough for white tablecloths, Catalan specialities, fresh market supplies.' The message, I think, is clear: a simple place doesn't mean poor food, any more than a smart place means good food.

It would be a shame to spend time in Barcelona and not take advantage of the excellent seafood, in which case you should head for Barceloneta, the old fishermen's quarters.

Though the area is almost exclusively working-class, many of the restaurants cater for a wealthy clientele. Yes, bring your Amex. Obviously, if you plump for lobster you will pay more than you will for a *paella*. The following all serve good seafood dishes: **Salamanca** and **Bar Ricart**, both on Carrer Almiral Cervera; **Can Sole**, Carrer San Carlos 4; **Casa Costa**, Carrer Baluarte 124; **Casa Tipa**, Passeig Nacional 6.

On the way back to town, opposite the Llotja, there is the venerable old **Set Portes** at Passeig d'Isabel II 14: panelled walls, solid furniture and excellent Catalan food. The *paella* is especially good. Two great favourites with tourists are almost next to one another on Carrer dels Escudellers. **Caricoles** at number 14 is a vast place with a maze of corridors and rooms. On the way in you go through a medieval kitchen. The staircases are winding and narrow; hams hang like stalactites from the ceilings; the walls are either tiled or covered with signed photos of actresses, bullfighters, artists and others who have eaten here. There is a large menu (in several languages) and specialities include *cargots* (snails), *sarsuela*, suckling pig, lobster and barbecued chicken. The food is good; the service rather too swift and peremptory. Unfortunately, there is 'ethnic' music played by a small band of imitation troubadours: meals cost quite enough without subsidizing this sort of thing. The **Grill Room**, a few yards back towards the Ramblas, is smaller and provides similar food with less ostentation at lower cost. I recommend a lunchtime visit and a plate of mussels at the bar. The décor is appealing art nouveau. Not far from here, at Carrer d'Avinyó 9, is **El Gran Café**: good Catalan food in pleasant *fin-de-siècle* surroundings.

Behind La Boqueria market are two restaurants worth a visit. The more expensive, and the smaller of the two, is **Bar Egypto**, where I have eaten a splendid dish of langoustines. Down the street, at Carrer Jerusalem 12, is **Restaurant Egipte**. This used to be considered one of the best reasonably priced restaurants in the city. I have eaten both well and badly there. The atmosphere is distinctly 'Islingtonish'. The chicken stuffed with prunes and cheese is recommended. Not far from here, in the murky Carrer Sant Pau, a reasonable meal can be had in the great dining room of **Hotel España**.

Back across the Ramblas and a little way inland from Plaça Reial is the famous **Can Culleretes**, founded in 1786 and still going strong. Good Catalan cooking at affordable prices. Much the same could be said of **La Cuineta**, just behind the cathedral at Paradis 4.

On the other side of Via Laietana is **Els Quatre Gats**, Carrer Montsió 3–5. This is one of Barcelona's most famous cafés. It was here that Casas, Rusiñol, Picasso and others met and hung their paintings; it was here that Albéniz gave concerts and Maragall read his poetry. And all this in a *modernista* building designed by Puig i Cadafalch. This is a good place for snacks. There is live music – mostly jazz – some evenings.

Perhaps one of the best traditional restaurants is the **Madrid-Barcelona** at Carrer Aragó 282. This is the old Passeig de Gràcia station restaurant, a large tomb-like building with mirror-lined walls, a gallery and a very Parisian feel about it. The food is honest and unfussy, as is the service. If you are not eating, it is a good place to drink. Further out in the Eixample is the admirable **Senyor Parellada**, Argenteria 37. This restaurant is renowned for its game stew and its fish.

For cheap, wholesome vegetarian food, try **Self Naturista**, Carrer Santa Anna 15–17. As its name implies, it is a self-service restaurant. There is a good tapas bar opposite. There is no shortage of fast-food restaurants in Barcelona: Burger King, McDonalds and Kentucky Fried Chicken are all to be found on or near the Ramblas.

Expensive Eating

The top restaurants in Barcelona are probably far too expensive for the majority of tourists. They are certainly well beyond my means and I must confess, somewhat sadly, that I have never eaten at places like the Ritz or Via Veneto, nor am I likely to. Consequently, the descriptions which follow are cursory and derivative.

The best Basque food is to be found at **Beltxenea**, Mallorca

275, 1st floor, and at the slightly less expensive **Amaya** at Rbla. Sta. Mónica 20. **Via Veneto**, Ganduxer 10–12, is said to be one of the finest restaurants in Spain, and almost as admired is **Florián**, at Bertrand i Serra 20. Both specialize in Catalan cuisine. Colman Andrews suggests that **El Dorado Petit**, which serves French and Catalan dishes at Dolors Monserdà 51, is 'arguably the best in town'.

USEFUL ADDRESSES

Tourist Information Offices
Generalitat de Catalunya, Gran Via 658; Tel: 301 74 43 or 317 22 46. Open: 09.00–21.00, Monday to Friday; 09.00–14.00, Saturday.
Sants Station; Tel: 490 91 71. Open: 08.00–20.00.
Ajuntament, Plaça de Sant Jaume; Tel: 318 25 25. Open: 08.00–20.00 (summer only).
Palau de la Virreina, Rambla 99. Open: 10.00–21.00 (summer only).

Foreign Consulates
UK, Avinguda Diagonal 477; Tel: 322 21 51.
Ireland, Gran Via Carles III 94; Tel: 330 96 52.
USA, Via Laietana 33; Tel: 319 95 50.

Crime
Barcelona City Police have set up special facilities for tourists (English and French spoken) at Rambla 43; Tel: 317 70 20. Open: 24 hours in summer.

Left Luggage
There are left-luggage lockers at Sants Station, open: 06.00–23.00, and at Passeig de Gràcia–Aragó Station, open: 06.30–22.30.

Hospital Services

In case of emergency, go to one of the following:

Hospital de Sant Pau, Av. S. Antoni Maria Claret 167; Tel: 347 31 33.

Hospital Clinic, Casanova 143; Tel: 323 14 14.

Red Cross Hospital, Dos de Maig 301; Tel: 235 93 00.

Ambulance Services; Tel: 329 77 66 or 300 20 20.

Traffic Accidents; Tel: 092.

Doctor (emergency); Tel: 212 85 85.

SELECTED READING

Andrews, Colman, *Catalan Cuisine*, London, Headline Books, 1989.

Arts Council of Great Britain, *Homage to Barcelona: the city and its art 1888–1936*, London, 1985.

Boyd, Alastair, *The Essence of Catalonia*, London, André Deutsch, 1988.

Ford, Richard, *Handbook for Travellers in Spain*, London, John Murray, 1845.

Hernández-Cros, Josep Emili *et al.*, *Guía de Arquitectura de Barcelona*, Barcelona, Ajuntament de Barcelona, 1985.

Macaulay, Rose, *Fabled Shore : from the Pyrenees to Portugal*, London, OUP, 1949.

Mackay, David, *Modern Architecture in Barcelona 1854–1939*, London, the Anglo-Catalan Society, 1985.

Orwell, George, *Homage to Catalonia*, London, Secker & Warburg, 1938.

Penrose, Roland, *Miró*, London, Thames & Hudson, 1970.

Pevsner, Nikolaus, *An Outline of European Architecture*, London, Pelican Books, 1943.

Pladevall i Font, Antoni, and Pagès i Paretas, Montserrat, *This is Catalonia : Guide to the Architectural Heritage*, Barcelona, Plaza & Janés, 1988.

Soldevila, Carlos, *Barcelona*, Barcelona, Ediciones Destino, 1951.

Thomas, Hugh, *The Spanish Civil War*, London, Penguin, 1968.

Tóibín, Colm, *Homage to Barcelona*, London, Simon & Schuster, 1990.

Torres, Marimar, *The Spanish Table : The food and wines of Spain*, London, Ebury Press, 1987.

Vergés, Oriol and Cruañas, Josep, *The Generalitat in the History of Catalonia*, Barcelona, Departament de Cultura de la Generalitat de Catalunya, 1986.

Most of the books listed above are available in Great Britain. Those which are not can be obtained in Barcelona. There are two excellent bookshops on the Ramblas with a broad selection of popular and academic works dealing with all aspects of Catalan life, from its history to its cuisine, from the arts to sport. One is in the Palau de la Virreina, Rambla 99; the other – run by the Generalitat's Department of Culture – is across the road on the ground floor of the Palau Moja. Both these bookshops – and many newspaper kiosks – sell *Vivir en Barcelona* and *Barcelona*, two glossy magazines about city life. Better than either of these is *Catalonia*, which is published in English and French, as well as Spanish and Catalan. For visitors the most useful publication is the weekly guide, *Guía del Ocio*. English, American, French, German and other foreign newspapers are widely available, often on the day of publication: try the newsagents and bookshops on the Ramblas and Passeig de Gràcia. For books in English, try Itaca (Rambla de Catalunya 81) and Come-In (Carrer de Provença 203).

INDEX

All places are in Barcelona except where stated otherwise.

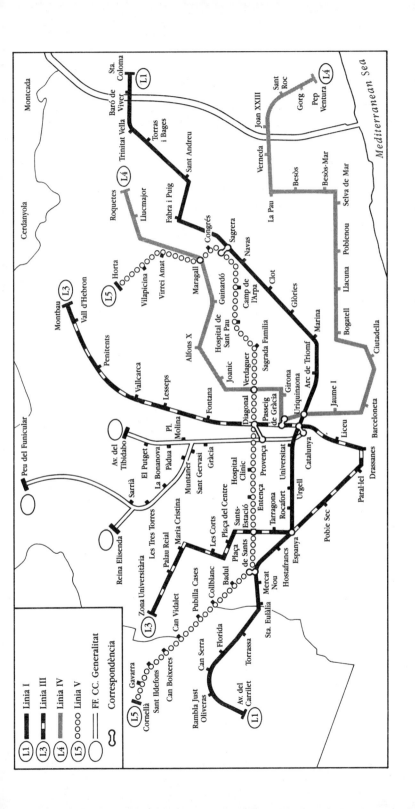

FOR THE BEST IN PAPERBACKS, LOOK FOR THE 🐧

In every corner of the world, on every subject under the sun, Penguin represents quality and variety – the very best in publishing today.

For complete information about books available from Penguin – including Puffins, Penguin Classics and Arkana – and how to order them, write to us at the appropriate address below. Please note that for copyright reasons the selection of books varies from country to country.

In the United Kingdom: Please write to *Dept E.P., Penguin Books Ltd, Harmondsworth, Middlesex, UB7 0DA.*

If you have any difficulty in obtaining a title, please send your order with the correct money, plus ten per cent for postage and packaging, to *PO Box No 11, West Drayton, Middlesex*

In the United States: Please write to *Dept BA, Penguin, 299 Murray Hill Parkway, East Rutherford, New Jersey 07073*

In Canada: Please write to *Penguin Books Canada Ltd, 2801 John Street, Markham, Ontario L3R 1B4*

In Australia: Please write to the *Marketing Department, Penguin Books Australia Ltd, P.O. Box 257, Ringwood, Victoria 3134*

In New Zealand: Please write to the *Marketing Department, Penguin Books (NZ) Ltd, Private Bag, Takapuna, Auckland 9*

In India: Please write to *Penguin Overseas Ltd, 706 Eros Apartments, 56 Nehru Place, New Delhi, 110019*

In the Netherlands: Please write to *Penguin Books Netherlands B.V., Postbus 195, NL-1380AD Weesp*

In West Germany: Please write to *Penguin Books Ltd, Friedrichstrasse 10–12, D-6000 Frankfurt/Main 1*

In Spain: Please write to *Alhambra Longman S.A., Fernandez de la Hoz 9, E-28010 Madrid*

In Italy: Please write to *Penguin Italia s.r.l., Via Como 4, I-20096 Pioltello (Milano)*

In France: Please write to *Penguin Books Ltd, 39 Rue de Montmorency, F-75003 Paris*

In Japan: Please write to *Longman Penguin Japan Co Ltd, Yamaguchi Building, 2-12-9 Kanda Jimbocho, Chiyoda-Ku, Tokyo 101*

The Other Nile

The Other Nile is rich not only in atmosphere, anecdotes and intriguing information but also in hard political fact. Here, describing the people he met – camel-herders, or diplomats, or refugees – Charlie Pye Smith gives the tragedies of civil war and famine vital, individual faces. 'No Man's Land is getting bigger every year,' he writes, 'and Waugh was right: it is no place for tourists. Nevertheless I'm glad that for a little while I ventured between the barbed wire.'

'Funny, thoughtful, warm-hearted, conscience-prodding . . . Like all good ecologists Mr Pye-Smith has an instinctive sense of history which gives an added depth to this remarkable book' – *Good Book Guide*

Travels in Nepal

From Kathmandu east to the fabled outpost of Namche Bazar, within sight of Everest, or west to the Kali Gandaki, the world's deepest gorge, Nepal is a country dominated by the other-worldly landscape of the Himalaya . . .

'It is refreshing to find a travel writer bothered to grapple with facts instead of simply gossiping about the view from the train window . . . This gives his account – which in itself is an attractive description of a beautiful, mountainous nation – a tough and interesting backbone' – *Independent*